How to Build
Dioramas

2nd Edition

Sheperd Paine

Acknowledgments

While many of the techniques described in this book are my own, many more were developed by fellow modelers. It would be impossible for me to acknowledge everyone who contributed an idea or suggestion, but special thanks are due to the following individuals who contributed directly to this book: Joe Berton; Bob Bihari; Rolf Brieger; Mike Cobb; Bruce Culver; Paul Decker; Roger Harney; Ron Hillman; Bob Reder, Bob Johnson and John Cather of Monogram Models; Ralph Muscente; Art Neckerman and Tom Ferris of Valiant Miniatures; Irv Radinger; Dave Reed; Philip Stearns; Jim Stephens; John Wager; Armand Bayardi; Bob Letterman of VLS ; Mike McCauley of Max Trax; Lewis Pruneau; Keith Gill of the Museum of Science and Industry; Bob Kauffman and Don Pomarenski of Custom Dioramics. Unless otherwise credited, all models and photographs are by the author.

Printed in USA

99 00 01 02 03 04 05 06 07 08   10 9 8 7 6 5 4 3 2 1

Visit our website at
http://books.kalmbach.com
Secure online ordering available

Publisher's Cataloging-in-Publication
(Provided by Quality Books, Inc.)

Paine, Sheperd.
    How to build dioramas / Sheperd Paine. — 2nd ed.
    p. cm.
    ISBN: 0-89024-195-3

    1. Models and modelmaking. 2. Diorama.
    I. Title.

TT154.P34 1999   745.592'82
                           QBI99-1276

Book design: Sabine Beaupré
Cover design: Kristi Ludwig

Contents

Introduction

A diorama, in the strictest sense of the term, is a scene enclosed in a box and viewed through a small opening, something we more commonly call a "shadow box." In recent years, diorama has come to mean any scene executed in three dimensions, whether it is enclosed in a box or not. At its most basic, then, a diorama is nothing more than a model or group of models placed in a realistic setting. This setting almost invariably involves a landscaped base of some sort and probably a few figures to add scale and interest.

Once installed in a setting, however, any model undergoes a transformation. It becomes part of a three-dimensional picture, an image as vivid and informative as a painting or a photograph. This is because a model standing alone is limited to being just what it appears to be: a miniature replica of an object in real life. In a diorama setting the model is placed in context, and the context furnishes a frame of reference that amplifies and further illustrates the model's meaning and significance.

Here's an example. A model of a Sherman tank standing alone shows what the tank looked like but gives little indication of the role the Sherman played in World War II. But add a diorama setting that shows the tank rumbling down a dusty Normandy road, with battered fenders hanging loose and bone-weary crewmen slumped in the hatches, and your viewer will appreciate the rugged durability that made the Sherman a part of American history.

A scene that tells a story. The diorama provides a meaning and perspective that a free-standing model cannot. It can also offer more than just an historical context. In its most developed form, a diorama is a scene that tells a story. This does not imply a story in the narrative sense, it simply means that a diorama can show "something going on." In this sense, a diorama is not just a model of an object or a group of objects, but of an *event*. This event may be active and obvious, such as an infantry attack, or it may be passive and subtle, such as weary infantrymen resting after a battle, or a forlorn and derelict aircraft abandoned in the desert. When a diorama becomes narrative, figures become an important element; it is difficult to have something going on without people around. Even when there are no people at all, as in the case of the derelict airplane, it is their conspicuous

A good model standing on its own is certainly interesting, but a diorama provides a historical setting and a feeling of drama (upper left) that might otherwise be difficult for a viewer to visualize.

A diorama is more than just a model displayed on a base with a couple of figures. A diorama is a model that tells a story, but it doesn't need to show a specific event. In a simple scene like this one (lower left) by John Rosengrant, there is no real "story," but, like a camera snapshot, it captures a moment in time.

Although dioramas can be large scenes with buildings, vehicles and dozens of figures, they can also be small and simple. This single figure (right) by James Welch could arguably be called a diorama: the "scene" is the painted reflection on the astronaut's visor!

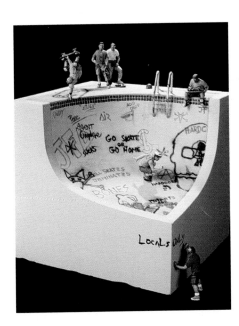

Although the majority of the scenes in this book are of military subjects, some of the most memorable dioramas are not. "Locals Only," a scene by Joel Frisch showing skateboarders in an old swimming pool, is a wonderful example of what you can come up with if you let your imagination run free.

absence that tells the story and makes the scene work.

The size of a diorama is not important; in fact, some of the most effective dioramas are quite small. Small dioramas, often called vignettes, gain visual strength from their compactness; because the story is compressed into a small area with a minimum of distractions, the viewer can absorb it immediately.

Although dioramas have long been an accepted form of display for museums, their popularity as a hobby is a relatively recent development. Museums have featured dioramas of all sizes and descriptions for many years. A diorama of the 1796 Battle of Lodi was commissioned by Napoleon himself shortly after the campaign and is still on display today in the *Musée de l'Armée* in Paris. The many dioramas in the Science Museum in London and the Smithsonian in Washington are world famous. Natural history museums make frequent use of full-size dioramas to display animals in their natural habitat. Museum displays are well worth seeing and can give you ideas for your model work.

The fellow who builds dioramas in his basement or on his kitchen table is of necessity working on a much smaller scale than a museum. He must tailor his efforts to his much more limited display space once the work is completed. But even within these practical space restrictions the hobby is quite a recent development.

As a hobby, diorama building has grown out of other model-making hobbies—model

aircraft, armored vehicles, ships, and figures—while remaining a distinct branch of each. In a sense, diorama building really does not exist as a hobby in its own right, but only as part of these other hobbies. Aircraft modelers build aircraft dioramas, armor enthusiasts build armor dioramas, ship modelers build ship dioramas, and figure painters build figure dioramas, with little or no crossover between them. None of the four groups seems to have much awareness of what the other three are doing.

This book is for all modelers who wish to use dioramas to display their work. Regardless of the type of models, the techniques involved are very much the same, and I hope that the modeler working in one area will bear with me and tolerate specific attention given to the other three.

Your approach to dioramas will vary, depending upon your modeling experience and area of primary interest. If you're an aircraft or armor modeler, you'll want to focus attention on the machines you are modeling, and you'll want to use the dioramas to set them off. If you're a figure modeler, you'll probably want to tell a story. Your approach to dioramas will depend not only on your own attitude toward your hobby, but also may vary from one project to another. A favorite aircraft or vehicle may qualify for a simplified treatment that focuses attention on the centerpiece, while other models become minor players in story dioramas.

For armor and aircraft enthusiasts, dioramas offer a chance to place a subject in a historical context or to illustrate an aspect of the real thing that is not easily discerned from the model itself, such as a hand-started prop on an aircraft. To the figure painter, tired of doing individual figures on individual bases, there is the opportunity to put several of them together in a related grouping.

The skills you'll need. The diorama builder must not only master the skills of his particular area of interest, but must also learn landscaping, weathering, figure painting, simple scratchbuilding, and working with new materials. If he ventures into shadow-box dioramas, he must learn some basic electricity, too. This broad area of new skills often scares away would-be diorama modelers. With no previous experience, the first diorama seems to present a formidable obstacle indeed.

This need not be the case. A few basic techniques, which can be mastered in an evening or two, are all that you really need to get started. From there you'll be building on your foundation techniques by adding a few new tricks to your repertoire with each new project. You'll be surprised at how rapidly your abilities expand this way, and in six months you may well find yourself doing things that

you never dreamed of being able to do when you started.

No techniques in this book are beyond the ability of an average modeler, but this is not a book for outright beginners. It describes how to place models you have already built into a setting, not how to build the models themselves. If you are just starting out in plastic modeling, you would probably be better off to get a few models under your belt and learn the basic techniques. Soon you'll be ready to try your hand at dioramas.

If you've never built a diorama before, relax. This book is for you. The dioramas described in the seven step-by-step chapters are introduced in the order of their difficulty. You can start with a simple scene, and as you gain experience and confidence in your ability, you can proceed to more complex projects. Just putting a finished model on a landscaped base is a good start, and more important, it's the first step along the road to more ambitious projects. You'll be pleasantly surprised how quickly your skills develop once you start working.

It is important to point out that there is no single way to do things. Modeling is always a very personal endeavor, and methods that work well for one person may not work at all for another. I know capable modelers who have trouble getting results the way I do things, while some of their methods are equally baffling to me. For this reason I will try to give alternate techniques whenever possible. If one way seems to be giving you trouble, try the other. Any method that works for you is the right one.

You don't need to be an artist to build fine dioramas. Although some viewers consider dioramas an art form, few people who build them have any formal art training. If you can assemble and paint a plastic kit, you can build a diorama—you needn't be a sculptor, illustrator, or designer. People trained in these areas may have a momentary advantage in some aspects, but they also have a lot to unlearn. Basically, building a diorama is a process of taking existing elements from plastic kits and elsewhere and combining them into a scene. A diorama is only as complicated as you care to make it. All that is required is basic modeling skill, a bit of self-confidence, and some imagination.

Imagination, more than any other ingredient, is the key to building successful dioramas. Imagination comes into play in many areas—choosing a subject, layout and planning, and selecting and using materials. You have much more imagination than you give yourself credit for, but it may never have been exercised. If you make an effort to seek innovative solutions to problems as they arise, you will find that your ingenuity and imagination grow with experience.

CHAPTER ONE

Ideas and Planning

Of all the steps in building a diorama, planning is most important and most frequently overlooked. Most dioramas that miss the mark usually do so because of critical planning errors before construction is even begun. Designing a diorama is not difficult, but it's always worthwhile to make sure that the basic concept of your diorama is well thought out and that the way you intend to carry it through is practical and sound. Planning is the foundation on which your diorama is to be built, and whatever time you devote to ensuring the strength of that foundation is time well spent.

Ideas. All dioramas begin with an idea. How do you find an idea? A good way to start is to ask yourself just what you want to do with your model. First, what kind of idea are you looking for? Is this a favorite subject that

you want to show off on a simple landscaped base, with as few distractions as possible? Does it have any unusual features that ought to be shown off? Or do you want to show an event or do a story? Sort out which of these goals you want to achieve in the beginning, because they will affect your thinking throughout construction. While it is possible to achieve several goals in a single diorama, one goal must dominate the others, and you will have to be careful not to allow the supporting ideas to usurp its importance.

Keep your primary goal in mind as you work, even after construction begins. When obstacles arise to interfere with your original idea, don't hesitate to make adjustments to compensate for them. You may find that figures have to be rearranged, added, or subtracted, vehicles repositioned, or buildings enlarged or reduced. If you keep your basic goal in mind as you work, you can make such adjustments comfortably as you go along.

Having decided what kind of idea you

want, there are more questions to answer. What are the characteristics of a good idea? How can you tell if your idea is practical? How do you develop it into a diorama?

The simplest diorama is a base that is used to display a particular model. Developing this idea consists of deciding what sort of ground-work you want and how many additional details to include. A single figure is always a good addition. It will not compete with the model for attention and provides a readily understood measure of scale. Moreover, because a viewer's eye will eventually be attracted to the figure, you can position it in such a way as to draw attention to a feature of the model that you want to be noticed. A figure standing near the drive wheels of a tractor,

---

A diorama can simply show off a model (top, model by D. C. Ryan), or it can tell a story (lower left). Your subject will often have special features that you want to show, such as the folding wings on the carrier aircraft at lower right.

1 Show your subject doing its thing. The German sturmpanzer Brummbär was designed for street fighting, so this setting is particularly appropriate.

2 The TBD-1 Devastator was a notoriously unsuccessful aircraft, usually meeting the fate shown here, so in a sense the plane is in its natural habitat in this diorama.

3,4 Scenes like these are natural diorama ideas. Left, "I thought the lines were THAT way!" Right, "Mail call."

Avoid trying to copy a photo exactly. Doing so will only hamper your search for an idea and can severely reduce your flexibility once you start construction. Instead, try to take ideas and details from photographs and combine them into a scene of your own.

Evaluating your idea. Once you have an idea you think might work, evaluate its effectiveness as a diorama. The first thing to bear in mind is that you are working for an audience. Whether you are aware of it or not, you are trying to put your idea across to a viewer. What effect will the idea have on the viewer? Can the idea be put across visually? Certain ideas fail to work in a diorama setting because they are too difficult for the viewer to comprehend just by looking at them. A fighter pilot testing his engine, for example, is difficult to carry off successfully because the action of the pilot is lost in the cockpit. Even if you can get the prop to spin, there is no motion that is characteristic of a pilot testing his engine as opposed to preparing for takeoff or shutting down after landing. However, if the figure in the cockpit is clad as a ground crewman, and another figure is operating a piece of support equipment, the idea, slightly modified, can be put across.

Most ideas have to be carefully thought out to make the action obvious. Consider a scene of a tank crewman trying to clear a jammed .50 caliber machine gun. Basically a good idea for a story diorama, it could lack narrative strength if not handled properly. Just placing the man's hand on the cocking lever is not enough to carry the idea across—after all, he could just be cocking it. But if you emphasize the jam by opening the feed cover and making the figure really strain to pull back the cocking lever, the idea begins to click. Placing the tank at an awkward angle in a ditch with a dead crewman slumped over in one of the hatches dramatically sharpens the urgency of the situation, and all of a sudden you've got yourself a dynamic idea!

Artistic license. Occasionally, you have to take a few liberties with the facts to put your point across. Call it artistic license. The degree to which you are prepared to do this is

for example, will serve to emphasize how massive they are. Positioning a figure next to the odd-shaped tail of an aircraft can help ensure that viewers notice this peculiarity.

You can take this a little further by having one or more of the figures engaged in action that shows off some characteristic of the model that might otherwise be missed. For a fighter armed with an unusually large cannon, you might add ground crewmen loading ammunition. For a German armored vehicle with overlapping road wheels, a scene of crewmen trying to change an inner wheel could graphically demonstrate the disadvantage of that design.

When searching for ideas, try to come up with something that shows your subject "doing its thing," performing a task it was designed to do, or otherwise engaged in characteristic action. For armor, this means nothing more than showing scout vehicles scouting and

assault vehicles assaulting. This approach is roughly analogous to museum dioramas that show animals in their natural habitat.

The natural habitat of an airplane is the sky, and any diorama you do of a plane on the ground will show it out of its element. Unfortunately, airborne aircraft dioramas are grossly impractical and very difficult to build. The only things that airplanes do on the ground are get serviced or crash, so the "doing its thing" idea doesn't have much application to aircraft.

If you want to do a story diorama, the search for an idea becomes more involved. Most often, inspiration comes from things we have seen or read in books, so the best place to start is your own reference library. The local public library is also a good source. Local libraries often have unpublished histories of local combat divisions with many unusual pictures.

EMPHASIZING THE STORY LINE

A

B

C

Make sure that your story line is forcefully carried over to your viewer. In **A,** it is not clear that the machine gun is jammed (the soldier could just be cocking it). In **B,** the open cover and straining figure make the jam more evident. In **C,** the location of the vehicle and the dead crewman add urgency and drama, and the jammed gun becomes central and obvious.

very much a matter of personal taste, but even the most straitlaced modeler has moments when he is sorely tempted! I generally don't mind stretching the truth if doing so explains the scene more clearly. In the diorama of the B-24 assembly ship the garish color scheme is an essential part of the aircraft, but it is doubtful that the crew would have started painting the polka dots until they had finished spraying the overall white. I felt it was important to show both operations, so I fudged a little. The spray painting operation without the polka dots would have been dull and uncharacteristic of the assembly ship, while showing only the detail painting would have meant eliminating the technical interest of the spraying equipment.

Bear in mind the sophistication and knowledgeability of your prospective audience. If you are building just for yourself and other modelers, you can delve into some

pretty esoteric stuff, but if your diorama will be loaned to a local library or displayed in your family room where people unfamiliar with your subject will see it, you are better off to keep things simple.

Your idea may have to rely on a caption to put its idea across, although the most effective dioramas, like the funniest cartoons, are those with no caption at all. The tank with the jammed machine gun mentioned above would not be hurt by the simple title "Jammed!", but it really doesn't need it, either. Some ideas may require explanation in the form of a small card placed next to the exhibit. Such a card should, however, be supplementary; if everyone has to read the card to understand what is taking place, the idea itself is probably weak.

Next, there should always be one center of attention, with the rest of the action supporting it. This is true whether the central focus is

an object, such as a vehicle or aircraft, or an event. Too often, modelers go overboard in adding little "scenes within the scene" until the overall impression becomes one of total confusion. A maintenance scene, for example, is always a good subject as long as the various activities of the mechanics support the main action. Even a subplot, such as a crap game in a corner, is acceptable as long as it remains in the background. If there are too many subplots, the main action is lost and confusion sets in. Always select a single major focus of attention with no more than one or two subplots, put it near the center of the diorama, and subordinate everything else to it.

Is your idea practical from a standpoint of size? Many ideas develop size problems when you start working with them. In a photograph or painting you have the option of "cropping down" to your subject, but in a diorama this option is severely limited. Two pilots in conversation next to the nose of their B-24 makes a nice photograph because you see only enough of the big bomber to recognize it for what it is. If you tried a diorama of the same scene, similarly cropping off all but the nose of the B-24, the effect would be ludicrous. The section of airplane would look just like what it is—a section of an airplane. You can usually crop off sections of buildings, fences, and similar features and maintain the impression that they continue beyond the edge of the diorama, but you can't crop vehicles or aircraft. All you can do is select a smaller vehicle or reduce the conversation to a subplot. If your diorama idea depends upon a large vehicle as a *supporting factor,* you can anticipate trouble with size.

Space problems will also arise because, except in shadow boxes, you don't have the luxury of perspective. At first glance, a fighter plane up on blocks to zero its guns seems to be a good idea for a compact diorama. But if the idea is going to work, you have to show the target the plane is firing at, and that would be 50 yards away. Even in 1/72 scale that comes to 24″ of open, empty space between the plane and the target, and your compact diorama has suddenly grown out of control! Similarly, a scene showing a single partisan cutting telegraph wires seems simple until you realize that supporting the wires requires another pole the proper distance away on either side. The net impression changes to a long section of telegraph poles with the partisan thrown in as an afterthought. One solution might be to scatter additional partisans around the base of the pole to restore balance. Another might be to crop the scene back to one pole by using stiff wire that could be cut off a short distance to either side of the pole. This might turn out to look like a television antenna, so you'd better experiment before going ahead with it.

5 All of the painting operations on this assembly ship probably would not have been done at the same time, but the painting idea comes across much more strongly if the operations are shown that way.

6 A busy aircraft scene requires a lot of activity to fill the space around the model. I posed Monogram's B-26 on a factory assembly line to provide justification for plenty of detail.

7 Small humorous touches are easy to add. Note the patch of yellow snow at the base of the trees.

8 The preliminary layout for a simple diorama is done by using the model, a ruler, and a few cardboard strips to establish the rough borders around the main subject.

Large airplanes create a problem of a different sort. A model with a length of 19" and a wingspan of 24" will cover very little of the large base it requires, leaving vast open areas in front and in back of the wings. If you want to create a busy impression such as a maintenance scene, you'll need a lot of figures and equipment to fill the empty space. Sixteen figures may overwhelm a P-51 Mustang, but they don't have much effect at all on a B-29.

Humorous ideas. Do you want to be funny? Humorous ideas are among the most difficult to carry out; they require thoughtful planning if they are to work. There are three kinds of humorous dioramas: the major gag, where the humor is the central theme; the minor gag, which plays a supporting role, either to a major gag or in an otherwise serious scene; and the delayed-reaction gag, which depends upon the viewer not seeing the humor immediately.

A major gag diorama is a cartoon in three dimensions, but there is an important difference. A cartoonist, working on paper, can eliminate distractions and simplify details to focus attention on his joke—as a diorama builder, you can't do either. Major gags are difficult to carry off successfully. If you're doing a major gag, make sure that it dominates the scene—the joke must be the first thing the viewer sees. Keep your scene as small and simple as possible, because jokes that are funny as

quickly drawn cartoons are out of place done in oils on a large canvas. Finally, if a joke is your major attraction, it had better be funny. Nothing looks more foolish than a joke that has gone flat!

Minor gags, on the other hand, are not overly difficult and can add a lot of fun to your dioramas. Be careful that these touches are

DEVELOPING A STANDARD THEME

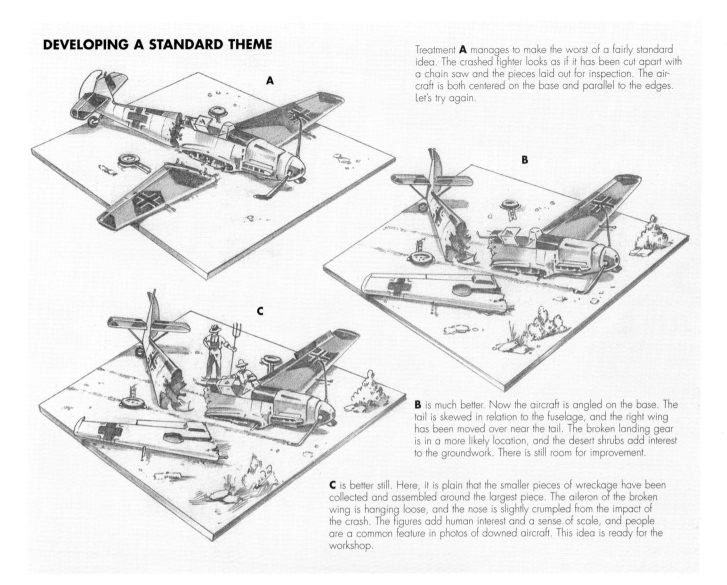

Treatment **A** manages to make the worst of a fairly standard idea. The crashed fighter looks as if it has been cut apart with a chain saw and the pieces laid out for inspection. The aircraft is both centered on the base and parallel to the edges. Let's try again.

B is much better. Now the aircraft is angled on the base. The tail is skewed in relation to the fuselage, and the right wing has been moved over near the tail. The broken landing gear is in a more likely location, and the desert shrubs add interest to the groundwork. There is still room for improvement.

C is better still. Here, it is plain that the smaller pieces of wreckage have been collected and assembled around the largest piece. The aileron of the broken wing is hanging loose, and the nose is slightly crumpled from the impact of the crash. The figures add human interest and a sense of scale, and people are a common feature in photos of downed aircraft. This idea is ready for the workshop.

neither so subtle that nobody notices them, nor so strong that they overshadow the main idea. Ensure, too, that the main diorama idea is compatible with humor; funny touches are out of place if the main theme is very serious.

The delayed-reaction gag is the most difficult humorous diorama to pull off. This is a joke that the viewer does not catch immediately, but that hits him suddenly as he looks closer. To work successfully, this kind of idea requires what comedians call timing. The joke must be arranged in such a way that you have some control over how long it takes the viewer to spot it. What you must do is hide the joke, then give the viewer clues to find it. The more clues, the quicker he finds it, the fewer clues,

the longer it takes. You can never predict viewer reaction with much accuracy; all you can really hope for is that the viewer will not spot the joke immediately, and that he will see it before he loses interest and walks away.

The only way to test humorous ideas is to show a mock-up to several friends to see if it elicits the correct reaction. If it doesn't, discuss the idea with your test viewers to determine how it can be improved, then test it again on someone else.

If your idea meets all of these criteria, it will make a good diorama. But it is still only an idea—and probably a rather vague one at that. The next step before construction is to develop the idea in detail and test it in a three-dimensional format.

Layout and composition. Layout and composition involve recognizing the important features of the subject and arranging the elements of the diorama in a way that sets them off. They are the process by which we translate our abstract idea into physical reality. *Composition* is determining the overall design of the diorama, while *layout* is arranging various parts to fit that design. In practice, all this means nothing more than shuffling the pieces around until things look right. There are, however, a few ground rules and tricks of the trade that simplify these steps. Let's start with composition.

The purpose of composition is to arrange the elements of the diorama so that they direct the viewer's eye smoothly from one part of the design to the next, ensuring that he sees everything and sees the important things first. A good way to begin thinking about how to accomplish this is to analyze how an average viewer looks at your diorama. Generally speaking, viewing is a three-stage process. First, as the viewer walks over to look at your piece, he will glance quickly over the whole scene. If your diorama is properly designed, this glance should be enough to tell him what is going on. He will also see the general arrangement of the larger parts (buildings, vehicles, etc.), but will not have time to notice individual figures or details.

In the second stage, the viewer's eye travels systematically across your diorama, absorbing smaller items missed on the first pass. This second pass will not be very systematic because of the numerous distractions that will catch the viewer's attention. It is probable that his eye will move from left to right, because we are all conditioned that way by reading. An interesting effect caused by this conditioning is that when a column of troops or vehicle is moving from right to left, against the grain, the eye is more likely to pause and notice small details than if the objects were headed in the other direction. This also means that, other things being equal, the right side of the diorama (where the eye stops) is visually stronger than the left.

In the third stage, having had a chance to get his bearings and see what there is to see, the viewer will return to details that caught his attention to examine them further. Awareness of how this viewing process works will be helpful as you develop and arrange the parts of your dioramas.

Designing a simple diorama. Laying out a simple diorama such as an airplane on the tarmac or a vehicle on plain ground is an excellent way to illustrate composition and layout. Since we have only one piece—the airplane or vehicle—there is a distinct limit on the variety of arrangements open to us. All we have to do is figure out how big the base is going to be and at what angle the model will be placed on it. Always make the base to fit the model; never allow the size of an available base to make this decision for you. Bases are easy to make, and nothing looks more awkward than a model on a base that is either too large or too small.

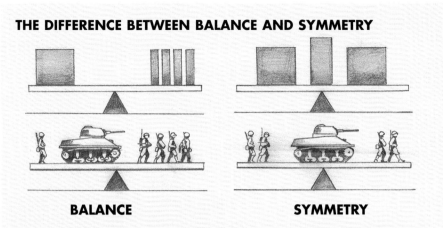

THE DIFFERENCE BETWEEN BALANCE AND SYMMETRY

BALANCE   **SYMMETRY**

While artistic balance is desirable in a diorama, symmetry looks artificial and contrived, because it rarely occurs in real life.

9 A good illustration of a diorama with no element parallel to the edge of the base. The aircraft, concrete panels, and runway markings all run at different angles. Model by Dave Smith.

Set your model on a flat surface. Place it at an angle that you like and use books, rulers, or anything handy to establish a border around it. Give the model some breathing room, but don't overwhelm it with space. For vehicles, 1″ or 2″ of space all around is about right; for airplanes, wingtip to wingtip is fine, but never allow the wings to extend beyond the edges of the base.

In positioning your model on the base you will want to observe an important rule: NEVER PUT ANYTHING PARALLEL TO THE EDGE OF THE BASE. You want to maintain an illusion of snapshot spontaneity to give the impression the groundwork extends beyond the confines of your base. If any element in your diorama is parallel to the edge, it convinces the viewer that the scene was constructed to fit the confines of the base, rather than the base made to fit around the scene. This may seem unimportant, but it is vital. It is also easy to do—*remembering* it is the trick.

Arrange your airplane so that it is at an angle, and unless you are showing a moment just prior to takeoff, angle the seam lines in the concrete a different way. With aircraft it also helps to move the model an inch or so back off center, leaving more room in front of the nose than behind the tail. This provides the impression that the airplane is more likely to go forward than backward. Armored vehicles can run at all sorts of odd angles; even if you show a tank moving down a road, the road should not parallel the edges of the base. Even a slight angle, as little as 5 degrees, is enough to do the trick.

Once you have the model angled the way you like it and have established a perimeter for the base, measure the size of the base with a ruler and you are ready to start work.

Planning a story diorama. Laying out a diorama with more pieces requires considerably more thought. Here, even if we don't have a story to tell, we have certain aspects of the scene that we want to attract more attention than others. We want to control and guide the viewer's perception, and in some cases, we want the viewer to notice things in a particular order. The crap game in the maintenance

BASIC IDEA DEVELOPMENT

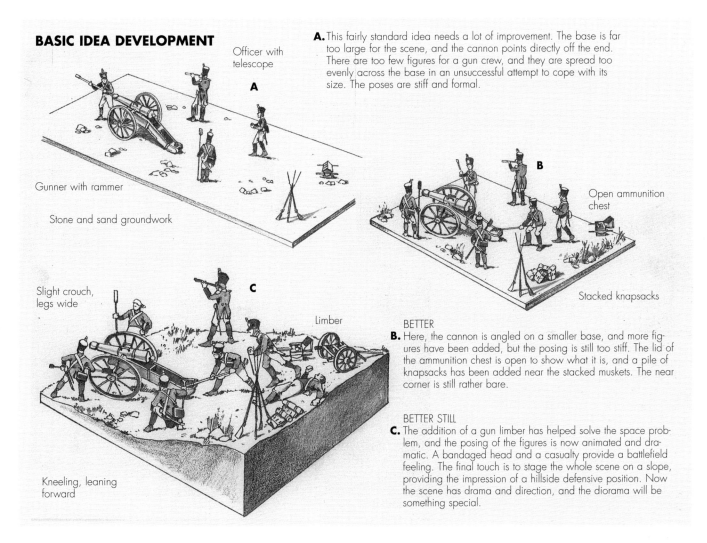

Officer with telescope

A. This fairly standard idea needs a lot of improvement. The base is far too large for the scene, and the cannon points directly off the end. There are too few figures for a gun crew, and they are spread too evenly across the base in an unsuccessful attempt to cope with its size. The poses are stiff and formal.

Gunner with rammer

Stone and sand groundwork

Open ammunition chest

Stacked knapsacks

Slight crouch, legs wide

Limber

BETTER

B. Here, the cannon is angled on a smaller base, and more figures have been added, but the posing is still too stiff. The lid of the ammunition chest is open to show what it is, and a pile of knapsacks has been added near the stacked muskets. The near corner is still rather bare.

BETTER STILL

C. The addition of a gun limber has helped solve the space problem, and the posing of the figures is now animated and dramatic. A bandaged head and a casualty provide a battlefield feeling. The final touch is to stage the whole scene on a slope, providing the impression of a hillside defensive position. Now the scene has drama and direction, and the diorama will be something special.

Kneeling, leaning forward

scene mentioned earlier is a good example: we want to ensure that the subplot is noticed, but not so quickly that it interferes with the main event. Arranging plots and subplots may sound a bit like trying to impose order on a cat fight, but it is not as hopeless as it seems. While we can never predict viewer reaction with 100 percent certainty, we can arrange things so that they work most of the time.

We discovered that there is a pattern in the way most viewers look at things. Now let's look at the ways we can make that knowledge work for us. The best way to develop a design is to start laying out the pieces. You can make some rough sketches if you want to, but don't waste time working a sketch out in great detail, because what looks good on paper has a way of falling apart in three dimensions. Start working with the actual models as soon as possible. If the models are already built or in progress, you can use them to establish rough positions and base size. Even if construction has not begun, you can lightly tack the major parts together to provide a representation of sizes and shapes. If the wheels or landing gear are not yet installed, use blocks, paint bottles, or anything handy to raise the model to the proper

height. Mock-ups of buildings or other major props can be made up quickly from cardboard and later used as patterns.

If your idea includes figures, be sure to include them in your planning, and if you are going to do any pose converting, this is the stage at which you'll want to start working on it. Tack the figures together with modeling clay to establish basic positioning. Take your time with the figures, because in many ways, they are the most important element in your diorama. Don't bother adding equipment or other details, but get the posing just the way you want it.

Don't be afraid to experiment with all sorts of things at this stage. Rearrange the figures and vehicles to see what develops. One idea leads to another, and you may stumble onto a better design than the one you originally had in mind; many of the best dioramas develop that way. You may come across ideas that look terrific, but don't really fit into your current project. Don't force them in where they don't belong; file them away for use in a future project.

Your first concern when laying out your pieces for a story diorama is to think your idea through, item by item. Make sure every figure

and accessory fits comfortably without conflicting with the central theme. There should be a logical reason for everything in the diorama being where it is and doing what it is doing. Why is that figure bending over? Who is that soldier shooting at? Why is this man shouting? To whom? Why would someone put those oil drums there? Is that really the best place to stand while repairing that engine? Why are those weapons stacked over there? Is that mechanic holding the proper tools for what he is supposed to be doing? By asking yourself these questions and others like them, you can tie off many of the loose ends of your diorama before you begin work. Your design will be "tighter" and more logical, and your viewer will readily understand your idea.

Another major consideration is the relative size of the elements in your diorama. If your main event is relatively small, take care that background buildings, vehicles, and subplots do not overpower it. The viewer should not only see your main event first, he should see it immediately. If you find background items are too large, cut them down. If a vehicle is too big, replace it with a smaller one. Bear in mind that the cumulative weight of a lot of little items can be as overpowering as

DEVELOPING AN AMBITIOUS IDEA

A

In this urban combat scene, **A**, no consideration has been given to ending the diorama. The buildings are large, dominating the scene, and the structure in the foreground hides the action. There are not enough figures to show what is going on, and the streets are too narrow to see the action anyway.

B

B is better, but eliminating the foreground building leaves a dead space. The additional figures are another improvement, but they are going off in all directions.

C

C is better still. Pointing the gun at the viewer dramatically indicates the direction of the enemy, and the infantrymen are all shooting and moving in this same general direction. The wrecked jeep effectively fills the dead space, and the overall scene has immediate dramatic impact.

10 Building sizes can be deceptive. The structures in this diorama are scarcely two stories high, yet they appear much taller.

11 Here, the figures provide dramatic urgency, emphasize the purpose of the vehicle, and imply an enemy that is not modeled.

12 A good example of off-center balance in a diorama. The fence and antitank weapon balance the tank, while still creating an interesting and natural scene. Diorama by Dave Smith.

13 It usually doesn't take much effort to fill empty areas. Here, empty ammunition canisters and rough ground vegetation have both been used effectively. Model by Dave Smith.

14 A figure can be an important scale indicator when there is nothing else around to demonstrate the size of an object. In the case of this Civil War naval cannon, I had the figure kneeling, further emphasizing the enormous size of the gun. The ship's cat came about because I needed a reason for the figure to kneel. More important from a diorama standpoint, it provides a simple "story line" for the scene.

one or two big ones. If there is too much going on, don't be afraid to weed some of it out. Even if your diorama shows as much action as a three-ring circus, the act in the center ring should still be the main attraction. If lesser acts will detract from the main event, save them for another project.

Once your viewer has located and identified the main event (phase one of the viewing process) you must guide his eye around the rest of the diorama (phase two). You don't want him to miss anything. The left-to-right viewing sequence is one thing to bear in mind, but there are other ways of guiding the viewer that are even more effective.

Placing and posing figures. Figures are your strongest allies. Pay close attention to where your figures are looking, pointing, or moving. Viewers will instinctively glance in the same directions, and you can use this to great effect. If you arrange the figures in your scene properly, you can direct a viewer's eye from one point to the next—figure A is shouting to figure B, who is standing next to C, who is looking in the direction of D, and so forth. You can also use this effect to direct attention back toward the center of your diorama. By having your figures look back into the center of the scene you can ensure that your viewer does not wander off the edge. This is not to say that all figures at the edge of your diorama should be looking back toward the center, but if they are looking off the edge, there should be a perceptible reason for it. Without such a reason, your viewer will

instinctively try to find one and be confused when he doesn't. For example, one figure looking off the edge is a riddle, while a man shouting and beckoning to someone outside the diorama makes more sense.

If you show troops in combat, don't have them shooting or attacking in several directions at once unless they are clearly supposed to be surrounded. Troops attacking in the same general direction provide a dramatic sense of motion and leave no doubt as to where the off-base enemy is. Watch out for figures standing alone, isolated from the main action. A figure standing alone becomes a one-man subplot, and must have a valid reason for being where he is. A way to link a solitary figure to the main action is to have someone nearer the center talking or shouting to him. Be sure to keep the two figures close enough that the viewer can see the connection; 4″ is about the limit. Often, crewmen on top of a large vehicle or aircraft appear isolated from the main action. This can be corrected by having one figure lean over and talk to someone on the ground, and the connection can be strengthened further if the talking figure points to something (on or off the diorama) and the other figures look in the same direction.

You can also use background details and clutter to channel your viewer's attention. The eye has a natural tendency to travel along long, slender objects. A fallen log, for example, can be used not only to fill up empty space but

also to guide a viewer around a corner and back into the diorama. The log can point to something you want to be seen or can serve as a connector between two objects separated by open ground. You can make this ruse a little less flagrant by pointing the log slightly away from the target so that it serves as a tactful suggestion instead of a direct order. The eye also is drawn toward the tallest and highest objects in a scene, so if an important element of your diorama is getting lost, move it to higher ground.

Balance. Another consideration in laying out your diorama is one that is not likely to affect the telling of your story, but that will have a lot to do with its visual appeal. This is *balance.*

What balance means in a nutshell is this: every diorama has a right side, a left side, and a center, and there should be something to engage the viewer's attention in each part. If you look upon your diorama as a teeter-totter, the weight of visual attractions on one side should be about equal to the weight on the

15,16 To get your story across, you will sometimes have to provide visual clues to what is going on. Don't be too subtle, or the idea will be lost on your viewers. During the planning stages, show your scene to some friends or family members and ask them to explain what they see; if they can do this easily, you know you are on the right track. In this scene set during the early days of the M-1 tank, the clues are the open engine compartment on the M-1, the crew members standing around helplessly, the officers consulting the manual on the hood of the jeep, and the crew of the passing M-60 colorfully expressing their opinion of the situation. Little details can further the story, even if they are not seen right away: the firing simulators on top of the gun tube of the M60, the temporary "aggressor" markings taped to the hull, and the road sign clearly indicate that this scene is taking place on maneuvers on Germany.

17,18,19,20 "On the Green Line" shows an Israeli Merkava on the streets of Beirut in 1982. The idea was inspired by film footage on TV, but I think what really intrigued me was the challenge of doing a scene that was taller than it was wide. I also wanted to show off some of the unusual features of the vehicle, such as its ability to depress the main gun and the large trap door at the back of the tank, which served as both an escape hatch and an emergency entry for wounded or stranded crews from other vehicles.

21 The assembled model is posed on blocks of wood (or anything else handy, in this case a videocassette box). I knew I wanted the road angled to show off the depression of the main gun, and it quickly became apparent that because of the tall building the action need to be moved higher up into the scene. The switchback in the road provides the necessary excuse.

22 The base is now completed (see the closeup picture in the next chapter for its construction) and the figures are posed around the tank. The figure climbing up the wall in the foreground helps to connect the main level visually to the one below it.

23 Always try to place figures at different levels in your scene. All the figures in this case could easily have been at ground level, but it would not have had the visual interest that it does with two of the men standing on top of the turret. The man tying his boot on the right is there primarily to fill what would otherwise be empty space, but I wanted to have him doing something.

24 I liked the idea of showing cavalry and tanks working together in the early days of the World War II, and the mounted officer shows how small the tanks were.

other. If you have a big event on one side, you need a couple of smaller events on the other side to balance it. The same applies to shapes: if you have a large vehicle or building on one side, you need a number of smaller objects on the other. Open space is also a factor in balance. A small object standing conspicuously alone can have as much visual weight as a larger object with less space around it; a single figure can often balance a large vehicle. The ingenious and subtle ways objects can be balanced against each other is something that cannot be learned overnight. Experimentation and observation are your best teachers.

It is important to understand that balance does not mean *symmetry*. In fact, you should go out of your way to avoid symmetry except where it occurs in real life. This is closely related to the "nothing-parallel-to-the-edge-of-the-base" rule. Few things in real life are laid out with a T-square and calipers, so you'll have little use for right angles and exact measurements in your dioramas. Don't be afraid to try unusual angles, shapes, or designs, even with your bases. There is no law that states bases have to be round, rectangular, or square. Trapezoids, ovals, and kidney shapes work well and provide novel and unusual touches. Don't hesitate to experiment with different ground levels in your dioramas. Often, all a conventional idea needs to make it spectacular is one or two elements shifted up to a higher level. There is a wide variety of landscaping excuses for doing this.

Another visual consideration when laying out your diorama is what to do with "dead space"—open ground with nothing on it. You don't want to leave it empty, but don't overfill it, either. Put in just enough to keep your viewer's eye moving smoothly over the scene from one detail to the next. It doesn't take much to fill dead space; leaves on the ground or oil spots on the runway are often enough. Other convenient devices are small shrubs, runway cracks, branches and twigs, discarded

equipment, and irregularities in the ground. Small animals can also be useful. If you can find them, snakes and lizards are good for desert scenes and are relatively easy to make with epoxy putty.

When laying out these minor details, be careful that their arrangement does not appear arranged. Make sure your discarded equipment and fallen branches are strewn about in a random, careless manner. Avoid even spacing and parallel alignments. This is harder than it sounds; it requires a conscious effort to be random. I have seen excellent battlefield scenes that looked artificial because the battlefield debris was as carefully selected and laid out as the stones and flowers in a Japanese rock garden. The arrangement, though seemingly random, was just too perfect to be natural.

Finalizing your design. Don't hesitate to spend a week just fiddling around with the pieces, rearranging them to ensure the design you finally settle on is something you'll like.

25 It's hard to make a vehicle look as if it is moving, because it is not. The best you can do is to pose the figures as if they were in motion. In this case having the jeep turning the corner on two wheels helps to get the idea across, too.

26 To give the action a dramatic sense of direction, have most of the figures facing the same direction, even if one or two of them are looking back.

27 Composition is important, but it is more a matter of instinct than planning. Fill your space well, and use the direction figures are facing, pointing, and shooting to guide the viewer's eye around the scene. This little vignette by Bill Horan shows how cleverly this can be accomplished. Add figures one or two at a time as a pattern gradually emerges. As the concept develops, the original posing may change to adapt to newer groupings and poses that work better. This is the reason you pose all of your figures before doing any detail work on them. After an hour or two of experimentation, you step back to look at the results and realize, "yes, that has come together pretty well." As you gain experience with each diorama, the process becomes easier. In fact, it's the part of diorama building that I enjoy the most.

Many of the ideas we've discussed here may well be things you have been doing all along without being aware of them. If you are just starting out, you can use this chapter as a checklist, but as you gain experience, let your instinct and your eye be the ultimate judge. Then, if something doesn't look quite right, the principles discussed here may help you correct it.

Above all, be patient. No matter how long it takes, you must have your idea thoroughly worked out before moving on to construction. When the base size, building design and dimensions, vehicle location, and figure poses and positioning are all firmly established in your mind, you are ready to start building.

CHAPTER TWO

From the Ground Up

Many modelers who devote inordinate amounts of time to their model grudgingly spend only an hour or so working on the base and groundwork of the diorama on which it will be displayed. Neither of these two elements requires a great deal of time or skill. All that is necessary is an awareness of their importance and a few basic techniques. The base forms the frame for your diorama "picture," and just as you would not put a Rembrandt in a dimestore frame, neither should you put your model on a hunk of scrap lumber.

Types of bases. Once you have determined its dimensions, decide what kind of base you will use. Some are more elaborate than others, but none requires a woodworking shop to build. The easiest bases to construct are of plywood or particle board. Use a piece

$3/4''$ to $1''$ thick; thinner material may warp. It pays to buy good plywood, because cheap grades have knotholes and other imperfections that can spoil the edges of your diorama. If you don't have the facilities to cut the wood yourself, you can usually have the lumberyard cut it to your specifications for a nominal fee. You shouldn't have to buy an entire 4' x 8' sheet; most lumber-yards sell scraps.

Once the base is cut, use sandpaper wrapped around a block of wood to sand the edges. The sanding needn't be perfect because you are going to cover the edges, so just smooth down the rough spots. Walnut veneer can be purchased in 1''- or 2''-wide rolls at your lumberyard or hardware store. Standard length for a roll is 6', enough for one base. To apply the veneer, cut a strip the length of one of the sides, leaving an extra $1/8''$ at each end. Brush an even coat of white glue onto that edge of the base. The veneer manufacturers suggest contact cement, but I have found that this leaves too little time for adjustment. Glue

the veneer in place with white glue, aligning it with either the top or bottom edge but allowing it to overlap on the other three. Press out air bubbles with a block of wood and set aside to dry. Later, trim the excess veneer off roughly with a scissors or craft knife and use your sanding block to sand the edges of the veneer flush with the base. Repeat this process for the other three sides.

Your base is now ready to varnish. Any clear finish is fine, but I prefer clear lacquer in an aerosol can because it dries fast and is easy to apply. Proper finishing will require about three coats. With open-grained woods such as walnut, sand lightly between coats with fine sandpaper to help fill the grain.

There are several variations of the plywood and veneer base. The first involves applying veneer to the top edges as well as the sides.

Note the colors of the sand and the scrubby desert vegetation in this World War II North Africa scene.

STRIPWOOD EDGING FOR BASES

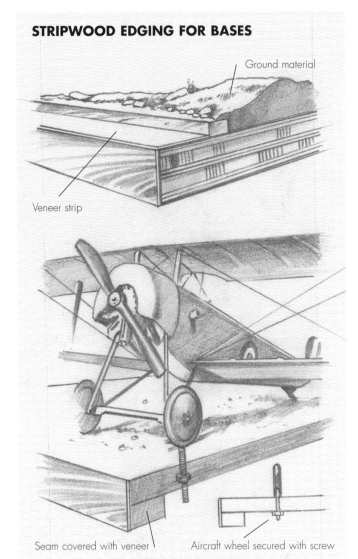

Ground material

Veneer strip

Seam covered with veneer

Aircraft wheel secured with screw

Veneer the edges in the usual manner, then cut a strip of veneer slightly longer than one side, hold in place, and trim to exactly the right length. Cut each end to a 45 degree angle with scissors. Glue this piece down, aligning it carefully with the edge. Lay the next piece in place and use the angle cut in the previous piece to draw the matching angle. Cut, test the fit, cut the other end to 45 degrees, and glue. Repeat the process for the third and fourth sides. You will have to match angles at both ends of the fourth piece, but if you take your time it is not hard.

Another variation is a small containing ridge on the base for your landscaping. Use the small strips of basswood available at most hobby shops—⅛" square is about right. Cut the strips to length, then cut the ends at an angle greater than 45 degrees. Since the landscaping will cover all but the vertical edges of the strips, there is no point in attempting a perfect mitered corner, and an angle of more than 45 degrees will ensure a neat joint where the strips meet. Stain the basswood to match the veneer and glue it in place.

You may find it useful to incorporate a similar ridge at the bottom of your base. This creates a hollow space under the base that is useful if you use nuts to attach your model to the base or when wiring must be run underneath.

The size of the ridge will depend upon how deep a recess you require. Install the ridge before applying any veneer. Cut the corners to more than 45 degrees to ensure sharp corners, and allow the strips to slightly overlap the edge of the plywood. Sand them flush after the glue has dried, then veneer over both plywood and ridge at the same time in the usual manner.

Yet another type of base is the picture frame, nothing more than a piece of thin plywood set into an ordinary picture frame. This type of base requires a frame with a raised center. Ready-made frames come in many standard sizes suitable for diorama bases. Don't try to save money by making your own frame at home—frame assembly requires precision cutting that calls for precision machinery. Custom-made frames are expen-

sive, but there are shops that specialize in do-it-yourself framing. They cut the wood to your specifications, and you nail it together in their shop using their clamps and materials (they'll even show you how). This is an inexpensive way of making an attractive base. Fill the center of the frame by tacking in a piece of plywood.

Glass or plastic display covers must be custom-fitted to the base, so you must decide whether you want a cover early in the game. A cover will keep your diorama dust and damage free, but it can be expensive, even if you build it yourself. Consult the Yellow Pages of your phone book for a supplier of acrylic plastic. Most plastic manufacturers provide booklets with step-by-step instructions on how to cut and assemble their product.

Earth and rocks. The first step in ground texturing is to prepare the base. If you have any significant terrain features, such as roads or trenches, mark their locations. Give the base a quick coat of varnish to seal it against moisture from the ground-making material.

1 This runway surface is sand-textured plywood. Note the oil stains and the tufts of grass growing up in the concrete expansion seams.

2 Dave Smith used mat board for the runway under his A-10. Note the subtle surface texture, the cracks, and the runway markings. The Tactical Air Command crest is a decorative touch.

3 The snow in this Battle of the Bulge diorama is Celluclay painted white. To simulate areas of bare ground, I sprinkled on small patches of sand, painted them brown, and dry-brushed white around the edges to make smooth transitions.

Although there are many materials that will produce satisfactory terrain, my favorite is a commercial papier-mâché called Celluclay. It mixes with water, is relatively clean to use, usually dries overnight, and has a nice, earth-like texture. It can be mixed with powdered color to pre-color it, but I don't often bother with this.

Prepare your Celluclay by piling a small amount of the dry material in the bottom of a mixing bowl. You will eventually develop a feel for how much material a given job will require, but in the beginning it is better to mix up too little and have to make more than to mix up too much and have a lot left over. Mix in water a little at a time. A drop or two of dishwashing detergent or window cleaner will serve as a wetting agent, overcoming the natural resistance of the dry material to the water. Knead the Celluclay with your fingers until it

is thoroughly mixed, adding water until the mixture has the solid, gooey consistency of bad oatmeal. Draw off excess moisture with a paper towel. If the Celluclay is thin and runny, it will shrink when it dries, showing the outline of blocks or figure bases underneath it.

The final ingredient in the Celluclay recipe is a generous dollop of white glue to help the mixture adhere to the base. If you don't add white glue, the Celluclay tends to curl up at the edges. The amount of white glue is not critical, but it is better to have too much than not enough. A tablespoonful is about right for a blob of Celluclay the size of a scoop of ice cream.

The easiest and most efficient way to mix Celluclay, either natural color or tinted, is in a food processor. Toss in the required ingredients, throw the switch, and a few seconds later you will have a smooth working paste. Clean

the machine thoroughly with water when you are done or your next milkshake may taste of groundwork!

When the mixture is at its gooey best, transfer it to your base and use your fingers or a rubber spatula to spread it to the edges, leaving slight rises and hollows in the ground. Smooth the material neatly down at the perimeter with your finger. Excess Celluclay can easily be wiped off the edges of the base while still wet, but you may want to cover the veneer with masking tape while installing and painting the ground, particularly on a large project. At this time you should install buildings, figures with bases, and any accessories that must be embedded in the ground. Work the Celluclay up to and around them with a small screwdriver or similar tool.

The next step is ground texture. Stay away from the sand, gravel, and earth sold in hobby shops, because these materials are far too uniform to be realistic. Unless you are modeling a crushed-gravel driveway, what you need is a natural assortment of sizes and textures. The best place to find this assortment is the gutter in front of your house. Mother Nature has conveniently deposited there a bonanza of sand, pebbles, and tiny rocks that are perfectly suited to dioramas.

VEGETATION PATTERNS

Trees are usually surrounded by under-growth, unless this is cleared away by man

Ground vegetation usually grows in irregu-larly sized and spaced clusters

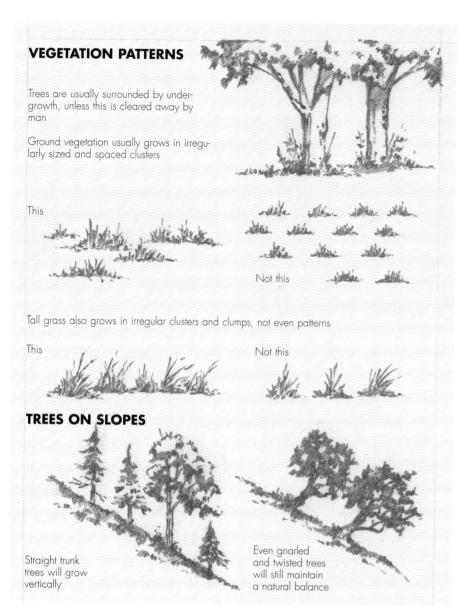

This

Not this

Tall grass also grows in irregular clusters and clumps, not even patterns

This

Not this

TREES ON SLOPES

Straight trunk trees will grow vertically

Even gnarled and twisted trees will still maintain a natural balance

4 Although lichen is difficult to use for trees in larger scales, I found it quite effective in this scene of the fighting in the Normandy hedgerow country.

5 Moss of various sorts makes excellent foliage and effective camouflage.

6 The TBD-1 Devastator diorama features rip-ples made by pressing crumpled aluminum foil into the final layer of clear resin and removing the foil when the resin is set.

Install the rocks first. Set them into the ground, not on top of it. Pay some attention to the topography of the area where your scene is set. Rocks vary in size, shape, and number from one part of the country to the next. If you are modeling farm country, stone walls or irregular piles of rocks should be placed around the edges of the fields. After the rocks are positioned, sift the sand into place using a coarse sieve and tamp lightly into the surface with your fingers. Leave the Celluclay bare to simulate packed earth.

Grass and low vegetation. Unless you are modeling a desert scene, rocks and sand alone will look too desolate. There are several commercial products available to simulate grass, including dyed sawdust and shredded foam rubber. While the foam products are adequate for smaller scales such as HO and 1/72, in larger scales they look like just what they are—foam. The best product I have found is Boyd Models "Static Grass," a form

of fiber flocking manufactured in Germany for model railroads. Static Grass consists of millions of little individual blades of grass, from $\frac{1}{16}$" to $\frac{1}{8}$" long.

To apply Static Grass, brush white glue onto the areas you want to cover, then sprin-kle on a generous amount. Gently blow off the excess; this action will also make the remain-ing fibers stand upright.

Dyed sawdust and shredded foam, while inferior in appearance to Static Grass, do occasionally have their uses. They are applied in the same manner as Static Grass. Sawdust, an old standby used by model railroaders, is effective in the larger scales. Be sure to buy brown sawdust sold as "earth" rather than the garish, phosphorescent green "grass." You are going to paint the stuff anyway, but if you should miss a spot, the brown will not be as obvious as the bright green.

Additional low vegetation such as bushes, crabgrass, and weeds can be made from a number of materials. This is one application

where shredded foam works well in all scales. Another possibility is to use the gen-uine article, some kind of natural growth. Check with your florist to see what he has. Asparagus fern, air fern, and other decorative growths make good vegetation and foliage.

When all of the ground cover and texture is in place but while the Celluclay is still wet, carefully position your vehicles and figures and press them firmly into place. You want your models to appear to have weight and to sit firmly on the ground. Nothing looks quite as foolish as a 60-ton tank delicately perched on a row of pebbles, with daylight visible under its tracks. On wheeled vehicles, cut or

6a,b,c
These are the steps in the resin and foil method. First, a shallow diorama tray is lined with aluminum foil. After the first resin pour, the model is embedded in it. The foil is pressed into the final layer.

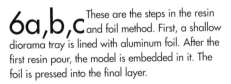

sand a flat onto the bottom of each tire to provide the illusion of weight.

While it is sometimes a good idea to leave vehicles and figures in place until the groundwork is dry to ensure a proper fit when they are replaced after the ground is painted, be sure that you will be able to remove them before painting.

USING STATIC GRASS

1 Sprinkle it on over wet glue

2–Blow gently across the surface

3 Paint when dry

7,8 These examples show water sculpted in epoxy putty. Cy Broman's 1/600 scale China gunboat (top) and my 1/1200 sixteenth-century carrack show how different colors are required for different situations. The muddy river water in photo 7 is especially effective.

When the Celluclay has dried completely (usually overnight, but during periods of high humidity it may take longer), you are ready to paint it. Always paint your ground texture unless you are using foam, which doesn't take paint very well. Bare groundwork and texture may look pretty good, but painting will always improve their appearance and also helps when you come to blend the vehicle with the terrain. Use oil- or lacquer-base paints because these will not soften the Celluclay.

Use an ordinary house-painting brush ½" or ¾" wide. If you have one, there is no reason why you can't use an airbrush for this initial painting. Begin by brushing a liberal coat of thinner over the entire surface. This breaks the surface tension and ensures that the paint will run into all the little nooks and crannies in the ground cover. Mix up a dark brown about the color of polished walnut, keeping the color slightly on the greenish side. Avoid reddish browns unless red clay is a particularly notable feature of the area in which your scene is set (such as Georgia or the central highlands of Vietnam), because the unusual color will attract undue attention. For desert terrain mix a lighter dusty tan. After you have applied the earth color, while it is still wet, mix up a dark green and apply it to the grassy areas. Don't worry if the green and brown blend together a bit where they meet; this is desirable.

Highlighting ground texture. When the first coat of color has dried, preferably overnight, you are ready to highlight the ground texture. Highlighting is accomplished by a technique called "dry-brushing." Dry-brushing is an important technique to master because it is used in many phases of diorama modeling, particularly weathering. Highlighting ground texture is its simplest application, and an excellent way to learn.

The best brush for dry-brushing ground texture is a 1"-wide white bristle artist's oil-painting brush. You will use finer red sable brushes for dry-brushing models, but a coarse brush is better suited to rough ground. Mix a color distinctly lighter than the base coat you applied previously, and dip only the tip of the brush into it. Stroke the brush back and forth a few times on a scrap of cardboard to remove most of the paint, then whisk it lightly across the surface of the ground, just touching the raised surfaces. There should be just enough paint on the brush to deposit color on the raised surfaces; no color should run into the recesses. It may take several passes of the brush to deposit sufficient paint, and in some cases you may even use a scrubbing motion.

Now mix a still lighter shade of the same color and repeat the process, brushing so lightly that you hit only the high spots. Repeat with an even lighter color if necessary. The net effect of this dry-brushing will be light color on the higher surfaces and darker shades in lower areas. This gives your ground a realistic three-dimensional quality. There is no rule that says your highlight color must be derived from your base color, but it's usually easier that way. To lighten earth colors you generally add white, but be sure you work toward a tan color rather than gray. If you find the color changing to gray, add tan. If necessary, start over with a fresh batch of color.

Dry-brush grassy areas just as you did the

• 24 •

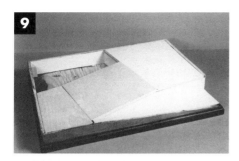

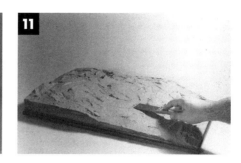

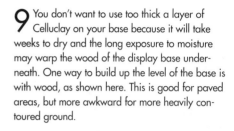

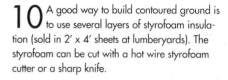

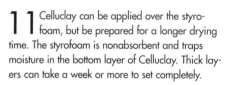

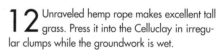

9 You don't want to use too thick a layer of Celluclay on your base because it will take weeks to dry and the long exposure to moisture may warp the wood of the display base underneath. One way to build up the level of the base is with wood, as shown here. This is good for paved areas, but more awkward for more heavily contoured ground.

10 A good way to build contoured ground is to use several layers of styrofoam insulation (sold in 2' x 4' sheets at lumberyards). The styrofoam can be cut with a hot wire styrofoam cutter or a sharp knife.

11 Celluclay can be applied over the styrofoam, but be prepared for a longer drying time. The styrofoam is nonabsorbent and traps moisture in the bottom layer of Celluclay. Thick layers can take a week or more to set completely.

12 Unraveled hemp rope makes excellent tall grass. Press it into the Celluclay in irregular clumps while the groundwork is wet.

13 Most ground in its natural state is covered with a mixture of grass and low shrubs. In this case, the grass is a combination of static grass and hemp rope, with small chunks of sheet moss from the florist for shrubbery. Remember that nature is seldom symmetrical, so scatter your shrubs at random.

earth, using yellowish green instead of tan. You want a lot of contrast, so don't hesitate to use almost straight yellow. Dry-brush a little of your earth color into the fringes of the grassy areas so your greens and browns fade into each other, leaving no sharp edge. This provides a subtle, natural effect.

Runways. Aircraft diorama builders face special problems in modeling runways and hardstands. One solution is to use Celluclay and roll it out flat with a rolling pin—use flour to keep the Celluclay from sticking to the roller. Sprinkle the surface with uniform fine sand (N scale model railroad ballast is ideal), let dry, and paint. This method makes excellent asphalt runways, which usually aren't

perfectly flat. To simulate concrete, apply the fine sand directly to the plywood base. Brush on white glue, sprinkle on sand, and blow off the excess. An alternate method is to use cardboard. Pebble-textured mat board works well; just cut it to size and glue it over plywood. Both sand and mat board surfaces are painted and dry-brushed in the usual manner. Remember that concrete is more often tan than gray, particularly when it gets older.

Concrete runways are made of panels with expansion gaps left between them. These gaps are usually filled with tar which permits expansion but seals out water. The tar seams have a distinct three-dimensional quality that simply painting them on fails to reproduce. Here's a better way. First draw the panel lines

lightly with a straightedge and pencil. Put a quantity of thick black or dark brown acrylic paint (the tube variety that artists use) into a fine-tip syringe and, using the straightedge as a guide, deposit a thin bead of paint along each line. Varying the pressure on the plunger will cause the bead width to be irregular, just like real tarred seams. When the acrylic paint dries, it will be slightly lumpy, just like the original. If it is too lumpy, tamp the seams down lightly while still tacky with a moistened finger, but bear in mind that the acrylic paint will shrink as it dries.

Unless your airstrip is brand new, weather it. As asphalt surfaces get old, they crack and crumble at the edges and display blotchy patches where potholes have been filled.

Concrete gradually cracks and discolors, and grass often pokes through the seams in lightly traveled areas. Cracks can be cut or scribed into the surface with a craft knife or scriber, and grass added with white glue and Static Grass. Simulate discoloration by allowing the initial concrete color to dry thoroughly, then giving it a liberal wash of thinner. While the thinner is still wet, brush on additional concrete shades, allowing them to feather out into a subtle effect. If your scene is posed where aircraft are serviced, add oil and solvent stains. These are made by lightly tapping a brush full of thinned black paint against your finger while holding it 6″ from the runway surface. The amount of paint in the brush, the force with which you tap, and the distance from the ground will determine the number, size, and spacing of the oil spots.

The easiest way to paint runway markings is to spray them, either with an airbrush or an aerosol can, but they can be hand painted if you are careful. When spraying, the easiest form of masking is a wet-paper mask. Position strips of really wet paper (any kind, as long as it's not stiff—even facial tissue will do) the requisite distance apart, soak off excess moisture with a paper towel, and spray. The moisture will hold the paper in place long enough to do the job, and it's easy to remove afterward.

Special terrain situations. The basic methods we have discussed are fine for fairly level ground, but what if you want something with more rugged contours? I'm not talking about mountains, or even foothills, but simple things such as gullies, foxholes, and shell craters. If these features will be no deeper than the thickness of your base they present no great problem; simply cut away enough of your base to make room for them. Use a router, power drill with a ¾″ or 1″ spade bit, or a hammer, wood chisel, and muscle. You are going to cover the holes with Celluclay anyway, so the cutout areas need not be neat. To accommodate deeper holes, add ridges to the bottom of the base. Drill or cut completely through the plywood and form the depression with wire screen or plaster-impregnated bandage tacked over the hole. Then landscape as usual.

A useful feature created by this method is a dry wash. These gullies are created where rainwater washes away the earth because there is no vegetation to prevent erosion. A dry wash is usually a shallow depression, often quite wide and with small "cliffs" at the sides. Its primary advantage as a design element is to provide a convenient excuse to put certain parts of your scene on abruptly different levels. A dry wash on a diorama can be made either by cutting a depression in the base or by adding higher terrain above it.

16

17

14 In Andrei Koribanics' "Eye deep in Hell" the ground work tells the story more than the figure does, showing the horrors of World War I trench warfare.

15 Alex DeLeon could have used simple landscaping on this figure, but the railroad crossing carries the concept to a far more interesting level.

16 Don't be afraid to break up the pavement in an urban scene as Bill Taylor did here.

17 Trees with foliage are a real modeling challenge. When you need a bunch of them, you can use model railroad lichen, which works adequately if you cut it up to avoid the telltale "lichen lumps."

the manner in which you assemble them. They should look as if they are all part of the same large section of bedrock. Model railroaders have developed a number of ingenious ways to build large rock faces. *How to Build Realistic Model Railroad Scenery* from Kalmbach describes these methods and includes other useful information that is applicable to dioramas.

Celluclay alone is often sufficient to model rich, smooth soil, such as plowed fields. Add a few small pebbles to simulate clumps of dirt, but avoid using sand. Plowed furrows can be made individually with a pencil for large scales or collectively with a comb for small scales. If you model armor, remember that tanks tear up the landscape, particularly soft ground and lush grass. Even the lightest armored vehicles completely shred sod, leaving pairs of deep brown furrows in their wake. You can simulate this on your dioramas by using the models themselves to impress track marks in the ground.

Snow. Snow has a powdery surface that plaster alone fails to duplicate. One traditional method for simulating snow is to sprinkle the surface of wet plaster with dry plaster or flour. Flour will yellow with age, but dry plaster works fairly well, although it often looks rather lumpy. I have achieved successful results using Celluclay. Just smooth it over carefully and paint it white. Small patches of sand sprinkled in a few depressions and painted muddy brown simulate bare spots in the snow cover. Use the dry-brush technique to feather the border between the mud and the snow because a sharp edge there is not realistic.

Tall grass. Unraveled hemp rope makes excellent ordinary grass in the large scales and buffalo and swamp grass in the smaller ones. The best material I have found for tall grass in 1/32 or smaller scales is theatrical crepe hair, a material used in the theater for making false

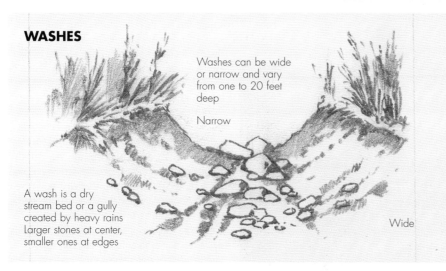

WASHES

Washes can be wide or narrow and vary from one to 20 feet deep

Narrow

A wash is a dry stream bed or a gully created by heavy rains. Larger stones at center, smaller ones at edges

Wide

Small rises can be made with thick applications of Celluclay, but thick sections can take weeks to dry. You are better off to build up underneath with blocks of wood or rocks. If the hump extends to the edge of the base, end it neatly with a simple plywood or basswood riser veneered on the outside. Prominent hillsides or other high features can be modeled with the plaster-impregnated bandage material used to make casts. Arts and crafts stores carry Pariscraft, a brand of plas-

ter-impregnated fabric used as an art material.

Large rocks are easy to model. You can use natural rocks, but be sure to select pieces that are rough and jagged, not smooth or eroded. Coal makes excellent stratified rock when painted, as does redwood bark. To be convincing, whatever you use to represent rocks must be carefully embedded in the terrain; rocks are revealed by erosion, not dropped by helicopters. If you want to model a cliff face, you will have to be careful in the rocks you select and

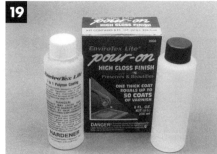

18 A single tree is going to attract more attention, and lichen and sheet moss won't do the trick anymore. Mike Good used an assortment of dried flowers and foliage for the background for Attila the Hun.

19 Envirotex is a thick clear plastic coating. It is simple to use—just mix the two parts, pour it on, and let it dry overnight.

20 Envirotex works perfectly for shallow streams. Just fill the stream bed with rocks and gravel. When the bed is dry and the paint has had time to cure, mix the material and pour it in (model by Bill Taylor).

---

beards and moustaches. It comes in a braided rope and is available wherever theatrical makeup is sold. Several years ago I found a really nice mousy blond color, ideally suited for grass. I've used it a lot and still have more than half the rope left.

To work with crepe hair or hemp rope, first straighten it. Unravel a generous length and soak it in warm water, then stretch it out on the floor with a book or similar weight at each end to hold it taut until it dries. For short scrubby grass you can use crepe hair without straightening.

Before installing tall grass of any sort, color the Celluclay. Otherwise, there will be small patches of natural gray color that are nearly impossible to cover with paint around the "roots" of your grass. Celluclay can be colored by adding a small amount of dry powdered color (available at model railroad shops, hardware, and paint stores). Add powder to the Celluclay mixture a little at a time until the desired color is obtained. The exact shade you end up with is not critical since you are going to paint over most of it anyway—the important thing is to eliminate the gray. A mixture of green and orange food coloring is an adequate substitute for dry pigment, but it may turn dark as the Celluclay dries. The final step before putting on grass is to sprinkle sand on the earth surface.

I have never cared for the traditional method of installing tall grass, which is to drill a series of holes and to push the fiber into them. Unless an awful lot of holes are drilled, this results in unrealistic small clumps that sprout from bare ground at regular intervals. The gluing method I use gives a more natural appearance with less effort.

Begin installation by spreading a generous amount of white glue over an area about 2" square. Using scissors, cut a tuft of crepe hair and press the end into the glue. Add more tufts until the patch of glue is covered, then apply more glue and repeat. Try to keep your grass about the same overall length; you can go back after the glue has dried and trim it to irregular lengths with small scissors. While the glue is still wet, you may want to stir the grass strands with a pencil so that it does not all appear to be growing in the same direction.

Trees. Low vegetation is rarely a problem in dioramas, but trees and bushes are another matter. The difficulty is primarily one of scale. In small scales, a general representation of the irregular shape of the tree and a certain transparent looseness to the foliage are all that are required to make a convincing tree. In larger scales, 1/48 and up, the viewer is able to make out individual leaves, and the traditional model railroad materials tend to look too little like trees and too much like what they are—lichen and foam.

Trunks and branches present no problem; small roots provide an excellent source of both. These can be gathered anywhere when the ground is soft. A single afternoon spent with a small shovel and a shopping bag should provide enough roots to last a couple of years. Look for small shoots and saplings about 2' or 3' high. The quality of the roots will vary from one species to the next. Bushy roots are best; the more branches and little tendrils the better. Be careful not to damage the roots. Wash off the dirt with a hose and let them dry thoroughly in the sun before storing them for future use.

The real problem with trees is foliage. Lichen and shredded foam with fiber matting to hold it together can provide adequate but rarely spectacular foliage, and both must be used carefully. Hobby shop lichen is usually a dreadful color and must be re-dyed in a weak solution of orange or brown fabric dye to tone down the green. Tear the lichen irregularly to break up its neat round shapes before gluing it to the branches. Foam is easier to work with, the colors are better, and the matting material can be pulled and stretched into irregular and realistic shapes.

The most effective foliage material for larger scales is a form of scraggly moss, but even this is better suited to scrub trees than mighty oaks and spreading chestnuts. Effective large trees can be built using a large root and several layers of this moss, but really good results require a lot of time. Each bit of moss must be carefully selected and glued in place. If you embark on a project like this, don't expect to finish it in an afternoon.

Fortunately, large trees are rarely needed on dioramas. In 1/32 scale, a 40' oak is 15" high, big enough to overpower any scene beneath it, so from a design standpoint, you are better off sticking to relatively small trees. You can avoid the foliage problem altogether by modeling dead or shell-splintered trees, or by setting your scene in winter or late fall when limbs are bare.

Evergreens present a slightly different problem. Mosses and ferns, especially asparagus fern, make good evergreen foliage, but it is difficult to find good trunks. For evergreens, you will have to make trunks. For small bushy trees this is no problem; since little of the trunk will be visible, a simple armature of twisted wire is adequate. Larger trees, particularly airy and open types of pines, are construction projects in their own right. A dowel will have to be whittled to a point and holes drilled for the branches. Bark texture can be added with acrylic modeling paste or epoxy putty, and branches cut from roots glued into the holes. Finally, add foliage. The results are spectacular, and you will not need many such trees for a diorama.

Modeling water—sculpting techniques. The traditional method for

modeling water is to form plaster or other material to the desired shape and texture, paint, and use a high-gloss varnish over the paint to achieve the wet look of water. The advantage of this technique is that you can carve or sculpt waves or ripples into the surface with great control. The base material you choose will depend upon the size of the area to be covered. Plaster is best suited to large (2 or 3 square feet), relatively flat bodies of water. The plaster should be distinctly goopy in consistency, easily poured yet still having some body. Shallow waves and ripples can be quickly worked into the plaster with a putty knife, pencil, rubber spatula, or any tools that seem to work. If you want to retard the setting of the plaster to give you more working time, a few drops of vinegar will do the job nicely. It's wise to run some experiments first, because the effect of vinegar on different types of plaster varies.

Epoxy putty or other sculptable materials are suitable for modeling rough water, but they are expensive and time-consuming for large areas. Epoxy putty is the most effective material for simulating heavy seas in ship dioramas. Sculpting epoxy is not terribly difficult, but it does take time. The best tool I have found is a round, blunt-pointed rod: even a pen cap can do the job. The shape of the tool will vary with the scale you are working in: the smaller the scale, the sharper the tip. Experiment with dif-

ferent sizes and shapes until you find the ones you like best. Be careful to apply only the amount of epoxy you can comfortably complete working with before it sets. Large areas may have to be done in several stages.

Sculptured epoxy putty is at its best for rapids and other fresh water applications. No other material is quite as good for violent white water, and the sculptability of the epoxy allows you great freedom and precision in achieving just the effect you want. The biggest disadvantage of epoxy for modeling shallow water is that the material is not transparent, but if you take care in painting you can fake depth quite effectively. Paint the deepest water dark brown, blending this gradually into yellowish brown or rock color where the water is shallower. The blending should be subtle, and is best accomplished with an airbrush or brushed artist's oils. When the colors are thoroughly dry, give the water several coats of gloss varnish and paint in the white water. White water is not all white, much of it is translucent, so the best way to simulate it is to thin white paint considerably, and use successively thicker paint as you work closer to the heaviest bubbles and foam. Use unthinned paint and a stabbing, stippling action with a stiff brush to simulate froth and foam.

If you are modeling oceans, you should know how they work. Ocean waves are caused by wind blowing across the water. These seas

21 Envirotex also works well for large bodies of standing water. Bob Letterman used it successfully for the river in this scene.

travel in the same direction as the wind until they lose their momentum and fade away, and the wind that causes the seas need not be in the immediate area. Seas are not the same as rollers on a beach; they tend to be higher, often much higher, and do not break at regular intervals. The ocean surface is an irregular series of parallel ridges crisscrossed by innumerable small ripples. There are no level areas; the water is always moving either up or down. The height of the seas can vary from 1′ to as much as 60′.

In ocean dioramas you only need to pay close attention to certain aspects of ocean waves. Since seas travel in the same direction as the wind, make sure that all flags are blowing in that direction, too. If your diorama includes sailing ships, make sure that the set of the sails is consistent with the wind direction. You can reduce the distance between seas by as much as half without making them appear grossly unrealistic, a good thing since even in 1/1200 scale, an 800′ interval is 8″.

Ocean water colors are shades of blue or green, depending upon the color of the sky. Stormy seas are gray. Keep at least a touch of green in your color; even the Pacific and Mediterranean, famous for their bright blues,

OCEAN WAVE TOPOGRAPHY

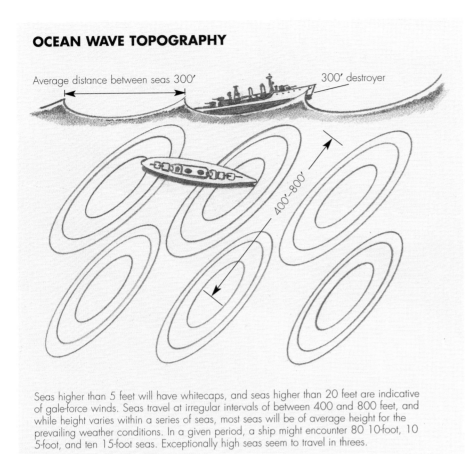

Seas higher than 5 feet will have whitecaps, and seas higher than 20 feet are indicative of gale-force winds. Seas travel at irregular intervals of between 400 and 800 feet, and while height varies within a series of seas, most seas will be of average height for the prevailing weather conditions. In a given period, a ship might encounter 80 10-foot, 10 5-foot, and ten 15-foot seas. Exceptionally high seas seem to travel in threes.

tend toward turquoise. Dark blue seas don't look realistic. I generally paint sculptured oceans with water-base paints and use an airbrush to add color variations, either to indicate shallows or just give a pleasing effect. When dry, I apply several quick coats of clear gloss spray lacquer.

Modeling water—pouring techniques. A technique for modeling water that is gaining great popularity is the use of clear polyester or polypropylene casting resin. This is sold in craft shops for embedding objects in plastic. The great advantage of resin water over sculptured water is that resin is transparent, providing a representation of depth. Objects can be partially or completely embedded in the resin, making them visible both above and below the surface. Resin is ideally suited to modeling slow-running streams, shallow pools, and other water where the bottom is clearly visible. The resin can be tinted with dyes, and an enhanced effect of depth can be achieved by tinting the lowest layer and then making each successive layer lighter until the top layer is perfectly clear. Murky, muddy water can be made by tinting the resin with ordinary hobby enamels.

Resin does have its disadvantages. Its shelf life is only a matter of months, so don't buy any more than you need for the project at hand. *Always work in a well-ventilated area.*

The material sets by a catalytic reaction that can generate a good deal of heat. Pouring it in layers thicker than $1/8$" can cause it to crack at the edges or, worse still, melt the models embedded in it. The resin is a powerful solvent, so test it out thoroughly on any paint or plastic with which it will come in contact. The resins I have used do not seem to affect bare styrene or models painted with water-base paints such as Polly S. Always run a few tests with any material that will be touched by polyester resin.

For applications where the bottom is to be visible, landscape the bottom just as if it were dry land, and paint it with water-base paint. When this is thoroughly dry (wait an extra day or two to avoid any possibility of trapped moisture), pour the resin in successive $1/16$"–$1/8$" layers, tinting if you wish. Whether you tint the water with dyes is a matter of personal taste. For fresh water shallows, a weak golden brown tint can be achieved by mixing small amounts of green and orange dye.

Mix the resin according to the directions. Use a paper cup (no Styrofoam—the resin will melt it!) about half full and add the appropriate number of drops of hardener. How long the resin takes to set will depend upon how much hardener you add. Too much hardener will speed up the reaction and generate heat, which can craze the surface of the resin or

melt a model embedded in it. Too little hardener can cause the resin to take as long as a day or two to set. A setting time of 45 minutes is about right. The second layer can be poured while the first is still tacky, but watch for heat buildup; feel for heat by holding your hand $1/4$" from the surface.

Small ripples can be worked into the top layer of polyester resin water with a rubber spatula or similar tool, but you will have to work fast because once the chemical reaction starts there is a swift progression from liquid to gel to solid. There will be only a few seconds when the resin is thin enough to take ripples yet thick enough to hold them. To eliminate stickiness on the surface of the final resin layer, subject it to a bit of warm heat. Positioning a 100-watt light bulb a few inches from the surface of the water or leaving your diorama on top of the furnace for about an hour is sufficient.

While casting resin can be used for large bodies of water, it is not well suited for modeling rough seas because its natural tendency is to level out. If your diorama calls for high seas with a distinct succession of waves, you are better off working with varnished putty or plaster. Low, choppy seas, however, can be simulated effectively with polyester resin. Here's how.

Begin by building a shallow tray to contain your ocean. This is best built as a permanent fixture part of the display base. Stain and varnish the base and carefully seal the inside seams of the tray with 5-minute epoxy. Paint the inside of the tray blue or green with water-base paint and pour the resin in the usual manner, tinting it to the desired color, usually a greenish blue. Mix in a little less hardener than usual and allow more time between layers to ensure that the resin will not shrink away from the border. Insert your model at the appropriate layer.

The final layer of resin can be textured in two ways. The first is the same poke-and-pull method used for epoxy putty. This method is adequate for calm seas, but you have to work fast, and with an ocean scene you may have a lot of area to cover. In a ship scene, don't forget to add bow waves and wake. Foam and white water around the ship can be painted in once the resin has set.

A far more effective way of texturing the final resin layer is to use crumpled heavy-duty aluminum foil as a press-on mold. Crumple the foil to represent ripples in your scale—the smaller your scale, the more you should wrinkle the foil. Crumple enough foil to cover the entire surface of the diorama. Pour the final layer of resin and push the foil down onto it. The dull side of the foil will give your sea a matte, windblown surface, while the shiny side will give a glossy surface. It will probably

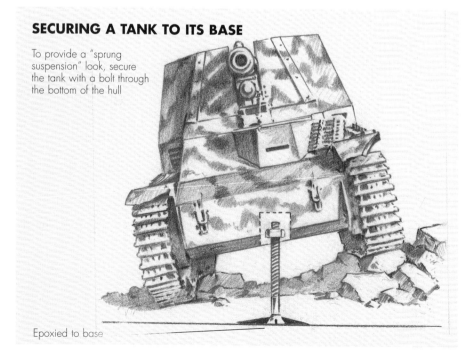

take several foil sections to cover a large base. If you use sections, tear the foil to avoid straight edges in your sea. Be very careful that no resin creeps over the edge of the foil, because if it does, when the resin sets the foil will be permanently embedded in it, a shiny silver reminder to be more careful next time.

When the resin has set, peel away the foil and examine the surface closely. Air bubbles, open spaces, and other imperfections can be patched with drops of resin and swatches of foil. Press the foil down securely to avoid leaving conspicuous circular patches. For scales larger than 1/72, brush on a final thin coat of resin to round out the bottom of the wave troughs for a liquid appearance.

When using the foil technique do not embed your models in the resin if there is a way to avoid it. Working the foil around the edges of the model, particularly small, delicate models, can be tricky. Instead, wait until the water is completely textured and position the model on the water surface. Trace the outline of the model with a scriber, grease pencil, or marking pen, and use a Dremel tool or other hand grinder to cut out a recess for it. For ship models with hollow bottoms, you need only cut a groove of sufficient width to accommodate the edge of the hull. A small amount of resin can be poured into the recess and the model settled in, or the model can be glued in with 5-minute epoxy. The final touch is to paint in white water where necessary.

The crumpled foil technique can also be used for swift-running streams, provided they are fairly level. Twigs and branches can be added by drilling holes in the finished resin and setting them in with resin or glue.

The simplest way of modeling small quantities of water is to use 5-minute epoxy glue. This is ideally suited to ultra-miniature ship model dioramas (1/2000 scale and smaller) and for small streams and rivulets in larger scales. Some epoxies leave a mottled, sticky surface, so you will have to experiment to find a brand that provides a smooth, glossy finish. For ocean scenes, paint the base with water-base paints and apply the epoxy. It is best to cover the entire base at once, but bear in mind that you will have less than 5 minutes to manipulate the material. If necessary,

SECURING A TANK TO ITS BASE

To provide a "sprung suspension" look, secure the tank with a bolt through the bottom of the hull

Epoxied to base

smaller areas can be worked and the entire surface then covered with a final thin coat to hide the seams.

As the epoxy begins to set, use a toothpick to pick out ripples and waves. At first these will gently fall back into the surface, but as the epoxy thickens this tendency will diminish and the waves will remain. Like polyester resin, epoxy is limited to fairly calm seas, and you can't use the foil trick. Epoxy is also good for other small areas of water-buckets, cups, and puddles. The biggest problem in these small situations is the natural tendency for epoxy to crawl up the sides of the container. This is called capillary action, and there is not much you can do about it, other than applying the epoxy in two or three layers.

Fastening models to the base. There are a number of ways of attaching your models permanently to the diorama base. The easiest is just to glue them with white glue or epoxy. If you use epoxy, be sure to touch up any glossy spots with flat varnish. While aircraft models can simply be glued to the base, because of their relatively small area of contact, they are likely to break loose when you can least afford it. For more secure attachment, install pins or short brass wire rods in the wheels of the airplane and drill matching holes in the base. The airplane can then be glued in place, or left secured by only the pins.

22 Clear silicone caulk makes an excellent ocean. For application, see the step by step description in Chapter 9. The foam wake in this case was painted onto the dry caulk with white artist's oil paint (it smears better than hobby paints).

23 The clear water surface for this museum display started with a sheet of clear ¼" plexiglass. It was formed by laying it on a water form sculpted in Celluclay and using a heat gun to relax it until it followed the sculpted contours. It was sprayed with transparent blue and green paint, and then textured with clear silicone caulk. The submarine is actually suspended under water by two brass rods: the periscope and a second rod hidden in the bubble trail of the missile.

24 The bubbles are tiny glass beads used for industrial bead blasting which I found being sold in small packets at a surplus store. The missile exhaust is cotton.

CHAPTER THREE

Weathering Techniques

Many modelers who have never tried weathering have needless misgivings about it. Weathering is not difficult, and careful weathering can cover mistakes in assembly and finishing. There is a lot of truth in the axiom that it is easier to build a dirty model than a clean one. This is not to imply that you can be careless in assembling your models; while weathering will hide certain errors made during assembly, it can emphasize others.

Preparing your model for weathering. During assembly, be sure to remove all visible molding lines and thoroughly putty over and smooth all seams. These flaws may not show on the assembled model, but dry-brush weathering will make them stand out, as it will glue stains and other surface blemishes. Give your finished model a primer coat and then inspect the surface carefully for flaws.

The paint coat on your model will be subject to a lot of abuse, both chemical and physical, during weathering. Both scrubbing action and the use of thinners can lift paint that has not adhered properly to the plastic. Using different types of paint (water-base, lacquer, and enamels) for the initial painting and weathering processes will help eliminate chemical lifting. Before painting, wash the assembled model thoroughly with detergent and a soft brush to remove silicone parting agents remaining from the molding process. Consider painting the base coat with a lacquer-base paint, such as Floquil. This type of paint has a solvent action that provides a "bite" on the plastic surface. Lacquer should be applied using an airbrush so the paint will dry before its solvent crazes the plastic.

An airbrush is an absolutely worthwhile investment for diorama work. There are certain jobs that only an airbrush can do, such as painting intricate camouflage patterns or achieving a smooth, even paint coat on delicate detail, but an airbrush is also an enormous time-saver. An armored vehicle that takes an hour to paint by hand can be painted with an airbrush in about 5 minutes. The dead-flat varnish oversprays so important in modeling can be applied effectively only with an airbrush. An airbrush also provides a slightly pebbled paint surface; such a surface has a property called "tooth" that facilitates dry-brushing.

The manner in which you apply decals will have an effect on your weathering. Using decal-setting fluid to snuggle the decal film down against the surface of the model is imperative, but even this step will not eliminate the tiny ridge of film around the edge of the decal. As soon as you start weathering, the

---

Dave Smith has used dry-brushing to bring out the wood grain in the cargo bed and the molding around the cab door on this transporter model.

1 The clean areas on the windshield of this jeep were made by masking them and overspraying the model with an airbrush.

2,3 Note the oil stains, grease residue, rust and other subtle weathering effects on Jim Stephens' exquisite scratchbuilt World War I Mark IV tank.

decal edge shows. Carefully trimming excess decal film helps, but whenever possible try to use "disappearing film" decals such as those offered by Micro-Scale. These require no trimming, and their application system effectively makes the film disappear. The surface over which you apply decals is especially important. While most model paints provide a flat finish, a glossy surface is best for decals. For this reason, I often paint my models with glossy paints. After applying decals, I then overcoat the entire model with matte varnish.

Matte varnish is also used to correct unintentional gloss finishes and to provide a uniform surface coating on a model prior to weathering. Unfortunately, I have yet to find a 100 percent reliable dead-flat varnish; even the best brands go bad occasionally. Whatever brand you use, never take it for granted. *Always test matte varnish on glossy scrap to make sure it still works before applying it to your model.* Matte varnish that has gone glossy, or worse still, turned white, can ruin any model, and

the damage is virtually impossible to correct.

Finally, you must never try to weather over paint that has not fully dried. This is important. After painting and decaling your model, allow time for the model to cure completely before weathering. A curing period of 2 or 3 days is usually long enough, but leaving the model alone for a week is even better.

Four basic weathering methods are sufficient for most situations: washes, dry-brushing, airbrush effects, and pastel chalks. We'll discuss each technique in detail, then go on to show how they are applied to different models. Once you understand the basic techniques, weathering is largely a process of experimentation. You'll find that the techniques you use will differ not only from one type of model to the next, but also among models of the same type.

Washes. The first step in weathering is often the application of a wash over the basic paint. This is nothing more than greatly

thinned paint that is flowed over the surface so that it accumulates in corners and recesses. Although the primary purpose of a wash is to accent surface relief and bring out detail, washes are often used to simulate oil, grease, and other stains and to alter base colors.

Certain types of paint and thinners are better for washes than others. It is usually wise to stay away from Floquil because Diosol is a powerful solvent that may lift or soften the paint on the model. Washes made from water-base paints have a peculiar habit of looking great when you first lay them on, but often dry to a blotchy, unattractive finish. Although they occasionally turn glossy, paints thinned with turpentine or mineral spirits are my choice for making washes. Experiment with hobby paints and thinners until you find the one you like best. Don't rule out artist's oils, either.

First give your model a light brushing overall with thinner to prepare the surface for the wash. While this dries, mix a small amount of color with a lot of thinner to make the wash. Exact proportions are not important, but what you really want is not thinned paint but tinted thinner. To accentuate detail, make your wash with a darker shade of the basic model color. You can use a black wash, but it is better to add a bit of the basic model color to black. Use a wide soft brush to flow the wash freely onto the model, letting it run

4

4 The faded upper surfaces on this Me109 were done by lightly overspraying them with a slightly lighter shade of the color used on the rest of the aircraft, then adding subtle variations of the basic faded color with pastel chalks.

5,6 My weathering treatment on this Tamiya 1/25 Tiger I includes bent fenders, blackened muzzle, and liberal use of ground color on the lower parts of the tank.

7 Rubber components in armored vehicle running gear won't rust, so carefully research the construction of your vehicle and paint rubber portions, such as road wheel tires, black. Metal parts subject to wear should be rusted bright orange.

into all the small cracks and crevices. Excess wash can be removed by soaking it up with paper towel, but be careful to leave a generous accumulation in the recesses. You may want to wipe some areas clean with a dry tissue or cloth. It is best to apply the wash to large, clearly defined sections of the model; doing small, undefined areas results in blotches with irregular borders of paint around them when they dry.

To simulate oil and grease stains, use more concentrated washes. Apply these stains with a brush in the appropriate areas, brushing the stains downward if they would run and leaving irregular blotches if they would not. You can apply several different colors to adjoining areas at the same time, allowing them to flow together at the edges for an interesting and novel effect.

When laying on your washes, be careful not to overdo it. You want a darker color in the recesses, not straight black. When you dry-brush the model later, the contrast between surface and recessed detail will be increased, and what may look like insufficient contrast after only the wash may turn out to be just right.

Dry-brushing. Dry-brushing is the technique of using an almost-dry brush to apply paint to the raised detail of a model by lightly whisking the brush back and forth over the surface. Dry-brush weathering is a refined version of the same technique we use on the groundwork. The brush we use should be softer, and the effect achieved more subtle and delicate.

The two factors that control the quality of the effect achieved by dry-brushing are the amount of paint on the brush and the consistency of the paint. If there is too much paint on the brush, it will leave a solid patch of color on the model rather than a light frosting. If there is too little paint on the brush, it will leave nothing at all. You can regulate the amount of paint on the brush by lightly stroking the brush back and forth a few times on a scrap of card or cloth before touching it to the model. The second factor, the consistency of the paint, is also important, because if the paint is too thin, even if there is the right amount of paint on the brush, the brush may leave streaks. If the paint is too thick, it will be reluctant to leave the brush, and the brush will deposit rough, chunky blobs of paint on the model.

The desired result of dry-brushing is a smooth and subtle gradation of color, and the type of paint you use can have a lot to do with how well you achieve this. I suggest you experiment with several paints until you find something you like. I get some of my best dry-brushing results with artist's oils, but they take longer to dry than hobby paints. Others mix oils half-and-half with hobby paint, while some modelers use straight hobby paint. Water-based paints can also be used.

The colors you use for dry-brushing will vary from one model to the next. If your model has a camouflage pattern, you will have to dry-brush each of the different colors separately. A good color to start with is a lighter shade of the basic color on the model. Add white to the basic color, adjust the amount

and consistency of paint on your brush, and stroke the brush lightly back and forth over the surface of the model. After you have dry-brushed the entire model, add a bit more white to the paint and repeat the process, this time stroking more lightly and catching only the higher raised detail. Step back, examine your work, and dry-brush again with an even lighter color if necessary. Engraved detail which was barely visible under the basic color should now be highlighted beautifully.

The next step is to repeat the dry-brushing treatment with some of your terrain base color, gradually lightening it as you did the basic model color. Apply the earth shade in subtle irregular blotches, bearing in mind that dirt splotches are most prevalent near the ground. Vary the color of these blotches, adding a bit of brown to the color here, a touch of green there. This avoids a monochromatic look and gives the model realistic "spark." This dry-brushed ground color provides a direct visual connection between the model and the terrain beneath it. This is important, because you want the vehicle to look as if the dirt on it came from the ground.

Effective dry-brushing, more than any other weathering technique, is a matter of "fiddlin' around" until the model looks right. You may find yourself dry-brushing the same area half a dozen times before you get just the effect you want. Don't be afraid to experiment; it is the only way to learn any weathering technique.

When you are satisfied with the dry-brushing effect, allow several days for the paint to dry. When the dry-brushed color is completely cured, you can apply washes over it to tone it down if there are areas where you feel the dry-brushing is too harsh or the color isn't quite right.

Airbrush hazing, feathering, and fading. Most of my weathering is done with a brush, but the airbrush does come in handy once in a while. The forte of an airbrush is applying evenly colored stains with

5

feathered edges, such as soot around exhaust pipes, powder burns around gun muzzles, and grease stains with faded, indistinct edges. The airbrush can also be used as a substitute for a wash to tone down exaggerated dry-brushing. An often-touted use for the airbrush is for applying "dust," but I find that unless the situation calls for a very recent, even dust coating, the effect is unrealistic. Real dust accumulates in corners, crannies, and crevices, and is wiped or blown off exposed surfaces, and this distribution can't be simulated adequately by a couple of passes with an airbrush. While it is not a good duster, the airbrush does do an effective job of "fading" painted surfaces, an operation that calls for a smooth, somewhat transparent coat of color—just what the airbrush is designed for.

To use your airbrush for weathering, thin the paint more, and set your air pressure higher than for ordinary painting. Coverage and opacity are not factors at all, and you want soft feather edges wherever one color meets another. Always experiment on a piece of scrap to be sure the paint consistency and air pressure are correct before using the airbrush on the model. For grease and other stains, simply mix an appropriate color and spray it on in the desired pattern. Simulating faded paint is a little trickier. Light tan or gray is the best color for most situations, and the paint should be even thinner than is usual for weathering. Spray a very light frosting over all upper surfaces of the model, including decals, gradually increasing the coverage until you achieve the desired degree of fading. Be careful not to get carried away and overdo it—it

6

7

TYPICAL WEATHERING FOR A TANK

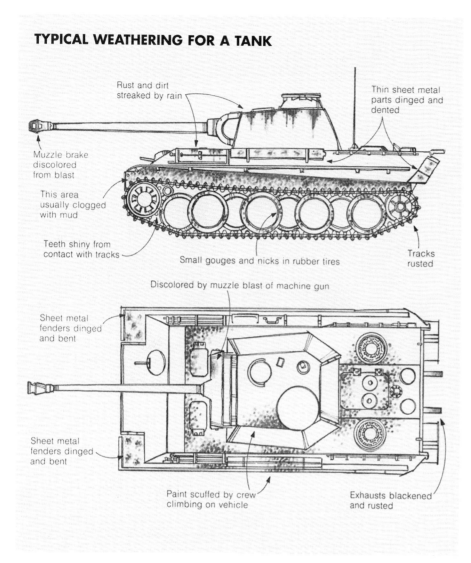

Rust and dirt streaked by rain

Thin sheet metal parts dinged and dented

Muzzle brake discolored from blast

This area usually clogged with mud

Teeth shiny from contact with tracks

Small gouges and nicks in rubber tires

Tracks rusted

Discolored by muzzle blast of machine gun

Sheet metal fenders dinged and bent

Sheet metal fenders dinged and bent

Paint scuffed by crew climbing on vehicle

Exhausts blackened and rusted

can't be "un-faded." Use the same method for toning down dry-brushing.

Airbrushing exhaust stains and powder burns on aircraft takes a bit of practice. These stains start out strong at the source and fade out as they are carried back along the fuselage by the airstream. To duplicate this, adjust the spray pattern down to a fine line. Start spraying at the source of the stain, holding the airbrush close to the surface and gradually pulling it away as you move aft along the fuselage. Practice this effect on scrap until you are confident of your ability to duplicate it on the model. If the stain accidentally becomes too wide, you can thin it by overspraying the edge with the fuselage color.

Using pastel chalks. Pastels are colored chalks which, when ground on a scrap of sandpaper, provide fine powdered color that can be applied with a brush for delicate weathering effects. Many of the effects possible with an airbrush can also be achieved with pastels, and many of the subtle colors and tones possible with pastels are far beyond the capabilities of an airbrush.

Pastel chalks can be obtained at any art supply store. The chalks you are looking for are soft artist's pastels, not hard blackboard sticks. Some shops stock pastel sticks individually, but they are more often sold in sets. A wide range of colors is available. The colors you'll need for weathering are black, white, yellow ochre, burnt sienna, raw sienna, burnt umber, and raw umber. You may want to pick up a few intermediate shades of these, but you can easily mix the powders to make lighter or darker shades.

Grind the chalk to powder by rubbing it on sandpaper, then apply the powder with a soft brush. Don't use an expensive brush, because rubbing it against the sandpaper to pick up the powder will ruin the tip. Broad strokes with a wide brush provide wide, even areas of color, while a scrubbing action gives a blotchy appearance. Using a small brush or the edge of a wide one makes narrow streaks of color. Tapping a full brush against your finger a short distance from the surface gives a spattered effect. You'll be surprised and delighted at the subtle feathered edges and delicate shadings you can achieve. Pastels

work better over matte finishes than glossy ones because the matte surface gives the powder something to grip.

Nothing duplicates dust so perfectly as pastels, and nothing is so simple. Just brush the powder on, blow it around a bit, and—because it's essentially dust itself—the material does the rest.

The primary disadvantage of pastels is that they are not permanent. Artists working with pastels usually spray their finished work with a clear fixative, but this is unsatisfactory for models because the fixative spray can drastically alter the colors, particularly light ones, and subtle effects can disappear altogether. Although unfixed colors will not change with age, the powder rubs off easily and shows fingerprints if you handle the model. For this reason, I apply pastels last; in fact, I usually wait until the model is permanently attached to its base so that the model itself will never have to be handled at all.

Weathering armored vehicles. Tanks and other armored vehicles seem to attract dirt like small children; grubbiness is an essential aspect of their nature. Even a freshly washed tank gets dirty driving the 50 yards from the washrack back to the motor pool. Whenever possible, refer to photographs of tanks in the field to see how tanks weather. These are your best source for information, and will ensure that your weathering is realistic. If something doesn't look quite right when you are done, go back to the photos to see what is wrong.

Since tanks are made of steel, let's start our discussion with rust. The vehicle is painted to preserve it, but areas that are subject to wear lose their paint and quickly start to rust. Where the climate is damp, rain running down the sides of the vehicle will carry streaks from the rusted areas. The areas most likely to wear are edges, corners, and projections where objects strike the vehicle. Similar damage is done by crew members climbing aboard; there are usually two or three routes which will be badly scratched and scuffed. Because of constant wear, these areas are less likely to rust, but they will show up as bare metal. Shiny metal can be duplicated by gently dry-brushing gunmetal paint (mixed silver and black) onto the surface. Keep the brush drier than usual and use a scrubbing motion. Rusted areas are treated the same way, using a dark burnt-orange color. One or two small spots of bare metal and rust are more than enough.

Tracks are the only parts of a tank that are not painted at all. These quickly take on the color of dark rust, except where the rust is worn down to bare metal by contact with the running gear and the ground. These bright spots will rust bright orange overnight if the tank is not in motion. The best way to rust

8 This battle-weary B-17 has finally seen one mission too many. Note the faded paint on the wings, the oil and exhaust streaks, the mismatched paint covering old wounds, and the chipped paint around the extensive flak damage.

tracks is to paint them overall dark brown, then dry-brush brighter rust onto the raised surfaces. Finally, dry-brush gunmetal where the rust would wear off. An excellent substitute for gunmetal paint is powdered graphite applied with a brush; rubbing with a soft (No. 0) lead pencil also works. Don't forget the rims of metal road wheels and teeth on the drive sprockets, all of which would be worn bare by the tracks.

Another aspect of weathering armored vehicles is adding terrain texture to them. In dry country the tracks will be covered with dust, and where the soil is moist the entire undercarriage will be clogged with mud. The sides of the hull will be encrusted with a mud layer several inches thick, as will the road wheels, idlers, drive sprockets, suspension arms, and anything else less than 4′ from the ground. If the vehicle has recently crossed a field, chunks of turf will be pasted throughout the system. The mud can be duplicated with Celluclay mixed with more white glue than usual and gooped all over the suspension before the model is painted. Don't overdo it; 2″ of mud in 1/32 scale is only ¹⁄₁₆″. Sprinkle Static Grass over the Celluclay and mush it into the "mud." Paint and dry-brush the mud and turf as if they were on the base, but remember that mud is much darker than dry earth.

Dry-brushing is particularly effective in armor modeling for applying the overall coating of dust and dirt to vehicles. Start out by giving the entire model a wash of dark green,

brown, or black, then dry-brushing with a lighter shade of the base color used on the vehicle. Continue dry-brushing using progressively lighter shades until you are satisfied, then dry-brush again with several variations of the terrain color to add dirt, dust, and general grime. You want a rough, splotchy effect, so use a scrubbing action with the brush.

Add black pastel smoke stains around the exhaust system and powder residue on the muzzle brake if the tank has one. Mufflers and exhaust systems rust badly from heat; dry-brush these with rust. You can get an effect of encrusted rust by painting the muffler and, while still wet, dipping it in baking soda. Then repaint and dry-brush. Pastel dust can be added as a final touch, but don't dust a muddy tank.

Aircraft weathering procedures.

Airplanes do not get nearly as dirty as tanks, but neither are they as clean as they often appear at a distance. They may not get covered by mud or dust, but oil leaks out, surfaces get scratched, and paint fades, stains, and chips. The next time you fly on a commercial airliner, take a close look at it. Although it looks immaculate from a distance, when you get up close you can see that the wing surfaces are streaked and the landing gear is dirty and oily. Only private planes and the colorful U.S. carrier planes between the wars were maintained to a really high standard of polish, and even today's private planes are not perfectly clean.

The dirt on aircraft reflects their operating conditions. Combat aircraft which see long service with only sufficient maintenance to keep them flying are pretty well battered, while peacetime aircraft that don't log a lot of flying time remain quite clean. Aircraft stationed in arid areas will fade and accumulate

dust more quickly than those operating in temperate climates.

How quickly paint fades also depends on paint quality. Certain aircraft were more prone to fading than others. The olive drab used by the U.S. Army Air Corps early in World War II not only faded badly in sunlight but even discolored, gradually shifting almost to purple. Fading and color shifting are best accomplished with an airbrush or pastels.

Worn paint takes two forms: scuffed paint, where abrasion has gradually worn through, revealing bare aluminum underneath (usually found alongside the cockpit and other areas where crew members walk), and flaked paint, where the finish has pulled off in irregular chunks. Scuffed paint is easy to simulate by dry-brushing with silver or gunmetal. Scuff only those areas where foot traffic is likely (beside the cockpit, near the fuel tanks and ammo hatches) and avoid areas where walking was not permitted ("no step"). Flaked paint is most often found around the engines, where heat gradually weakens the paint and frequent removal of access panels causes paint to flake off around panel edges, screws, and fasteners. Paint also tends to flake along the leading edges of wings, cowlings, and stabilizers. This phenomenon was particularly common in the Pacific, where the prop blast would blow up loose coral from the runway and scour the wings with it. Japanese aircraft were particularly vulnerable to this form of weathering, and planes with nearly half their finish blasted off were not uncommon.

There are several ways to model flaked paint. The simplest is to carefully paint the chipped areas with silver or gunmetal. This is the method I usually use. Another method is to underpaint the aircraft with silver, allow several days to dry, and then dab on tiny

TYPICAL AIRCRAFT WEATHERING

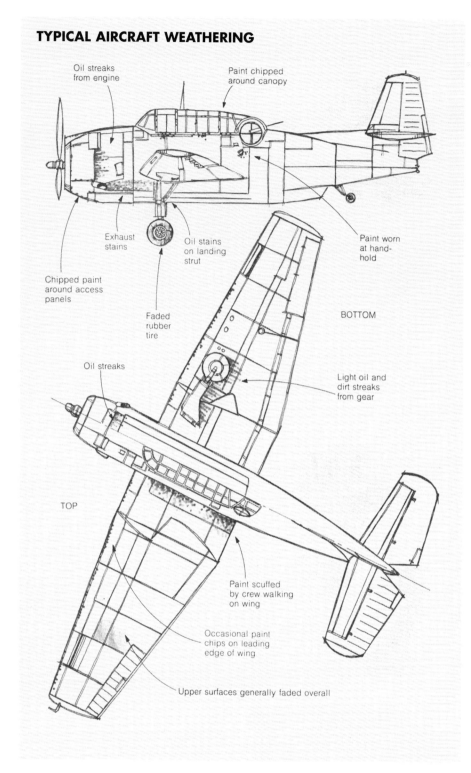

Oil streaks from engine

Paint chipped around canopy

Exhaust stains

Chipped paint around access panels

Oil stains on landing strut

Faded rubber tire

Paint worn at hand-hold

BOTTOM

Oil streaks

Light oil and dirt streaks from gear

TOP

Paint scuffed by crew walking on wing

Occasional paint chips on leading edge of wing

Upper surfaces generally faded overall

hydraulic systems. Such stains are caused when a small amount of grease or oil leaks from a hinge or fitting. There are a number of ways of making stains and streaks, but all involve applying a small spot of black or brown and using a moist tissue to streak it back. You can use a spot of hobby paint and wipe with thinner or a black felt tip pen and wipe with water. The felt tip pen method has the advantage that you can wipe the streak off and try again if you don't like the result, but the final streak should be oversprayed with a matte or gloss varnish so that it won't smudge.

Exhaust stains, when present, come in two different colors. Some are mostly black, while others have a brownish gray color; some aircraft show both at once. The gray shows most prominently on black and dark blue aircraft. When both colors are present, the stain is usually black near the source, gradually shifting to gray. These stains are best made with pastels or an airbrush. Powder residue stains from gun muzzles are common only on aircraft where the muzzles do not project from the wings or fuselage, and even then, they only extend back a few inches from their source. Similar stains may be found behind the rectangular casing ejection chutes under the wings.

Don't forget to weather the landing gear on your aircraft. Small amounts of grease and oil inevitably leak out of the gear, even on the best-maintained planes. This leakage is easily duplicated by a black or dark brown wash splashed over the entire gear, accented by a few vertical streaks applied with a brush. The strut itself is cleaned by its motion and should appear bright silver. Don't overlook the wheels on your aircraft, either. Dust and age fade black tires to dark gray, and the tire treads will almost always be dirty (look at the tires on your car). Many World War II fighters flew from natural turf fields; such planes would have mud and dirt on the wheels. Desert-based aircraft would have dusty gear.

Even in the desert, in-service aircraft seldom show much dust. Airflow during flight keeps surfaces clean except for the landing gear, which is hidden from airflow in the wheel wells. Avoid the incongruity of a heavily weathered aircraft with immaculately clear plexiglass. Plexiglass scratches easily and clouds over quickly in active service. Bring the clear surfaces into line with the rest of the plane by very lightly overspraying them with matte varnish, or by polishing with fine steel wool before assembly.

Weathering steel or wooden ships.

It's a long-standing joke among sailors that they spend half their lives painting their ships. The corrosive effects of salt water and salt air on iron and steel are so severe that any ship that has been at sea more than a week starts

irregular blobs of rubber cement (from the stationery store) where you want the paint to chip. Overpaint in the appropriate colors and allow to dry overnight. Use a strip of sticky tape to peel off the rubber cement, revealing the silver color underneath. This technique is particularly effective with larger scale models such as 1/24, because the actual chipping is visible. Don't make the mistake of flaking the paint off the black surfaces along the leading edges of wings. These areas were unpainted inflatable rubber de-icer boots.

Whatever kind of paint scuffing or chipping you do, check out the real airplane you are modeling, and try to duplicate the weathering visible on it. Remember that a little bit of silver goes an awfully long way. It is altogether too easy to get carried away with weathering effects you are creating, and overweathering is a far greater sin than underweathering. When in doubt, it is better to do too little than too much.

Aircraft also display stains and streaks caused by lubricant leaks from the engine and

9 The heavy weathering on this derelict B-25 was done almost exclusively with pastels. Pastels are far better suited to aircraft and small scale models than dry-brushing.

10 Typical oil and grease stain patterns around the cowling of an Me109.

weather a ship with pastels after it is permanently attached to the diorama (the powder will mess up your "water"), you will have to use the chalks beforehand, and handle the model with tissue until it is added to the base.

Wooden sailing ships don't rust, but they are subject to weathering of a different sort. In the days of sail, men-of-war were better maintained than merchant vessels, but all ships displayed hulls that were green below the waterline with bottom vegetation, and often their sails were stained, discolored, and heavily patched. The snow-white sails of today are the result of modern artificial fibers, but the flaxen sails of old sailing ships varied from elegant buff to dingy brownish gray, with patches of different colors depending on their ages and sources.

All of the four standard weathering techniques apply to ship models. What methods you use will depend largely on your personal preferences and the scale of the model. In smaller scales, you are more likely to work with pastels, while in larger scales dry-brush, airbrush, and wash techniques are applicable.

showing rust, and after several months it becomes heavily rust streaked. Even the most scrupulously maintained luxury liner will inevitably show some rust on her hull. Look at photos to determine where rust stains are most prevalent on the ship you are modeling. Long vertical streaks on the hull are not uncommon, but they must originate from a logical source, such as an anchor hawsepipe or

scupper. Be careful not to overdo these streaks. A stain 6′ long, enormous to a viewer standing alongside the ship, is less than ¹⁄₈″ long on a 1/700 scale model.

The best way to rust steel ship models is with pastels, because the effect must be subtle, but the color must be strong. Because of the small scale of many ship models, dry-brushing often looks coarse on them. Since you can't

11 The easiest way to simulate dust is with ground pastels. The earth in certain parts of the world is sometimes a distinctive color. In the central highlands of Vietnam and much of the State of Georgia, for example, the ground has a rust-red color that those who have lived there never forget. Be sure to carry this color up onto your vehicles and the boots of your figures (and anything else lying on the ground).

12 As Yogi Berra once said, "You can observe a lot just by watching." There may not be many tanks in your neighborhood, but there are often construction sites. Jim Stephens used what he learned from construction equipment near his home to achieve the subtle and realistic effects on this construction crane. The dust is ground pastels.

13 Little touches can really "make" your model. Notice the chunks of rubber missing from the solid tires on Jim's crane.

CHAPTER FOUR

Posing and Painting Figures

igures play a pivotal role in the success of most dioramas, because as the most familiar things in the scene, they catch and direct the viewer's attention. The figures are often the visual glue that holds the scene together, the way interrelationships between the elements are firmly established. Unfortunately, badly done figures can ruin a good diorama. Nevertheless, there is no reason for the terror that painting figures seems to inspire in most modelers. Nothing is involved that anyone can't master, given patience and experience.

The most difficult thing about working with figures is that each is slightly different, so there is no precise set of steps that you can always follow to pose and paint them. Successful figure painting boils down to careful analysis of each figure, followed by the proper steps to deal with it; in fact, the vast majority of mistakes made in painting figures

are mental mistakes. Figure painting is 90 percent mental and only 10 percent physical. A minimum of manual dexterity is essential, but most of the hard work is done by your eyes and mind. What I hope to do here is to provide enough information so that you can at least avoid embarrassing yourself with your first figures, and at best produce some pretty good ones. When the techniques vary for different scales, I'll point out how.

Assembling stock figures. When you prepare figures, be especially careful to trim off all flash, molding lines, and circular molding marks. Use a sharp knife, employing a fine scraping motion to smooth over the surface. Plastic figures sometimes have sink holes in their chests caused by shrinkage during molding. These should be filled with body putty and smoothed over.

Check the fit of figure parts carefully. Make sure that hands that are supposed to be gripping something actually grip it. Watch out

for sleeves. Limitations of the molding process often force manufacturers to round off the ends of the sleeves at the wrists. If necessary, cut off the hands, square the ends of the sleeves, and replace the hands. Hollowing out the sleeves slightly is also a nice touch. Watch out for the fit of headgear and equipment; examine photos of real troops wearing the equipment, and make yours fit the same way. Once your figures are assembled, make sure you fill all seams and gaps, particularly those between the body and equipment. Plastic body putty works well for this, and can be thinned and brushed smooth with acetone or nail polish remover.

When your figures are assembled, install them in the mock-up of your diorama, both to recheck the overall design and to ensure that

Although the tank is the main subject in this scene, the charging infantrymen, not the vehicle, provide most of the feeling of drama, motion, and direction.

those intended for specific positions will actually fit there. Pay special attention to seated figures. Make sure that they sit solidly, giving an impression of weight. Sand their bottoms smooth or build them up with putty until they fit properly. I usually keep the mock-up close at hand as I work on the figures, checking frequently as I go.

Use pins to mount the figures permanently in your diorama. Glue will often held them in place, but pins are more secure. Drill a hole up into the figure's leg past the ankle, which is the weak point. Cut a straight pin, paper clip, or piece of brass rod so that it will fit into the hole and stick out about ¼ the height of the figure, and glue it in place. One pin per figure is usually enough, but a second pin is sometimes advisable. Drill a corresponding hole or holes in the base.

Posing. The ability to pose your figures frees you from the shackles of having to use commercially available poses and vastly increases your freedom of design. Posing is very much a process of experimentation, and the major requirement is the courage to pick up the razor saw and start cutting figures apart. Even the cutting is becoming less necessary, due to the wide variety of plastic figure kits on the market. Many parts—arms, legs, heads—are interchangeable, allowing an almost infinite number of poses without doing anything more than swapping around the parts.

Effective posing is largely a matter of deciding what looks right and what doesn't.

1 These figures caught in midair are an effective (if somewhat extreme) example of the use of imbalance in posing figures to imply dramatic action.

2–7 The best way to learn how to paint figures is to examine the work of other modelers, so study these examples carefully.

The best way to learn about posing is to have friends or relatives pose for you, or to strike poses yourself in a full-length mirror. Pay particular attention to subtleties; an extra turn of the hand, a slightly different angle for the head, or a subtle shift of balance can bring an otherwise conventional pose to life. Experiment with every figure in your diorama until you are sure that you have the best pose for each.

Avoid stiffness, particularly in relaxed poses. People at ease are round-shouldered, with the head slumped forward. This is particularly apparent in sitting figures. Notice, too, that people rarely sit bolt upright, nor do they bend straight from the waist; the spine is almost always curved in a gentle arc from the buttocks to the nape of the neck. Standing people have a natural tendency to support their weight on one leg, leaving the other leg bent and relaxed. This throws the hip outward on the supporting side, and, assuming the legs are the same length, the hip above the bent leg must be lower than that on the straight leg. For a nude figure, rotating the hips in this manner would require cutting, filing, and re-

Wrong   Right

Make sure hands grip the object they are holding

End of sleeve indistinct on molded figure

Cut off hand, hollow out sleeve slightly, glue hand back

PAY ATTENTION TO THE HANDS

sculpting, but in most dioramas the figure's uniform and equipment hide most of the hip area, so all we have to do is reposition the legs and return the upper body to an upright position. It is important to note that when a person carries his weight on one leg, the supporting foot is always located directly under

the neck and spine. In conversions, this usually means moving the supporting leg inward until it is directly under the head.

Feet rarely point directly forward; they tend to angle outward at a natural angle of about 45 degrees. Feet pointing inward are indicative of an unnatural pose or ungraceful activity, and can occasionally be used effectively for pathos or humor.

Because action poses depend less upon subtlety, they are actually easier to make than relaxed poses. There are a couple of tricks to good action posing. First, to achieve a successful impression of violent motion, throw the figure off balance. When the viewer sees a fig-ure in a pose that couldn't be held for more than a split second without falling over, he will immediately comprehend that the figure is in motion; the more extreme the unbalance, the more violent and dramatic the implied motion. The second key to action posing is exaggeration. By carrying motion just beyond the limits of normal body extension, you create a sense of muscular imbalance. As a practical demonstration, consider the calisthenic known as the "trunk twister," in which the upper body, with arms extended, is rotated swiftly back and forth. For a split second, momentum twists the torso farther than it can normally go, then the body springs back to within normal limits of motion. For the most dramatic impact, pose the body just beyond the limits of relaxed motion, but don't cross the delicate borderline between hyper-extension and contortion.

Figure conversions. While swapping parts is an easy way to change poses, sooner or later you will come across a situation where stock figure parts don't quite fit the way you want them to. Your first figure conversions will start out as nothing more than shaving down an arm joint slightly to get a better fit, but within a few months you will find yourself performing major amputations and transplants

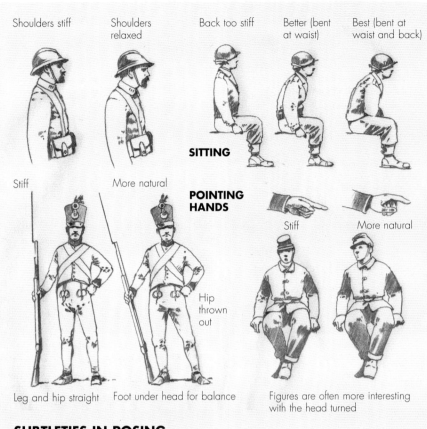

Shoulders stiff | Shoulders relaxed | Back too stiff | Better (bent at waist) | Best (bent at waist and back)

SITTING

POINTING HANDS

Stiff | More natural

Stiff | More natural

Leg and hip straight | Foot under head for balance

Hip thrown out

Figures are often more interesting with the head turned

SUBTLETIES IN POSING

that would horrify the most daring surgeon. There are a few things to bear in mind when you embark on radical figure surgery. First, while the human body can bend remarkably, the bones are not flexible, and they retain their original shape and length no matter what the pose. This is particularly important to remember when repositioning arms and legs. When a pose requires inserting scrap plastic to restore an arm or leg to its proper length, use other parts of the same type as convenient measuring devices.

The body bends at distinct joints (only the spine curves, and for model-work it can be considered to be two joints, one at the waist and the other at the base of the rib cage). This means that cuts should be made at the joints and the parts repositioned. To straighten an arm or leg, make a single saw cut from the inside of the joint, about two-thirds of the way through. Carefully heat the area over a candle or soldering iron until you can feel it give, then bend it to the desired angle. To bend a limb that is straight, remove an angled wedge, then use heat. Do not attempt major repositioning without making cuts, because using heat alone will result in "spaghetti" arms and legs. The torso can be bent forward, back, or to either side by angling the bottom of the torso piece or the top of the leg section. Which piece you cut depends on which section includes the fig-

IMBALANCE

Balanced figure gives little sense of motion

Off-balance figure really appears to be running

HYPER-EXTENSION

Figures at the extreme limits of motion are the most dramatic

KEYS TO ACTION POSING

ure's belt (change the body section without the belt). Gaps at the joints can be filled with either epoxy putty or hobby putty. Both materials can be filed and sanded when dry, but the epoxy putty has the additional property of being sculptable, so minor details lost during conversion can be restored.

Many figures that are grasping things never really look as if they are holding on to the object. A man holding a 25-pound machine gun has to grip it tightly just to keep from dropping it, so the open-palmed grip provided on so many kit figures just won't do the job. Fists make excellent grasping hands; simply remove a section the size of the hand from the object being held and glue the two remaining pieces on either side of the fist. When an object such as a rifle is held in both hands, the trick is to remove the hands from the arms and position them on the object first. Then arrange the figure's arms so the wrists meet the hands.

When a figure has an arm across the shoulder of another as in a walking wounded situation, the best approach is to glue the sections of that arm in position on the back of the other figure, and pose the rest of the figure to match it. Then glue the two figures together permanently and paint them as a unit.

Don't install any personal equipment or other nonessential detail on your figure until posing is completed. Again, check the figures on your diorama mock-up—certain flaws or unnatural positions that you had not noticed before may become apparent. When all posing is complete, your figures are ready for paint.

Scale distance, lighting, and painting positions. Although this chapter is primarily concerned with 1/35 and 1/32 scale figures, the basic principles hold true for all scales. Paradoxically, you will find small scale figures easier to paint, because although the detail may be smaller, there is less of it. On a 1/32 scale figure the insignia on a belt buckle is clearly visible and must be painted, but in 1/72 scale, the buckle can be a dot of plain silver.

This is an example of the principle of scale distance, an important concept in all model-work. The closest thing most of us can focus on is about 5" away; anything closer is a blur. Viewing a 1/32 scale figure from 5" away is the same as looking at a real person 12' away, and in 1/72 scale, the viewing distance approaches 40'. There is no point in including detail on a 1/32 scale figure that would not be visible on a man standing 12' away—if you can't see it in real life, you shouldn't be able to see it on a figure.

The light you paint under is important. If you find the lighting that is least flattering to your figures and paint under that, then any

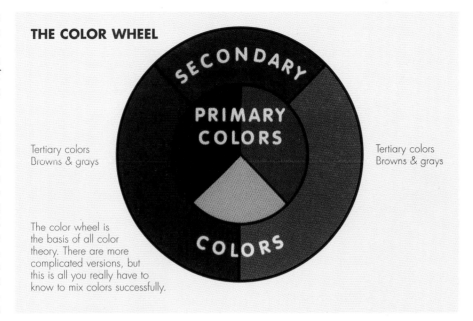

THE COLOR WHEEL

SECONDARY

PRIMARY COLORS

Tertiary colors
Browns & grays

Tertiary colors
Browns & grays

COLORS

The color wheel is the basis of all color theory. There are more complicated versions, but this is all you really have to know to mix colors successfully.

other viewing situation will be an improvement. Bright, diffuse light is best for painting, because it shows up all flaws in the figure and the paint. Sunlight is nearly ideal, but bright, diffuse "office-type" fluorescent light is a good deal more practical for modeling. Incandescent light bulbs rank a poor third. A few fluorescents have a strong greenish cast that can throw your colors off badly.

If you have trouble working at close distances, go to the drug store and buy some inexpensive reading glasses. A single lens magnifier is not good, because you need the depth perception afforded by binocular vision to judge how far the brush is from the surface of the figure.

Although the proper position for painting figures is a matter of personal comfort, the work requires a solid grip and steady hands. Rest both wrists on the edge of your worktable and hold your painting hand against the figure base. This should be enough support to keep your painting hand steady, since the only unsupported parts of your hand are the fingers. If resting your wrists on the edge of the table forces you to hunch over like a clerk in a Dickens novel, work at a higher table or raise the surface of your present bench to a more comfortable height with a box.

The first step in preparing an assembled figure for painting (always assemble the figure as much as you can before painting; if you can see it, you can paint it!) is to mount it on a temporary painting base. Use a piece of scrap wood or other material to make a convenient handle so you can paint the figure without touching it. Lightly glue or pin the figure to it. Give the figure a coat of primer if you wish, or if required by the paint you will use.

Paints and brushes. What kind of paint should you use? Unfortunately, there are no

magic ingredients. Paint is only a tool, and, like other tools, the manner in which it is used is what determines the result. A wide variety of paints has been used successfully on miniatures, and each type has inherent advantages and disadvantages. The most important characteristic of paint from the standpoint of painting figures is the time it takes the paint to set, or cure, because this is a critical factor in blending. Some paints cure as soon as they dry, while others have a certain working time after they are dry to the touch, during which they can be re-liquefied and blended together right on the figure. Setting times vary not only from one base (water, oil, or lacquer) to another, but also from one brand to another.

The paint you select is a personal choice. Try them all, and then settle on the one you like best (and there is no rule saying you can't use them all!). Here are the most common types:

· *Hobby paints.* Flat-finish hobby paints thinned with mineral spirits dry fairly quickly, but most have a working time of about 24 hours before they set. Because most blending is done after the paint is dry, good results require a delicate touch. Blending often turns hobby paints glossy, their primary disadvantage. Lacquer-base hobby paints, such as Floquil, are not suited to plastic figures because the amounts of thinner used during blending will dissolve the plastic. These paints can, however, be used on metal figures where the solvent action of the thinner is not a problem.

· *Water-base paints.* These include hobby paints, poster colors, and artist's caseins. Unless they are specifically designed for plastic models, such as Polly S, they require an undercoat of matte primer so they will stick. The advantages of these paints are convenience, bright colors, and ease in painting fine

detail. The disadvantage of water-base paints is that they set as soon as they are dry, leaving little time for blending. You can get around this by shading with a series of glazes, as explained later in the chapter.

· *Artist's oil colors.* Once you get over the horror of using something prepared for "artists," you may find artist's oils the easiest paints to use. I use them almost exclusively. Their greatest disadvantage is their long drying time, but this is what makes blending them so very easy. Because their consistency is different from other paints, it may take you a while to get used to them. The disadvantage of long drying time can be solved by placing the figure near a source of low heat, such as in a low-temperature oven, a box with a light bulb, or on top of the furnace. Another advantage of oils is that in the long run they are the cheapest paints to use; a starter set of small tubes can last several years, and a set of standard tubes can last a lifetime. For this reason, it pays to go first class. Buy the best oil colors you can find—they only cost a few extra cents per tube, and the quality will be reflected in your work. I recommend the Winsor-Newton brand.

The key to all painting, figures or otherwise, is the consistency of the paint. If it is too thick it will be reluctant to leave the brush, and if it is too thin it will run all over the place. Never use any paint directly from its bottle or tube; always transfer a small amount of paint to your palette and either allow it to dry out a bit or add some thinner. Once you achieve the proper consistency, you can maintain it by occasionally adding a bit of thinner to compensate for evaporation. The right consistency for hobby and water paints is quite liquid. Artist's oils, on the other hand, should be thinner than they come from the tube, but not as thin as the hobby paints, perhaps the consistency of warm grease.

If you are painting with oils and the paint becomes gummy and difficult to blend, you may be adding too much thinner, or possibly too little. If the undercoat has a tendency to soak the oil out of the paint, giving the undercoat a swift coat of thinner before you start can help.

If the type of paint you use is not critical, the type of brush you use is. You can't make a silk purse from a sow's ear, and you can't expect to paint a masterpiece with her tail, either. For figure painting you want round red sable brushes, the best ones you can find. They are expensive, but fortunately you don't need many. One each of No. 1, 0, and 00 should be enough to get you started. The brush should hold enough paint for striping, and you will find that you can paint amazingly fine lines with the No. 0, while the vaunted No. 0000 and No. 00000 sizes hold so little paint that they are practically worthless. Always remem-

ber that what you are paying for is the point, so take good care of it and the brush will last a long time. Use your high-quality brushes only for painting figures, and wash them thoroughly in warm soapy water when you are done. Lick the bristles to a point, being careful not to twist them, and store the brushes where they will not be damaged.

Mixing colors. To paint figures well you will have to learn how to mix colors, and this entails a working knowledge of the color wheel. The basic assumption behind the color wheel is that there are three colors that cannot be made by mixing anything else—red, yellow, and blue. These are the primary colors, and all other colors are achieved by mixing these three. The primary colors form the center segments of the wheel, and each of the second ring of colors, called secondary colors, is created by mixing two of the primary colors. Blue and yellow make green, red and blue combine to make violet, and red and yellow make orange. The third ring colors are called tertiary colors. These are made using all three primary colors.

According to the color wheel, if you have the three primary colors on your shelf, you can mix any color you want. Actually, you will need two more, black and white. When mixing, treat black as a very dark blue or brown (most black paints are) and white as an all-

8 This finished pilot figure shows just how much detail and shading are possible on even a small scale figure

9,10,11,12 This sequence shows the basic steps in painting a tank commander figure. First, the face after initial blending, next, after the addition of pink and five o'clock shadow. Third, the uniform colors laid in, and finally, the finished figure, after detailing.

purpose bleaching or lightening agent. For many years I used only five colors—red, yellow, blue, black, and white—and rarely had to call on any others. The variety of colors possible using these five pigments is far beyond even the most extensive line of bottled paints.

Practice mixing some colors, and you'll find that the color wheel actually works. Try these:

· Brown—1 part black, 1 red, 1 yellow
· Tan—2 black, 2 yellow, 1 red, 8 white
· Khaki—3 black, 2 yellow, 1 red, 8 white
· Field gray—3 black, 1 blue, 1 yellow, 6 white
· Olive green—2 black, 1 yellow
· Olive drab—3 black, 1 yellow, 1 red

You should have little trouble mixing any of the tertiary colors, but you may occasionally run into difficulty mixing some secondary shades, particularly purples and violets. This is because the colors you buy are rarely pure primary colors. If your red has even a bit of yellow in it, mixing it with blue is just like adding green and the result is a tertiary brown instead of a secondary purple. You probably won't need purples often, but when you do you will probably have to buy them.

Aside from saving you the money and bother of having to buy a bottle or tube of every color you need, a knowledge of color mixing can also solve problems that arise in

the course of painting. For example, if a face suddenly turns green during blending, you will know that the most likely cause is the accidental mixing of the blue-black in your shadow color and the yellow in your highlight, and you can adjust blending mixtures to compensate for it.

A final word about color mixing: Don't bother to clean your brush each time you dip from one color to another. This wastes an awful lot of time, and is not necessary. The amount of foreign color left by a dipping paintbrush is minuscule compared to the amount in the bottle, and the bottle will long since have been used up before this practice has any ill effect. Dip swiftly from one color to another, and don't worry about the consequences. When changing colors from red to white you can avoid the otherwise inevitable pale pink by taking a quick side trip into the blue. The blue kills the red, leaving your white clean.

You should definitely have a palette of some kind. The palette is necessary not only for mixing but also to control the consistency of the paint. For hobby paints I generally use white 4" x 6" index cards because they are disposable. For oil colors and water paints, I slip the card into a disposable clear plastic sandwich bag to keep it from soaking up the paint, then throw away the bag when I am done. A

piece of glass also works well, but must be cleaned after each session.

If you are working with turpentine-base paints, either oil or hobby paints, pour out only enough thinner for your immediate needs in a small cup, and throw it away at the end of the day's painting. A shot glass is ideal, or a rubber 35mm film canister is also good. Decanting your thinner keeps your main supply of thinner clean, and ensures that the turps you use at each session is fresh and unevaporated. Gummy turpentine can make hobby paints turn glossy. Don't worry if this small supply of thinner gets dirty—it has to get pretty badly polluted before it has any effect on the paint, and you are unlikely to manage that in just one figure painting session.

Basic painting techniques. Painting figures is a two-part process: The first part is figuring out where the colors go, and the second is putting them there. Let's start our discussion of shading and highlighting with a couple of questions: Why should we bother painting in supplementary shadows and highlights if it takes so much time and effort? Won't the room light cast its own shadows and take care of that for us? Unfortunately, the answer in both cases is "no."

If you look at a model figure painted in solid colors under normal light, the light is not

13,14,15 The face is the most important part of any figure painting effort. While a good face can often save a mediocre figure, a poor face can ruin an otherwise good one. Once you master the basics of painting faces, strive to give each figure character. Each of these faces has a personality that brings it to life.

intense enough to pick out the tiny shadows, and much of the detail is lost. This is because we have scaled down the figure, but not the light source. Unless we develop a special scale light source for each diorama, we must supplement the existing light with painted shadows and highlights. How do we determine where those painted shadows and highlights will go? Let's start by observing that there are two kinds of shadows: direct shadows, cast by a specific light source coming from a specific direction, and indirect shadows, which are cast by no specific source, just light from somewhere up above. The difference between these shadows is essentially the difference between a sunny day and a cloudy day. For painting figures, we'll let room light cast the direct shadows, and paint in indirect shadows, because indirect shadows are what

indicate an object's shape. Our eye automatically translates the patterns of light and shadow into shapes and forms. We can tell that an object is curved or bent by its shadows, even when we cannot see its profile.

To analyze where indirect shadows will fall on a figure, imagine a halo of light (see figure on page 52) about 12″ above it, with the light striking the top surfaces of the figure at an angle of about 60 degrees. The effect is the same if the light source is above and behind us, and we rotate the figure as we look at it. Surfaces revealed to the light source will be brighter, surfaces hidden from it will be in dark shadow. In the example of the ball, the color will be quite even down to the "equator," and will become progressively darker as it approaches the "south pole." Any other shape can be analyzed the same way.

Let's look at something less theoretical, a series of wrinkles on a sleeve. Note how sharp, deep wrinkles have dark shadows and make rapid transitions from light to dark, while shallower wrinkles have lighter shadows and make gradual transitions. Shadows on figures are not confined only to wrinkles. Let's consider a man standing at ease with one leg bent, theoretically clad in wrinkle-free clothing.

Notice that even without wrinkles, his body casts shadows that indicate his shape. The small of his back is darker than the area across the shoulders and buttocks, indicating the curvature of the spine. The lower front portion of the bent leg is darker than the upper surface, while the opposite is true of the back of the leg. When viewing from directly in front or behind, it would be impossible to tell if the leg is bent at all without these shadows.

Another way to explain this is to consider the octagonal cylinder shown in the figure at upper right on page 52. If this cylinder were placed under the halo of light, each surface would have a different degree of darkness, depending on the amount of light striking it. We can even assign numbers to each surface: the top, being the brightest, is 1, the upper slope 2, the vertical side 3, the reverse slope 4, and the bottom 5. By arranging these numbers around an end view of the octagon, we have a simple diagram that expresses the color change of the cylinder from top to bottom, from the lightest surface to the darkest. THIS IS THE STOP-SIGN RULE, the magic formula that tells you where the colors go. Compare the numbers on the shading chart with the numbers on the stop sign, and put

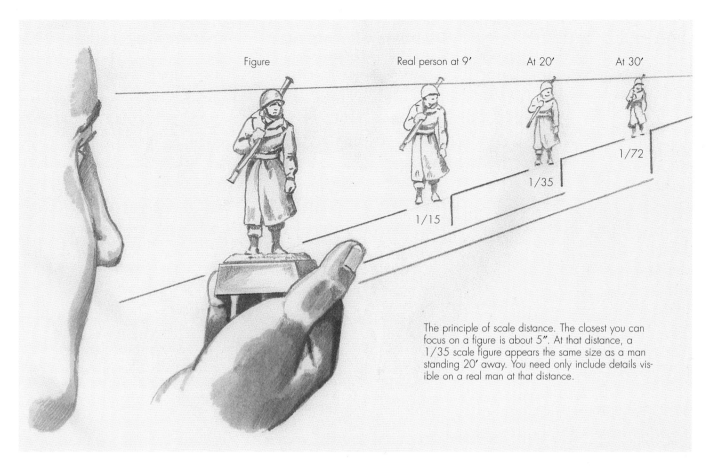

The principle of scale distance. The closest you can focus on a figure is about 5″. At that distance, a 1/35 scale figure appears the same size as a man standing 20′ away. You need only include details visible on a real man at that distance.

those colors on the surfaces of the figure that match the stop sign. If you are having trouble shading a figure, you have probably lost touch with the rule: go back to the diagram and figure out what you are doing wrong.

The first step in painting, then, before you even pick up a brush, is to completely analyze the figure in this manner. Each figure will be different. Pick up the figure and turn it around slowly, making mental notes of where the light and shadows fall. Do this twice, once for body shadows and once for clothing folds and wrinkles. The more thoroughly you think out the problems now, the fewer difficulties you will have once you start painting. Think constantly in terms of the 60 degree halo. If you are uncertain, position a light above and behind your head, and slowly rotate the figure. This provides a practical way to visualize the effect you are trying to achieve. This analysis, more than any other factor, is the key to success in painting figures. If you feel you haven't fully understood how to do it, go back and read the description again before proceeding. For your first few figures, you may have to spend as long as an hour analyzing each figure before you paint, but as you gain experience the analysis will become second nature and you'll scarcely be aware of it.

The first steps. The first step in coloring your figure is underpainting. Lay in the basic skin and clothing colors, hands, face, uniform,

boots, without shading, blending, or detail. Allow this paint to set thoroughly, preferably 3 or 4 days. If you under-paint with water-base paints as I usually do, you can proceed right away, since these colors set immediately and will not bleed through anything you put over them. The importance of underpainting will become clear later on when, while blending shadows and highlights, you accidentally wear through to the undercoat. The color revealed will be close to the one you are working with and will not show.

Now you are ready to take the plunge. If you are painting with oil colors, lay out the required colors on your palette. If you are using bottled paint, mix the paints thoroughly, and arrange them, the palette, and the thinner in a convenient working pattern. You will also want to keep some tissue handy to wipe your brushes.

The traditional method of painting figures is from the skin out, doing the face and hands first, and painting successive layers of clothing in order. This is not a bad practice to follow after you have gotten your feet wet, but for your first figure, doing the uniform first gives you a chance to practice blending techniques on wide areas before moving on to the smaller and more difficult areas of the face.

The initial step in painting the uniform is to mix a basic color, a highlight color, and a shadow color. The basic color is the actual color of the uniform, the highlight is a lighter

version, and the shadow is a darker version. The table provides a rough idea of how much contrast there should be among the various shades. The contrast should be strong—in fact, the most common error made by beginners is color timidity. Keep your contrasts strong, even if you have to exaggerate them the first few times. You'll soon learn that blending, not the colors, gives figure shading its subtle effect.

When you have mixed your three shades, begin to carefully lay them onto your figure. This is where shading analysis pays off. Take your time, work carefully, and think. Each time you add a color, ask yourself why you are putting it there. Is this area in light or shadow? Why? This process may be tedious at first, but it will soon become automatic. When you have all your colors laid in, stand back and look at your work critically. Get far enough away that the harsh borders between the colors are less distracting. Are the shadows and highlights in the right places? Is there enough contrast between the colors? It is better to make corrections now than later. When you are satisfied, you are ready to start blending.

Blending. Blending is feathering the edge between two colors to get a subtle and gradual transition between them. The specific technique will vary from one type of paint to another, but a few words of advice apply to all. Always blend with the biggest brush you can.

THE "HALO OF LIGHT"

Imagine your figure with a halo of life above it, striking the figure equally on all sides.

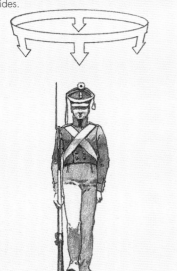

When we look at a figure, there is generally a light source above and behind our head as we rotate the figure before us. The effect would be the same if the figure were stationary and we moved around it, with the light moving with us. Or, you can imagine a halo of light about 12" above a figure, with the light shining down on it at an angle of about 60 degrees. This is the light in which the figure is seen, and this is the light we want to paint.

THE STOP SIGN AND THE FIGURE

Use the stop sign to assign color values to the surface of the figure below.

SHADOWS INDICATE THE SHAPE OF AN OBJECT

This is a flat disc

This is obviously a sphere

This block is flat

This one has a projection

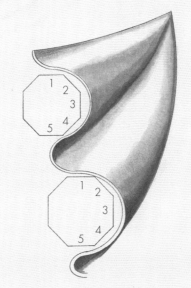

Clothing folds and wrinkles follow the same rule. In cross section, each fold is a small stop sign with a light top and a dark underside. Don't highlight the outer or projecting part of the fold and shade the depressions. According to the stop-sign rule it is the upper surface of the fold that is highlighted and the underside that is in shadow.

We can use the stop-sign rule to assign numbers to every part of the figure. The top of the cap and the top of the lower left arm are horizontal, like the top of the stop sign, and thus will carry a color value of 1; the area across the upper back is a 2; the stomach and vertical part of the leg are a 3, and so on. We can assign numerical values to any surface we see. This "paint by numbers" approach may seem a bit silly and tedious, but it works. As you get used to it, the process will become so instinctive you won't even be aware that you are doing it.

THE STOP-SIGN RULE

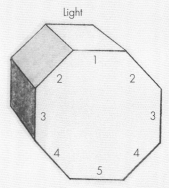

Light

By comparing any part of your figure with this drawing, you can assign a numerical color value to it, corresponding to the values in chart.

If we were to place an octagonal cylinder under the halo of light, each surface would have its degree of darkness. We can even assign numbers to each surface: the top, being the brightest, is 1, the upper slope 2, the vertical side 3, the reverse slope 4, and the bottom 5. By arranging these numbers around an end-view of the octagon, we have a simple diagram that expresses the color change of the cylinder from top to bottom, from the lightest surface to the darkest. THIS IS THE STOP-SIGN RULE. IT IS THE MAGIC FORMULA, THE FOUNTAINHEAD OF ALL FIGURE PAINTING KNOWLEDGE. If you understand the stop sign, you understand shading and highlighting. If you are confused, don't go any further until you understand it. Whenever you are having trouble shading a figure, come back to the stop sign and figure out what you are doing wrong.

This enables you to do the job with fewer strokes, avoiding the choppy effect caused by many little strokes with a small brush. *Blend only the edge between the colors;* don't blend all the way across them or you'll wind up with just one color.

· *Blending hobby paints.* When working with hobby paints, most blending will be done when the paint is already dry to the touch, but before it has set. Moisten a clean, soft-bristled brush with turpentine and stroke it across a folded tissue to remove the excess. There should be only enough thinner left on the brush to soften the paint on the figure. Gently stroke back and forth across the border between the two colors until the thinner "revitalizes" the paint and the border becomes indistinct. For a smoother effect, take an occasional stroke lengthwise along the border, too. Return your brush to the thinner occasionally and clean it. If the difference between adjacent colors is radical, you may have to work in stages, blending the border first, then in turn blending its edges with the colors on either side. Again, be careful not to go too far

16 Blood must be handled with taste. The trooper on the ground in this scene is gravely wounded, but the amount of gore has been kept to a realistic minimum.

17 If you include bodies in a scene, make sure they look dead, not just knocked over. Be sure to press them firmly into the groundwork. Note the way this figure's head is thrown back, and how the helmet tilts down over the eyes.

and blend the whole thing into one solid color.

· **Blending artist's oils.** Artist's oil colors are easy to blend because they do not dry for a day or so, giving you plenty of time to manipulate them. Use a clean, dry brush, and gently stroke back and forth over the area to be blended, lifting the brush away from the surface at the end of each stroke. For large areas, use a crisscross pattern for a smooth effect. Wipe the brush clean occasionally on a folded tissue. The subtlety of oils is truly amazing, and even the most delicate shadings are easy with a little practice.

One characteristic of oils that takes a bit of getting used to is the heavier consistency of the paint. This will often cause a gradual buildup of paint on the figure, and you can find yourself working with a thick, gooey

SHADOWS ON THE FIGURE

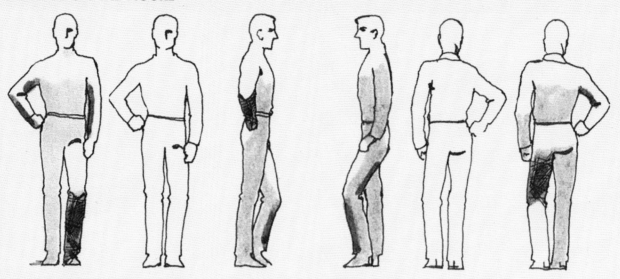

Shadows indicate both shape and pose. Compare the shaded and unshaded figures. These are the kinds of shadows and highlights you will be concerned with in painting your figure.

EFFECT OF LIGHT ON A SLEEVE

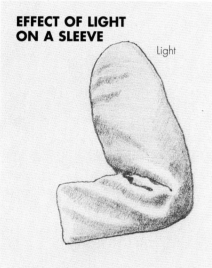

Light

Only the underside of each fold (not the entire hollow between folds) is in shadow, and the top of the fold is highlighted. Deep creases, such as at the elbow, make darker shadows than the shallow folds.

CHECK YOUR WORK CONSTANTLY

1. Up close, for smoothness of blending
2. At arm's length, for contrast. Painted highlights and shadows should be clearly visible at this distance. If you have blended them away, restore the colors and try again.

Hold the figure at arm's length and check your work to see that the colors are in the right place before blending. The contrast should be evident at this distance.

layer of paint, heavily textured with ugly brush marks. Attempting to correct this by thinning the paint will only cause it to dry faster and make it harder to blend. Instead, concentrate on applying a thin layer of the proper consistency and spreading the paint around a bit more.

When you have finished blending, very gently brush over the entire area with a clean, soft-bristled brush. This will soften the brush marks and add a final touch of subtlety to the blending.

One problem you may encounter in blending either hobby paints or artist's oils is "the glossies." Sometimes the paint dries to a glossy or mottled finish in the blended areas, particularly if you have done a lot of brushwork. The solution is to overspray the figure with matte varnish when the paint has thoroughly dried. Lacking that, just repaint the area and hope for the best.

• *Blending water-base acrylics.* As I already mentioned, acrylics are hard to blend because they dry and set too quickly. The way around this problem is to use a series of glazes. A glaze is like a wash, but more carefully controlled: rather than flooding the surface with thinned paint, we carefully brush a smooth, thin layer

across it, gently tinting the color underneath. Because the paint dries quickly, a series of glazes can be applied in succession, each one slightly deepening the color of the glaze underneath it. This requires patience. Keep the paint well-thinned, to the point where it is little more than colored water. If there is too much color in your glaze, a hard edge will show when it dries. Certain brands of paint definitely work better than others. The best, and in fact the one for which this technique was developed by modelers in Spain, are the Vallejo paints imported from that country. The glazes with this paint are extremely smooth, and the edges seem to soften and even disappear on their own. Whatever brand you use, the technique requires practice, but the results can be spectacular, particularly on the smaller 1/35 scale figures where oil paints tend to show too much texture.

Shading light and dark. The lighter the color, the more difficult you will find it to shade. The reason for this is that the range of colors from high highlight to deep shadow is very broad, in many cases running the full gamut from almost pure white to pure black. White clothing is the most difficult of all, because the shadow colors inevitably blend over into the highlights, turning snow white to dingy gray. The keys to shading white clothing are, first, to not over-shade it, and second to touch up the highlight areas after the shadows have set. Although the shadow colors you use will range all the way to a dark gray, the majority of your areas should remain white. Remember that the overall color impression of the figure will be the average of all the colors used to shade it. When painting

18 If you need to show blood, don't splatter red paint everywhere. It doesn't look like blood, it doesn't shock anyone, and it immediately marks you as a tasteless amateur. Far more disturbing to the viewer is seeing blood in unexpected places or situations, like the medic scrubbing down the stretcher in this aid station scene.

19 Large scale models mean more detail on the model, but also more detail on the figures. This can be a challenge, but it is also an opportunity. Note the wonderful faces and natural posing on the figures that Bill Hearne scratchbuilt to go with his 1/9 scale motorcycle and sidecar.

and shading white, remember that white uniforms are actually a very pale shade of some other color, usually gray or brown. Avoid using straight black when you shade whites. The ultimate (and rather shameful) answer to the problem of white uniforms is to avoid them whenever you can, particularly when you are just starting out.

Other light uniforms, such as khaki, are not as difficult to shade as white, but the range of shading colors is still a little intimidating. With most light colors other than white you have enough leeway that if the shadow color creeps into your highlight, it will not be too noticeable.

Dark colors are quite easy to shade; the trick is to avoid overshading them. The impression of the figure when viewed from a distance should still be that of a dark color, not

black. Since the base color is already pretty dark, it will not be too different from the shadow (usually jet black), so blending should be easy. Be sparing in your highlights to avoid lightening the overall color. One modest highlight shade should be enough, because dark colors often pick up sufficient highlights from room lighting alone. Black is the easiest color of all to shade because there are no shadows (there being no color darker than black), and only the faintest highlights. If you want easy uniforms to paint, stick to panzer black!

When blending is completed, step back and examine your work. Is there still enough

contrast in the colors? Have you blended too much away? Now look more closely. Is the blending smooth, with a gradual shift of color, or are there rough spots? Do the folds look natural? Have you shaded the body shape as well as the folds? Have you highlighted the top of the folds? A common mistake is to highlight the projecting parts of the fold and shade the depressions when actually, the top of the fold should be highlighted, and the underside in shadow.

Go back and correct any flaws you have noticed. To restore lost contrast you can go back and add more color, but bear in mind

20 When posing figures, treat them as a group, not just individual figures. Make them interact with each other, talking back and forth, and show them working as a team, moving toward a common goal.

21 Sometimes changing the angle of a figure's head can make a big difference. In this case, the tilted heads give the impression of one man talking and one listening; in fact, you can even tell by the angle who is talking to whom.

22 Clever use of body language can add interest, expression and even humor to your work (model by Bill Horan).

that you will have to use lighter highlights and darker shadow tones to compensate for colors already on the figure, and that each additional layer will increase the buildup of paint on the surface. If the accumulation of paint becomes too great, you can sometimes wipe off the excess carefully with a cotton swab or rolled tissue and start again.

Faces and hands. The face is the most challenging, most frustrating, and the most satisfying part of painting a figure. The job that you do on faces will, more than any other factor, establish your ability as a figure painter.

I usually paint eyes at the same time and with the same paint as my undercoat, so the eyes will not accidentally get blended into the rest of the face. Our main concerns in painting eyes are to make them straight, the same size, and symmetrically located in the face.

Most diorama scenes are set outdoors, where men tend to squint in the sunlight. This makes their eyes little more than slits, even in 1/32 scale. Also, in all common modeling scales the whites of the eyes are not white at all, but essentially the same color as the rest of the face. This is an instance of scale distance in which the tiny blood vessels blend in with the white of the eye to make it appear pink. Painting pure whites in the eyes is the major cause of the notorious "popeyed look" that every modeler wants to avoid.

If you have trouble painting and positioning eyes, the drawing shows a technique that should help. It's called the "cross" technique and it allows you to separate the problems and concentrate on them one at a time. The last drawing shows the finished eye. Notice that there are no lower eyelashes (they are not visible at a normal scale viewing distance) and the lower edge of the eye cuts straight across. Contrary to popular belief, eyes are not almond shaped.

Now we turn to the face itself. Let's start by looking at the face in terms of the 60 degree angle of light rule. The deepest and consequently the darkest part of the face is the area between the eyes and under the brows, on

SHADING COLORS

1	2	3	4	5
HIGH HIGHLIGHT	**HIGHLIGHT**	**BASE**	**SHADOW**	**DARK SHADOW**
■	■	DARK BLUE ■	■	■
■	■	DARK GREEN ■	■	■
■	■	BROWN ■	■	■
■	■	BLACK ■	■	■
		WHITE	■	■
■	■	RED ■	■	■
░	░	YELLOW ░	■	■
░	░	FLESH ░	■	■
░	░	TAN ░	■	■

Having assigned numbers to the areas of the figure, it makes sense to assign colors to these numbers. Members of my painting class make up a reference chart like this one before they ever touch a brush to a figure. Prepare one up for yourself, making the highlight shades somewhat lighter and the dark shades somewhat darker than they appear here.

When blending, pay attention to the consistency of the paint. If it is too liquid, it is hard to control; wipe it off and try again. If it is too dry, add a drop of linseed oil to revitalize it. Go back and add the high highlights (No. 1) and dark shadows (No. 5). Remember that the stop sign numbers refer to the final color in each area on the figure, not to puddles of paint on the palette. To compensate for color already on the figure, you will have to increase the contrast of colors you add, and the numbered puddles are soon forgotten. Add whatever is necessary to do the job.

- Blend the border only.
- Sweeping the brush from side to side blends all the colors together.
- Keep the colors separate.
- Use a vertical, stabbing, snapping motion of the brush to blur the border between colors.

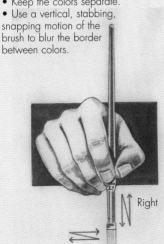

Right

Wrong

either side of the nose. Somewhat less dark will be the underside of the chin, under the nose, and under the upper and lower lips. The highlights fall across the forehead, down the bridge of the nose, on the cheekbones, and on the point of the jaw. These shadow and highlight areas are the keys that establish the shape of the face.

PAINTING EYES

The eye is more of a wedge shape than an oval. The colored iris is barely in contact with the lower lid, and partly covered by the upper lid.

RIGHT

WRONG

THE CROSS METHOD FOR PAINTING EYES

If you have trouble positioning eyes on the face, this should help.

1 Do not paint any whites at all in the eyes; at the normal viewing distance the whites appear the same color as the face.

2 Paint a wide band of light blue or brown through each eye socket, keeping each band the same distance from the nose.

3 Paint a narrow band of black or dark brown down the center.

4 Cut off the top of each eye band with a dark brown line. This is the upper eyelash. Concentrate on positioning the bottom edge of this line correctly, keeping the two eyes level from side to side, and let the rest of the line fall where it may.

5 Add half of a bottom lash.

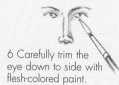

6 Carefully trim the eye down to side with flesh-colored paint.

SHADING AND HIGHLIGHTING THE FACE

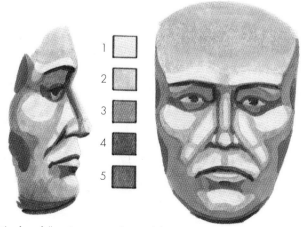

The planes of the face follow (no surprise by now) the stop-sign rule. You can assign color values 1 to 5 to the face, just as you did the uniform, although a bit of overhighlighting on the forehead, nose, and cheekbones doesn't hurt.

One of the biggest difficulties in painting faces is that there is so much to do in such a small area. In 1/35 scale, your entire working area is about the size of a large pea. For this reason it is not generally a good idea to lay in the full range of colors at once. Blending in such a small area is bound to result in a few colors getting lost in the shuffle, so you are better off to block in only the basic color, highlight, and shadow. Blend these first, then go on to lighter highlights and deeper shadows in a second stage.

The first step is to mix three basic flesh colors. Stay away from commercial "flesh"; it is invariably too pink. Remember that soldiers are out in the sun a lot, and their skin is tanned and weatherbeaten. What we are looking for is a sort of pinkish tan that is best achieved by mixing yellow ochre (yellow brown), burnt sienna (red brown), and white. Add some of this mixture to white for highlight and some to burnt sienna for shadow.

Now lay these colors onto the face. A No. 0 or 00 brush is as small as you should need for this job; don't go any smaller. Use the step-by-step pictures as a guide, and when you are done, step back far enough for the distance to do some blending and examine your work. Now clean your brush thoroughly and start to blend. Use short, delicate strokes. In such a small area it is especially important to restrict your blending just to the borders between colors. It is alarmingly easy to blend too wide an area, and this is where most of your problems are likely to set in.

When the blending is done to your satisfaction, mix up a darker shadow and a lighter highlight. The highlight should be almost pure white, and the shadow a dark brown. Carefully lay these colors in as shown in the drawing and blend them carefully. You are now working with really tiny areas of color, so the blending calls for an exceptionally delicate touch. Just whisper the brush across the surface, using something of a stabbing, stippling motion to avoid disturbing other colors nearby. Be particularly careful that your high highlight and deep shadow colors never meet. The highlight contains a lot of white and the shadow a lot of black, and if these two meet they will turn the face gray.

The final step is to add a touch of pink to the cheeks and lips. Use a darkish pink and apply a dash below each cheekbone and to the upper surface of the lower lip. Blend the cheek areas until just a subtle hint of the color remains. You probably won't have to blend the lip much at all, but do add a light pink highlight in the center.

A common touch for combat soldier figures is a 5 o'clock shadow. This effect is not too difficult (if you have gotten this far, you're ready for anything!). Just mix up a gray or grayish brown and apply it only to the shadow areas in the beard area. Blend this color in, feathering it lightly across the highlights. This will turn the highlight areas slightly gray without changing their essential color.

Moustaches and other hair should be painted last. The real trick to painting and shading hair is to treat it not as a group of individual strands, but as a solid mass. Analyze the hair as a single shape in terms of the 60 degree angle of light rule and go to work. Highlight the upper surfaces of locks and waves and shadow the undersides. If your figure has brown hair, avoid highlighting with a rich chestnut brown, since human hair rarely grows that color. Instead, use a standard brown for the basic color, and add white for

PAINTING FACES

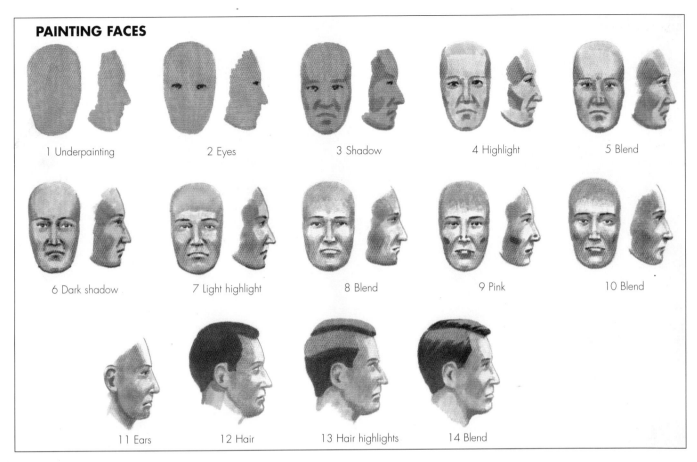

1 Underpainting
2 Eyes
3 Shadow
4 Highlight
5 Blend
6 Dark shadow
7 Light highlight
8 Blend
9 Pink
10 Blend
11 Ears
12 Hair
13 Hair highlights
14 Blend

the highlight. Remember, too, that blond hair is not really yellow, but more of a tan color, even in its palest forms.

Hands are painted with the same colors used for the face. The darkest shadows go between the fingers; be sure to feather them lightly to either side, simulating roundness. Use lighter shadow on the underside of the hand (depending upon which side is up) and across the fingers below each set of knuckles. Fingernails can be added with a drop of highlight color at the end of each finger, left unblended. Be sure your figure's hands are not too smooth. Men's hands tend to be rough and muscular, with veins showing prominently on the back of hand. Mottle the color on the back of the hand to indicate the muscles, and add veins with the highlight color.

Painting detail. When painting uniforms, I start with the widest areas and gradually work my way down to the smaller ones, saving the fine detail for last. As you work your way down in size, the blending becomes progressively easier. If you are working in oils, don't feel that you are limited to working with only one color per session for fear of bleeding. Oils tend to stay where they are put, and you should be able to paint adjoining areas with no problems. Although it is usually best to wait until the first color is dry, it is sometimes possible to overpaint oils while the color underneath is still wet.

The two keys to good detail work are the consistency of the paint and a good steady grip on the figure and the brush. These have already been mentioned, but they are particularly important in detail painting. If your grip is not steady, your hand will shake and you won't put the paint where you want it. If the consistency of the paint is not just right, it will not flow, or flow too freely, both of which can ruin fine detail. Proper control of the paint is 90 percent of fine detail work. With it, detailing can actually be fun, but without it, detailing is the very height of frustration.

Scale distance is an important principle in detail painting. A lot of modelers try to paint in details that would never be visible at all at the scale distance they are working with. This is losing sight of the forest for the trees. Don't try to paint individual feathers on an eagle so small that they would never have been visible anyway, concentrate instead on getting the head, chest, wings, and legs properly proportioned and readily identifiable. If the figure has a complicated piece of embroidery such as twisted-cord shoulder boards, don't try to paint each cord and twist. Instead, break the shoulder boards down into a characteristic pattern of lights and darks, then duplicate that pattern on the figure. This is an old trick copped from the great masters of oil painting. Look closely at an elaborately detailed helmet in a Rembrandt painting and you'll discover that all it really is

is a collection of carefully designed squiggles. The moral of this tale is that you will get a lot farther by suggesting detail than trying to duplicate it point for point.

For leather gear and other shiny objects, don't make the mistake of using a high gloss paint unless the material is patent leather. You can achieve a more realistic subtle sheen by mixing glossy and matte paints together, or by applying gloss or semigloss varnish over the matte colors. Polly S makes an excellent water-base gloss finish that won't disturb colors underneath it. One coat gives a soft, almost imperceptible, shine while additional coats gradually yield a high gloss. Bear in mind that gloss decreases in intensity as it is miniaturized: a high polish in real life becomes merely semigloss in miniature, even on the parade ground. The leather gear of troops in the field is rarely polished and usually has no shine at all.

Some detail painting will involve metallic colors. These touches add final sparkle to your work, and there are a few things you should know about using metallics. Metallic paints are nothing more than fine metallic powder suspended in a clear paint vehicle. The finer the powder, the better suited it is to modelwork.

There is one cardinal rule in working with bottled metallic paints: NEVER stir the paint. To do so is to lose control of the consistency of the paint, which is the key to painting

detail. Instead of stirring, transfer pigment from the bottom of the bottle to your palette, then add liquid or let it dry until the paint is the proper consistency. This will help you avoid the classic problem of applying a neat drop of silver to a button only to have it run across the uniform.

Buttons present no problem, but occasionally you'll encounter metallic areas that require shading. Weapons are easy as long as the engraved detail is good and crisp—paint the metal areas black and dry-brush over them with gunmetal and silver. For areas where this is not feasible, shade metallics the same way you would shade the uniform. Add black to your silver or brown to your gold for the shadow color, and use straight metallic for highlight. Block them in on the figure and shade and blend as usual. The slightly different characteristics of the metallics may cause some initial difficulty, but you'll get used to it quickly.

Don't assume that everything on a uniform is bright silver or gold. Metallic braid and lace do not have the same glitter and shine as smooth metal buttons, and even buttons are sometimes frosted. To achieve a dull metallic effect, paint the area with ordinary colors, and shade and blend them as usual.

When they have set, go over them with a light wash of metallic paint to add the right amount of flash and sparkle.

When working with metallic paints, be careful that they do not pollute your other colors. A small amount of metallic is all it takes to do this, and once the damage is done, it is irreversible. Never use thinner that has been used for metallics for any other paint, and clean your brushes especially carefully when you are done. Many painters keep a separate set of brushes for metallics.

Before leaving the subject of figures, I'll add a word about a somewhat distasteful subject. If your dioramas are military scenes, sooner or later you will encounter a situation that calls for blood. The way you handle this small detail can make or break the scene, and

23 Lewis Pruneau's Vietnamese bus shows how many figures can be crowded into a diorama (over a hundred in this case!), but that is the whole point of this scene.

24 Figure painters have been getting excellent results with the acrylic paints produced by Vallejo in Spain (the ones shown here are marketed under license by Andrea Miniatures of the same country). The technique for shading with these paints is not one of blending, but of applying a series of carefully controlled glazes (multiple layers of color thinned to the point of tinted water) which gradually build up to a subtle gradation of color.

far too many modelers overdo it. Unless shocking your viewer is your main intention, a little bit of blood goes a long way. Gory splotches of bright red paint all over your diorama quickly mark you as a tasteless amateur. A few well-placed drops are not only more discreet, but considerably more effective in the long run. Blood runs from wounds in fine ribbons, not broad bands of red, and it is rarely bright red.

The best way to paint blood is to paint it in first in crimson and then highlight with red. Then add high-gloss varnish to make the paint look wet.

CHAPTER FIVE

The Elefant's Dilemma

This whimsical diorama is a "delayed reaction piece"; it takes the viewer a moment or two to realize what's going on. Interestingly enough, the idea did not start out to be humorous at all. It started out during a bull session with friends about an intersection scene, with a harried MP trying to sort out a traffic jam. Two of the vehicles were to be a jagdpanzer Elefant and a horse-drawn supply wagon. While discussing subplots, the idea of having the Elefant run out of gas came up. The intersection and the rest of the vehicles were quickly forgotten, and the disgruntled tanker flagging down the wagon became the focal point of the scene.

Both models in the scene are 1/35 kits: an Italeri Elefant and an Esci supply wagon. Both are beautifully detailed and require little or no modification.

1 Here's the visual key to the Elefant's dilemma—a hapless German tanker with an array of four bone-dry gasoline cans.

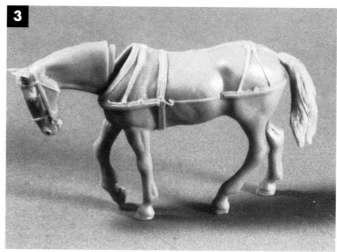

2 The initial planning stage: the kits have been assembled and the figures posed. A couple of pieces of scrap lumber simulate the raised roadway. Even in the mock-up stage it's easy to see how the figures direct the viewer's eye around the scene.

4 The only modifications made to the Elefant were replacement of the tow cables with ones made of solder wire, application of zimmerit, and the addition of periscopes in the river's hatch.

3 The wagon was built with no modifications at all, partly because it is such a nice kit and partly because I had no reference to check it against. One of the horses was modified by lowering the neck, to give it a stolid, "dobbin" look. The gap in the neck was filled with epoxy putty.

5 Zimmerit is an optional modification. The figures are pinned through the feet and glued to the vehicle with white glue so that they can be soaked loose if necessary.

6 After the base dimensions were established, the raised roadbed was added. It is a strip of plywood covered with veneer on the ends. The edge of the road was beveled and nicked.

7,8 The groundwork applied to the base. The path of the Elefant was made using the model, and the ruts in the road were made with a toy car. Although it doesn't look bad in this photo, the overall effect with the vehicles in place was quite disappointing. The ground looked too "manicured," and there was a vast empty space in the upper right corner. Even though the Celluclay was hard, I was able to soften it with water, scrape off the offending sections, and re-landscape it (right). The culvert is a piece of brass tube and the muddy water in the ditch is the painted and varnished base. Now the groundwork is not as smooth as before, and the ditch fills the dead space and adds interest to the scene.

9 A view of the wagon, showing how the reins fit the hands of the driver. The reins are paper, stained brown before installation and coated with white glue once in place. The rope traces are twisted solder wire. The hooks molded on the horse harness for the chain (I used ship model chain) and traces are inconvenient to work with, so I drilled holes and inserted wire hooks.

10 The other figures in the scene were converted from various Tamiya tank crew and infantry figure sets. This conversion work was so much a matter of trial and error that there is no way I could tell you which parts were used for which figure. Additional details, such as shoulder straps and pocket flaps, were made from epoxy.

11 The road sign was provided in the supply wagon kit. It establishes the locale as Italy, where most of the second model Elefants saw service. The wood grain was wiped on using a brown wash, then the lettering was applied with dry transfers. Final weathering was accomplished with pastels.

12 A back view of the finished diorama. The rusty color of the culvert stands out against the green water and foliage, making the pipe and ditch an excellent space filler.

13 The wagon figures were used as they came in the kit, although the rifle was removed from one and an epoxy loaf of bread—more appropriate for a field bakery unit—was substituted.

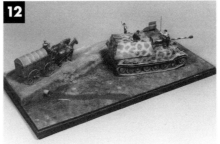

CHAPTER SIX

Details and Accessories

etails and accessories not only add interest to a diorama, they also fulfill the mundane but necessary function of filling space. You will often select a detail not because of what it is, but because you need an item of a particular size to fill dead space and balance your scene.

What kind of details can we use? For aircraft, the possibilities are pretty much limited to ground support and maintenance equipment, including work platforms, service units, bomb carts, tow tractors, wheel chocks, fire extinguishers, and aircraft parts.

For armor, the range is more varied, and useful items include bedrolls, ammo boxes, ration cases, storage lockers, vehicular equipment, discarded weapons, and other battlefield debris. Small structures and terrain features such as wells, water fountains, roadside shrines, signposts, telegraph poles,

fences, walls, and hedges can also be useful.

There is a wide variety of ready-to-use accessories available, with the promise of still more to come. Several companies offer plastic and metal accessory kits. Ready-to-use accessories can also be found in modeling hobbies using the same scale, an important source that is often overlooked. Armor enthusiasts will find metal accessories offered for model soldiers that will serve well for armor dioramas. A major resource for aircraft modelers is the model railroad field. Model railroad "O" scale is actually 1/48, and many accessories are available that can be used on aircraft dioramas. "HO" scale is by far the most popular model railroading scale and the variety of accessories available is wondrous. HO scale is actually 1/87, a bit small for 1/72 aircraft and 1/76 armor, but you will find that an awful lot of HO parts can be used to detail dioramas. Take the time to browse through a good model railroad shop to see what is available.

Wm. K. Walthers Inc. of Milwaukee is one of the largest model railroad suppliers, and its catalogs are excellent home references. Walthers publishes illustrated catalogs for both HO and O scale.

Creative scavenging. "Creative scavenging"—looking for likely items in areas outside normal hobby sources—is one of the best ways to find detail parts and accessories. Wherever you go—the hardware store, the toy store, the florist's, *anywhere*—be on the lookout for useful detail pieces. In some cases you may not know what a part might be used for when you first see it, but if you file it away

This diorama of a B-26 assembly line makes use of nearly all the materials and techniques discussed in this chapter. The factory effect is greatly enhanced by mirrors placed on each side of the scene. The mirrors generate the illusion of an assembly line that extends as far as the eye can see.

1 This photo shows how a tissue-paper tarp looks after painting.

2 To make bedrolls or tarps, wet some tissue, fold its edges toward the center, then roll and tie it.

for future reference, either physically (if it's cheap) or mentally (if it's not), months later you may find a use for it. Such creative scavenging is a challenge to your ingenuity.

Other sources for accessories are the hobbies of radio control and dollhouse miniatures. The workmanship on many items in these areas is often too coarse for application to smaller models, but every so often you'll find something worthwhile. It's always worth browsing through these areas at your hobby shop.

Tarps, blankets, and bedrolls. Some of the easiest details to make from scratch are rolled tarps, blankets, and sleeping bags.

These are made from tissue paper, and you'll need little or no practice before you can turn them out by the dozen. Start with a piece of facial tissue (don't use toilet paper—it dissolves in water), about 2″ by 4″, dip it in water, and fold the two long sides into the center. Now, starting at one end, carefully roll the strip up and tie it with thread where the straps will go. Use long pieces and cut off the excess when you are done. Paper or card straps can be added later when the piece is dry. The tissue rolls can be painted by first giving each roll a quick coat of thinner to ensure proper coverage and eliminate white spots. When the paint is thoroughly dry, dry-brush as usual and use white glue to hold

the rolls in place on the vehicle or diorama.

Tissue paper is excellent for duplicating all kinds of cloth: tarpaulins, discarded clothing, even drapery on figures. Wet tissue folds just like real cloth, and the secret to using tissue realistically is realizing that thin cloth such as a cotton shirt will have many more folds than thick cloth such as a heavy blanket. Use additional layers of tissue to simulate thicker material; as many as ten plies of tissue may be required to duplicate a thick blanket or heavy overcoat. When using multiple layers, it is best to layer the tissues, cut out a rough shape, wet carefully, and then cut to the exact shape.

Drape your tarp, discarded jacket, or blanket in position, carefully arranging the folds with a toothpick or paintbrush. Use extra tissue to soak off excess moisture and then brush on a heavy coat of white glue. After this initial glue coat has dried, brush on more glue to eliminate the telltale texture of the tissue, then paint.

Simple scratchbuilding. In spite of the variety of commercially available accessories, sooner or later you'll find yourself faced with

3 A B-24 spotted on an open hardstand leaves a lot of space around it to be filled, and accessories are a good way to hold viewer interest and create an impression of activity.

Feldlazarette 4

Adolf Hitler Strasse

Jacques Pepin
BOULANGER

**BASTOGNE
15 km**

SHELL, H.E.
155MM HOWITZER
578990326

If you have a home computer, it can help a lot with your modeling. Making road signs, insignia, name plates for the diorama base, and artwork for photoetching (see Chapter 12) used to be painstaking projects, but they are all a snap with a computer and printer. If you have a laser printer, you can even print your own decals on blank decal paper (available by mail from Micro Mark). An inkjet printer works nicely for signs (color yet!), but it won't do decals, because the ink is water soluble. Some samples of what you can do are shown here.

the requirement to scratchbuild something special that you need. The mere mention of the word "scratchbuilding" is enough to start shivers down the spine of many modelers. It shouldn't be. Scratchbuilding doesn't always have to mean building an airfield control tower complete with full interior and working lights; it can be as simple as making bedrolls out of tissue paper. If you've never scratchbuilt anything, start with small projects and gradually work your way up to more ambitious ones. Knowing how to build things from scratch opens up many diorama subjects that would otherwise be beyond your ability.

One of the first steps in becoming a competent scratchbuilder is to learn how to use *all* the materials available to you. I emphasize "all" because some modelers work exclusively with one or two materials, ignoring others. This is a severely restrictive approach that often results in unnecessary work. Each material—styrene, wood, brass, and epoxy—has its own strengths and weaknesses; each is more suitable for some jobs than others, and each is

easy to use once you know a few simple tricks of the trade.

Working with sheet styrene. Although most modelers have built plastic models, few have scratchbuilt with sheet styrene. Sheet styrene plastic is usually white. It is commonly available in thicknesses of ten (.010″), twenty (.020″), thirty (.030″), and forty (.040″) thousandths of an inch. Five (.005″) and sixty (.060″) thousandths are also available. Evergreen Scale Models makes styrene strips and scribed sheets. Small strips are not particularly useful unless you need a lot of them, since you can easily cut your own, but thicker pieces, up to ¼″ square, are useful and can save a lot of time that would be spent laminating thinner stock. Plastruct offers a line of ABS sheet and structural shapes that is compatible with styrene if you use Plastruct's special Plastic Weld cement.

Sheet styrene is easy to cut and cement, and thin stock is flexible enough to make curved surfaces. It can be sanded and polished

smooth, carved easily with a knife, and permanently formed by the application of moderate heat. Its disadvantages are that thin sections not supported from behind will warp, and sections thicker than the standard sheets must be laminated or constructed hollow. Small, delicate fabrications such as antennas are very fragile.

Cutting styrene is easy. Using a straight-edge as a guide, scribe the surface once or twice with a knife and snap the pieces apart. Even curves can be cut in this manner. Thicker sheets may require two or more passes with the knife. Thin sheets may be cut with scissors or a paper cutter, and holes punched with a paper punch; styrene strips can be cut with flush-cutting nippers. Styrene can be sanded using fine sandpaper wrapped around a small block of wood, and cosmetic emery boards also come in handy.

Styrene, like the plastic in kits, is cemented with solvents that dissolve the plastic and form permanent welds. Methyl ethyl ketone and ethylene dichloride are the best solvents; they can be purchased by the pint or quart from hardware stores, plastics supply houses, or industrial chemical distributors. Liquid plastic cements sold for plastic models also work well. Many of these solvents evaporate too fast to be used like other glues. Instead, the procedure is to align the two pieces to be glued and carefully touch a brush full of solvent to the seam. Capillary action will carry the solvent down the length of the seam, and the bond will be almost instantaneous. Both simple and more complex box shapes can be easily assembled in this manner. Simple curves are made by cementing thin sheet to curved back braces.

Styrene can be glued to other materials with 5-minute epoxy or alpha cyanoacrylate (ACC) "super glue." Do not use white glue or other adhesives meant for porous surfaces such as wood; the bond may hold momentarily, but it will soon give way.

The simplest technique for heat-forming styrene is stretching sprue to make plastic rod and wire. This is done by holding a piece of scrap runner frame over a candle or other heat source until soft, then stretching it to the desired thickness. Stretching very hot plastic yields hair-thin "wire," excellent for aircraft antennas; letting the plastic cool a second or two before stretching makes thicker plastic rod.

Another simple heat-forming method is to wrap styrene strip around metal tubing or a wood block. The styrene is held in place with rubber bands or clamps and immersed in boiling water for 5 or 10 seconds. This is a fast and easy method for making plastic rings, rectangular frames, and straps. Complicated shapes can be heat-formed by carving male and female dies out of wood, clamping a piece of

4 Ingenuity is important in creating accessories. This water pump was built from the pipe from a bazooka, the base from a truck transmission, and the handle and swivel posts from a 60mm mortar. The concrete base and wooden trough were made from sheet styrene.

5 If you work in 1/48 scale or smaller, model railroad parts such as these are extremely useful for detailing all kinds of diorama scenes.

styrene between them, and immersing the sandwich in hot water until the die halves come together. A low-temperature oven is a good substitute for boiling water, although water is more convenient.

A more sophisticated heat-forming technique is vacuum-forming. This involves heating a sheet of plastic until it is flexible, laying it over a wooden form, and using a vacuum pump to pull the rubbery plastic down tight against the form. A toy vacuum former was made years ago by Mattel; it was perfect for modelwork, but has been off the market for some time. A company called Idea Development makes an assemble-it-yourself machine that works off a home vacuum cleaner.

Because it has no grain, styrene is best suited for modeling metal, but it is also useful for modeling wood, particularly heavily weathered wood. Wood grain detail can be scribed into the surface with a scriber or knife. Scratchbuilt styrene parts can be painted with any model paint suitable for plastic kits.

Scratchbuilding with wood. In this age of plastic, there is a tendency for modelers to overlook the classic modeling medium, wood. Wood is an excellent choice when the job calls for a lot of strip material in a variety of thicknesses and sizes, or when the thickness of walls or other features would make construction in plastic awkward. Wood is easily cut, sanded, and finished, and can even be curved slightly. Its disadvantages include visible grain (which can either be used to advantage or eliminated) and lack of strength in thin sections.

Several woods are suitable for modeling: old favorites include birch, pine, basswood, apple, cherry, boxwood, and pear. Stay away from open-grained woods such as oak, walnut, or mahogany for very small work. Balsa is excellent for flying model aircraft where weight is an important consideration, but it is too soft and flimsy for precision miniature work.

Basswood is probably the best all-around wood for model building, and it is readily available in hobby shops in a large variety of sizes and shapes. Strip basswood sizes range from $^{1}/_{32}''$ square to $^{3}/_{4}''$ square, and structural shapes and various thicknesses of sheet wood, both plain and scribed, are also offered. Plywood is also useful. Most hobby shops stock special plywood for model planes and boats. This comes in a variety of thicknesses, and is excellent for structure walls and other applications that call for thick material. If you are building something that calls for a large quantity of structural shapes, such shapes are a lot cheaper in wood than they are in plastic, particularly in the larger sizes.

The first step in working with wood is to eliminate its natural fuzz. Even if you can't see it, sawing fuzz is there and will become visible as soon as you paint the wood. Spray all wood parts with fast-drying clear lacquer to raise the grain. When this is dry, give each piece a quick rubdown with fine steel wool. This treatment provides a smooth surface for painting, staining, or varnishing, but leaves the wood sufficiently porous to be cemented with standard wood glues.

Wood can be cut with a razor saw, knife, flush-cutting nippers, or even scissors. A simple miter box for cutting 45- and 90-degree angles is useful. Ordinary white glue such as Elmer's is more than adequate for joining wood parts. I also use an aliphatic resin glue called Wilhold. Epoxy will also work well on

6 This scene called for a lot of sandbags, so I made one out of epoxy putty and made a one-piece RTV mold and a bunch of quick plaster castings.

7 Here is a soldering aid in use while making a delicate "crow's foot" radio antenna assembly from wire.

8 Alumilite is a quick-setting casting resin available in most hobby shops. In fact, it sets so fast, you sometimes don't have time to pour it. I keep mine refrigerated, which helps retard the setting time.

wood (useful when gluing wood to plastic or metal) but standard super glues will not, since they are designed for nonporous surfaces. There are cyanoacrylate adhesives (super glues) designed for wood now on the market, and these are excellent. Hot Stuff, Jet, and Zap are brands sold in hobby shops.

Working with wood can proceed almost as fast, sometimes faster, as working with plastic. The glue dries rapidly in small applications, and precutting stripwood parts can make even the most complicated assembly go together very quickly. A set of clamps, either screw or sliding wedge type, is useful but not essential. Wood can be painted with any standard modeling paint—oil-, water-, or lacquer-base.

No special preparation or priming is necessary. Wood can be stained for a variety of interesting and attractive effects. Stains accent the grain of the wood beautifully, and there are some excellent "weatherbeaten" stains available in the model railroad field. Most glues are stain-resistant; staining the model after assembly will leave ugly glue marks at all of the joints, no matter how carefully you work. This problem is easily avoided by staining all parts before assembly.

Working with brass. Brass is the ideal material to use when a structure calls for a framework with many curves and bends, or when you must build a delicate assembly with a lot of strength such as a "crow's foot" antenna. Brass is a relatively soft metal and can be cut with saws, tin snips, or clippers. It can be sanded or filed smooth and takes a high polish. Brass wire can be *annealed* (made softer and more flexible) by heating it with a propane torch until it glows dull red and then allowing it to cool.

Brass can be glued with super glue or epoxy, but no glued joint will ever approach the strength of a soldered one. Miniature soldering is not difficult once you learn the basic principles. The first principle is that solder will stick *only* to those parts of the metal that have been cleaned and prepared with flux. Excess

solder will ball up on a fluxed area instead of flowing to any unfluxed portion of the work. The second principle is that both pieces being soldered must be heated to the flowing temperature of the solder for the process to work. It is the heat in the joint, not in the solder, that makes the solder flow and provides a strong bond. If you are soldering big pieces, it may take a while to heat them up even if the area of the joint is small. If you have difficulty soldering, it is probably because you have failed to observe one of these two principles.

The tools you'll need for soldering are quite inexpensive. You'll need a soldering iron, preferably one with replaceable tips. Any type of 60/40 tin-lead solder is fine, although the small-diameter solder sold for electronics work is best. You will also need flux; the best kinds are acid-base liquids or pastes. Don't try to use cored solders that include flux in the solder wire. These are convenient for electrical work, but too sloppy for modeling. You can use cored solder as ordinary solder without any problem, but don't count on the core for fluxing. To heat the work to the proper temperature without burning your fingers, you'll need something to hold the pieces in position while you work.

Miniature soldering is different from electrical work. Here, the neatness of the joint is important, so you need precise control over

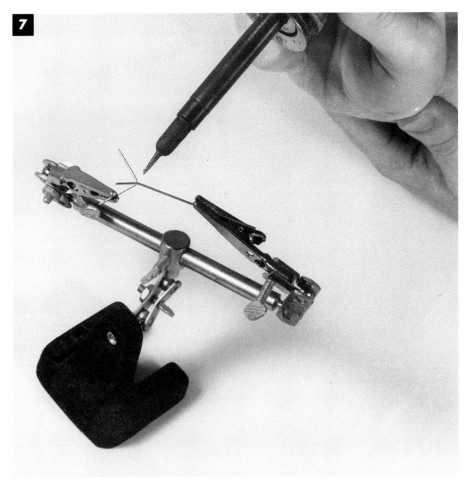

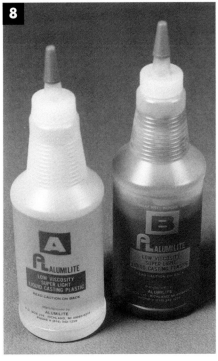

the amount of solder applied. Plug in your soldering iron, and while you are waiting for it to heat up, put your pieces in the fixture and align them. When your work is positioned and the iron is hot, brush a small amount of flux into the joint. Then cut off a small bit of the solder, just enough to do the job, and pick it up with the tip of the iron. In order to get the solder to stick, you may have to clean the tip of the iron by filing or scraping away the oxide. If this doesn't work, dip only the tip of the iron into the flux. Carry the little ball of solder to the work and touch it to the joint. Let the heat flow from the iron through the solder to the work. When the parts reach the right temperature, the solder will suddenly flow into the joint. Pull the iron away, and the job is done. Allow the joint to cool naturally, because hastening the cooling can weaken the joint. In small joints the solder cools in seconds, and with a bit of practice you will find that you can solder almost as fast as you can glue.

Soldering large pieces or multiple joints is more challenging. Large pieces call for more heat, so you may find it easier to solder heavy brass parts with a torch. The standard Bernz-o-Matic propane torch sold in hardware stores will do. It may be a bit clumsy at first, but keep the torch on the lowest setting and it will work quite well. The trouble with multiple joints is that heat applied to one joint may

melt the one you just finished. This problem is cured by the use of heat sinks, small metal clamps placed between the joint that is already soldered and the one that is about to be. The heat sink draws off enough heat to prevent the previous joint from melting.

Working with epoxy putty. Epoxy putty is ideal for jobs calling for detailed shapes or compound curves that would be awkward to carve in wood or plastic. It is excellent for making vacuum-form patterns, seat cushions, parachute packs, duffel bags, knapsacks, and figure conversions. This is a material few hobbyists are familiar with, since it is not commonly sold in hobby shops. It is a two-part epoxy material that comes in sticks that are kneaded together to form a putty with the consistency and workability of modeling clay. Its primary uses are sealing automotive pipes and body work. A plumber's or automotive supply house is where you are most likely to find it. (Brookstone Company, Peterborough, New Hampshire, sells it by mail. You can also find sources for it on the internet.) Since it is not formulated specifically for modeling, each brand has a little different consistency. One brand, Duro E-pox-e Ribbon, is widely available in dime stores.

Epoxy putty holds the shape it is molded into, and sets in about 2 hours. Applying low

heat can reduce the setting time to about 15 minutes. The putty is water soluble, sticks to itself quite well, and can be made even stickier by the application of a little water. Putty work is best done in stages: make the basic shape, and when the first part has cured, apply a little water to the hardened epoxy and add the new detail. The hardened putty can be filed, sanded, machined, carved, sawed, and even polished with fine steel wool.

Boxes, crates, and tubs. Let's put all this newfound knowledge to work by scratchbuilding some simple boxes and crates. It makes no difference whether you use wood or plastic. The drawing shows the basic assembly procedure. Note how the binding pieces at each end of the box are cut longer than necessary, glued on overlapping one another, and trimmed to size after the glue has dried. This simple principle is worth repeating: *Never cut anything to exact size if it can be glued in place oversize and trimmed to size later.* This little trick will give your work the appearance of precision craftsmanship without any of the bother.

Metal toolboxes can be made from sheet styrene. Add handles and other hardware with wire and bits of plastic. Since metal boxes are pretty flimsy, add a few nicks and dents with a knife, file, or Dremel tool and

BUILDING A CRATE

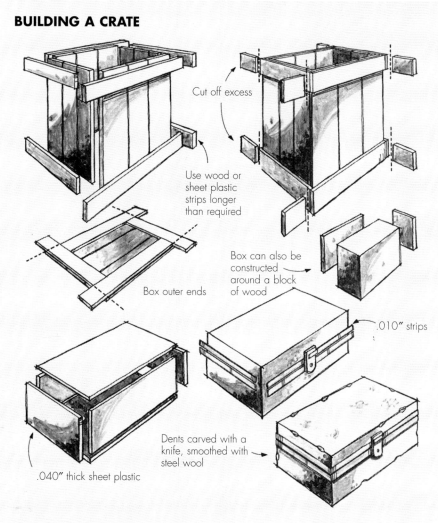

Cut off excess

Use wood or sheet plastic strips longer than required

Box can also be constructed around a block of wood

Box outer ends

.040" thick sheet plastic

.010" strips

Dents carved with a knife, smoothed with steel wool

BUILDING A METAL STORAGE BOX

SIMPLE FURNITURE

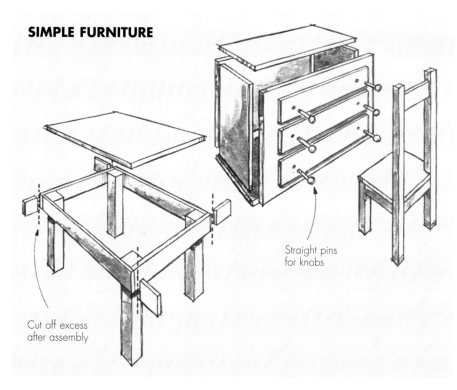

Straight pins for knobs

Cut off excess after assembly

9 Little touches like the stenciled lettering (taken from aircraft decal sheets) on these wood crates are what make the difference between average dioramas and really good ones.

10 The workstands on the B-26 assembly line are made of brass wire, soldered together. The air hose hanging limply from the overhead is shaped solder, and the air wrench is a model railroad part in disguise.

round off the edges of the box by rubbing with fine steel wool.

Furniture and work platforms.

Simple furniture can be made in much the same way as crates. The drawing shows some workable designs that can be thrown together quickly when nothing elaborate is required. Workstands are an important part of aircraft maintenance scenes and are not hard to make. The real stands are usually made of light steel pipe, formed structural steel, or a combination of the two. Dig into your research library to see just what the work platform you require looks like. It was not uncommon for field units to whip up special items of their own in their welding shops.

The simplest workstand is a pipe frame. This can be made out of brass wire, soldered together. Most modern workstands have non-skid metal flooring, but it is not unusual to see plain plywood sheets bolted to the pipe frame. If you choose to simulate plywood, don't make the sheets bigger than a scale 4' x 8'. Safety tread metal flooring is easily duplicated by rubbing a piece of aluminum foil over a piece of fine wire screen with a pencil eraser. Miniature brass screen is sold in hardware stores as "furnace mesh." The textured aluminum foil is then glued to a plastic sheet, painted, and—presto—safety tread!

More complicated work platforms and ground-support equipment require more effort and planning, but essentially use the same techniques. The engine hoist shown in the drawing is a typical example—the hardest part of building one is figuring out how it fits together and what kit parts can be used. Most

PIPE FRAME WORK PLATFORM FOR AIRCRAFT MAINTENANCE

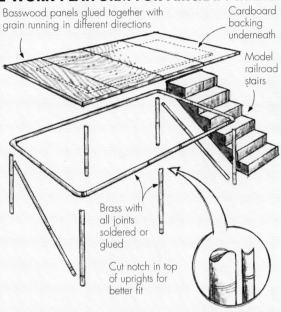

Basswood panels glued together with grain running in different directions

Cardboard backing underneath

Model railroad stairs

Brass with all joints soldered or glued

Cut notch in top of uprights for better fit

AIRCRAFT ENGINE HOIST

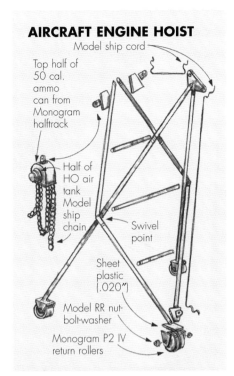

Model ship cord

Top half of 50 cal. ammo can from Monogram halftrack

Half of HO air tank Model ship chain

Swivel point

Sheet plastic (.020")

Model RR nut-bolt-washer

Monogram P2 IV return rollers

10

workstands, particularly standard issue, had wheels. Tail wheels from 1/72 or 1/144 aircraft work pretty well in 1/48 scale, until you realize that each platform calls for at least four of them! Airliner wheels from 1/144 scale models offer a less-expensive alternative, since each kit contains many of them, but even this is not a real solution to the problem. When you need many identical parts, one way to obtain them is to cast them yourself.

Casting your own parts. Casting is a technique that is indispensable to professional modelmakers, and with the proper materials, it is not difficult at all. The first thing you need is a pattern. This can be an original kit part, a

modified kit part, or something you have made up yourself. If the item you need is a complex assembly, you may have to break it down into several parts for casting.

The mold is made from RTV (room-temperature vulcanizing) rubber. The major manufacturers are General Electric and Dow Corning. There are many types; the material you want is the kind that requires no special scales for mixing, will cure against any pattern material, and is of sufficiently low viscosity to form an air-bubble-free mold without the use of a vacuum system. The GE rubber I use is RTV 11, which comes in one-pound containers and includes a small tube of catalyst. The mixing proportions for the catalyst are not

critical; the more catalyst you add, the faster the material cures. Low, humid heat can also speed curing, which normally takes from 4 to 24 hours.

Successful castings can be made with plaster, but I prefer two materials—Alumilite and Smooth-On. The disadvantage with Alumilite is that it sets in less than five minutes. Smooth-On has a longer working time. This means that you can pull your castings almost immediately, but it also means that you may not have enough time to eliminate air bubbles before the material starts to set. A neat trick is to store the bottles in the refrigerator; the plastic doesn't set up as quickly at lower temperatures.

CASTING YOUR OWN PARTS

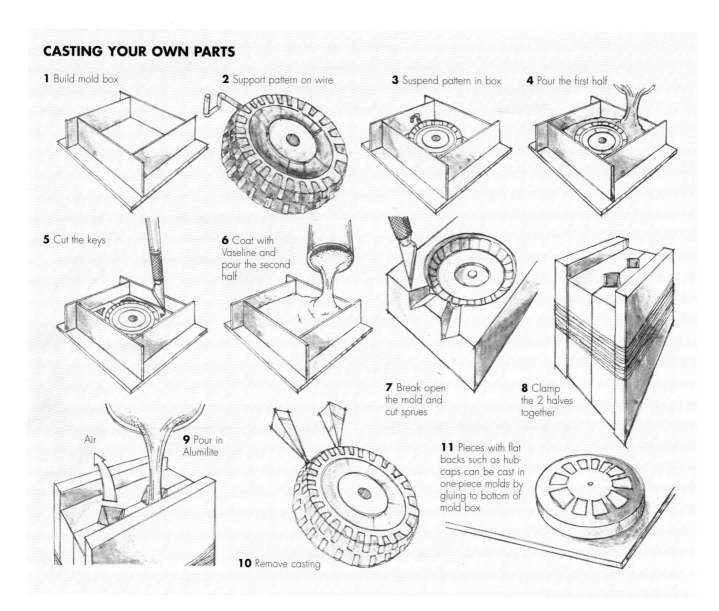

1 Build mold box

2 Support pattern on wire

3 Suspend pattern in box

4 Pour the first half

5 Cut the keys

6 Coat with Vaseline and pour the second half

7 Break open the mold and cut sprues

8 Clamp the 2 halves together

Air

9 Pour in Alumilite

10 Remove casting

11 Pieces with flat backs such as hubcaps can be cast in one-piece molds by gluing to bottom of mold box

The first step is to build a mold box. This serves only as a dike to hold the liquid rubber until it cures, so even a crude wall of modeling clay will do. The usual material for the box is wood or styrene, and the box should be large enough to surround the pattern with about ½" to spare on three sides, 1" on the fourth.

Support the pattern on a piece of bent brass wire. Insert the wire in a hole drilled in the side of the pattern, and glue the bent part of the wire to the side of the box with super glue, leaving the pattern suspended in midair in the center of the box.

Mix up the RTV as directed and pour it slowly into one corner of the mold box until the rubber level is halfway up the side of the pattern. When the rubber has cured, use a sharp knife to cut a chunk of rubber from each corner. When the second half is poured, these recesses will form locking keys to keep the halves in proper alignment.

Coat the first half of the mold with a thin layer of Vaseline, and pour the second half. When the second half has cured, break open

the mold, remove the pattern, and cut pouring sprues into the thick end of the mold. Cut two sprues, one to pour in the resin, the other a vent to allow the air to escape as the mold fills. Make the pouring sprue as large as possible.

Sandwich the mold between two blocks of wood and clamp it securely with rubber bands. Mix the resin and pour it slowly into the mold, allowing the air to escape from the vent. You can eliminate surface air bubbles in the casting by brushing a coating of resin over the two mold halves before they are mated. Leave a generous amount of resin in the sprue to take the place of any air bubbles that rise to the surface. You can squeeze the mold with your fingers to "burp" out large air bubbles.

When the resin in the sprue has cured, open the mold and remove the casting. Check for air bubbles. Not all of your castings will be perfect, but with some experience under your belt a rejection rate of one casting out of five is achievable. The RTV has a tendency to inhibit the surface cure of polyester resins, so your castings may be a little sticky or have sur-

face blemishes when they are first removed from the mold. The stickiness goes away in a day or two, and surface goo can be wiped off with acetone or liquid plastic cement.

This system is simple enough that even a beginner can get good results on the first or second try. Simple pieces with flat, undetailed backs can be cast in one-piece molds by gluing the flat surface to the bottom of the mold box. Both special parts, the pilaster and the rows of books, made for the shadow box in Chapter 15 were cast in one-part molds.

Detailed furniture and complex equipment. When your diorama includes residential buildings, you may need furniture that is a little more elaborate than simple sticks. Building such pieces could be complicated and time-consuming if you had to make each item entirely from scratch, but there is no reason to do it the hard way.

This is an excellent opportunity to exercise your ingenuity as a creative scavenger, and the best picking grounds are, as usual, the model

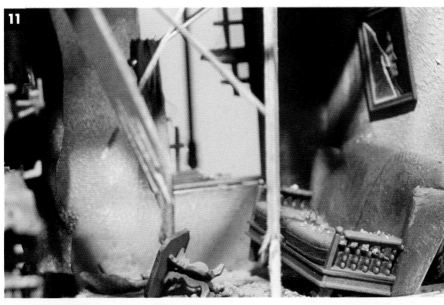

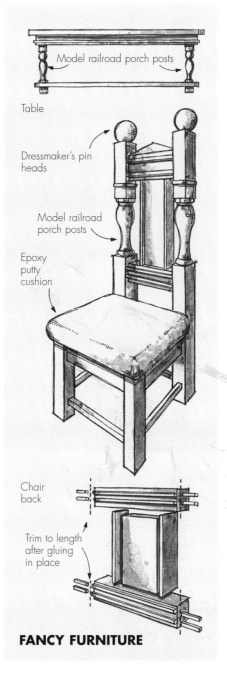

FANCY FURNITURE

railroad section of your hobby shop. Several companies make metal or plastic porch posts that can easily be modified into nifty table legs. By varying the sheet styrene top, you can swiftly put together round and oval tables, dining room tables, coffee tables, and even drop leaf tables. They'll even be a matched set! Porch posts can also be modified to make chairs, with epoxy putty upholstered seats. There is a wide variety of model railroad architectural details—eaves, braces, cornices, corbels, roof ornaments, windows, and doors—just waiting to be turned into fancy furniture.

Ground support equipment, particularly equipment appropriate for modern jet aircraft, is a sore point for diorama builders. A few

pieces are available, but most equipment still has to be built from scratch. You can convert HO or O scale roadworking or farm equipment to make a few of the less specialized items, but you'll have to build most service units from sheet styrene and settle for detailing them with scrounged parts. The heavier Evergreen Scale Models styrene strips are really handy here. Working with nippers, you can put together the blocks that form the basic shape of a power unit or other service module in fairly short order. Piping, valves, gauges, and other details can come from the model railroad department, and even the cheapest toy cars and trucks will furnish well-detailed wheels.

11 This sofa in the wrecked building on the sturmpanzer IV diorama was built from the back seat of a car kit, and detailed with HO balcony railing and Plastruct shapes. Note the broken spring and the stuffing coming out of the seat.

12 The air compressor for the B-24 polka dot painting scene started out as an HO scale tractor model. The seat and large wheels were removed, and a simple ABS (Plastruct) frame and railroad air tanks were added. The air hose is solder.

CHAPTER SEVEN

Superdetailing, Battle Damage, and Interiors

Superdetailing is a subject that could fill a whole book. Here, we are concerned only with the kinds of superdetailing that are most frequently called for in dioramas. If you are interested in more superdetailing tips, read Mike Ashey's books *Detailing Scale Model Aircraft* and *Model Aircraft Tips & Techniques*. My own *Modeling Tanks & Military Vehicles* may also help. All are available from Kalmbach Books.

Articulating aircraft control surfaces. One of the most frequently called for modifications to aircraft is repositioning the rudder, elevator, ailerons, and flaps. While it is standard procedure in peacetime to lock control surfaces in their neutral positions,

this practice was often allowed to lapse in wartime. Since the controls have individual locking systems, you can choose which ones you allow to hang loose. If the pilot's foot pedals are unlocked, the rudder will swing to one side or the other depending upon which way the pedals are pushed (if the pedals are visible on your model, make sure that the pedal is pushed forward on the side to which the rudder is swung). The elevator will be down if the stick is forward, and the ailerons will shift if the stick is to one side or the other (stick to the right-right aileron up, left down). The landing flaps will most likely be down on aircraft that have just landed, and the trim tabs (the small control surfaces built into the trailing edges of the larger ones) are often seen at odd angles when the plane is on the ground.

Most kits come with the control surfaces molded in the straight position as parts of the wings, fuselage, or stabilizers. To articulate them, you will have to cut them out with a saw or knife and replace them in the desired position. The most efficient way to do this is with a thin 1″ circular saw mounted in a hand motor tool. The plastic cuts easily, you have excellent control over the tool, and the cutting line is thin enough that both pieces are salvageable. The alternate methods are to cut through the plastic with a knife or to use a razor saw to cut through the two accessible edges of the flap, scribe the third edge halfway through with a knife, then snap the panel free.

Cutting and repositioning control surfaces such as flaps and ailerons is a subtle way to add realism to aircraft models.

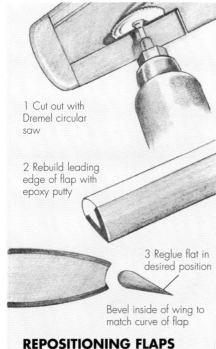

1 Cut out with Dremel circular saw

2 Rebuild leading edge of flap with epoxy putty

3 Reglue flat in desired position

Bevel inside of wing to match curve of flap

REPOSITIONING FLAPS

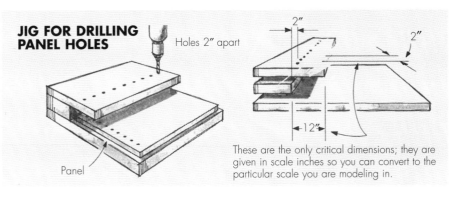

JIG FOR DRILLING PANEL HOLES

Holes 2" apart

Panel

2"

2"

12"

These are the only critical dimensions; they are given in scale inches so you can convert to the particular scale you are modeling in.

Before cementing the control surface back in place, you may have to build up and round off its hinge edge. Do this rebuilding with sheet styrene, epoxy putty, or a combination of the two. Use a sanding block to round off the edge. Seal off the ends of flaps with sheet styrene. On large-scale models, you may want to add bracing or other detail on the flap ends.

Now bevel the inside edges of the areas on the fixed structure of the aircraft until they mate properly with the curved edges of the control surfaces. Sand, carve, and file for a few minutes, then check the fit. Continue until a good fit is obtained. It needn't be perfect—a scale 1" gap is quite acceptable as long as it is consistent along the length of the movable section.

Don't forget the actuating rods, the operating devices connected to the cables that lead to the controls in the cockpit. On the larger control surfaces they are mostly internal, but the trim tab actuators are usually outside the wing. The small arm on the tab can be made from sheet styrene, and the rod that pushes it fashioned from wire or stretched sprue.

Removing access panels. Most aircraft maintenance scenes call for access panels to be removed, revealing the hardware that is being worked on. The first step in removing a panel, whether it is a cowling, engine nacelle, or fuselage panel, is to make sure that it was removable on the original aircraft. Access panels are removed in the same manner as the control surface pieces. Again, the best method is to use a thin-bladed circular saw in a motor tool, since this leaves the panel salvageable. The alternative methods are to cut out the panel with a knife, or to drill a series of holes around the edge of the panel, then cut away the plastic between them. Once the panel is removed, carefully trim the edges of the opening and carve away the inside edge so that the aircraft skin appears thin. Use narrow strips of .010" styrene to add the framing around the edges of the opening, and drill a series of fastening holes in it with a pin vise or Dremel tool running on very low speed.

Don't forget the panel you removed. The plastic piece is far too thick, but you may be able to bevel the edge to make it look thin. A

1 Any aircraft maintenance scene requires that one or more access panels be removed. This diorama of a P-61 in the South Pacific is a fairly complicated example: both the engine nacelles are stripped, one engine is removed, the gun bays are open, and the nose fairing is removed to service the radar.

2 Most folded-wing carrier aircraft can stand some extra detailing in the wing roots. Here's an example.

simple alternative to using the kit part is to vacuum-form a thin plastic panel over it. This provides a thin version of the original, accurately curved to match the contour of the plane. Don't forget to drill the fastening holes around the outside edge of the panel. Be careful to space the holes evenly; if you do a lot of this sort of work, it is worth the time to build a simple drilling jig (drawing above).

If you are ambitious enough to remove more than one panel, you'll have to model some of the exposed framework. This is easier than it looks. Before you do any cutting,

3

4

5

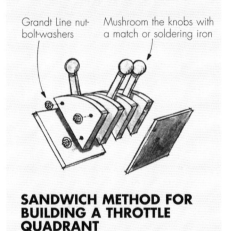

Grandt Line nut-bolt-washers   Mushroom the knobs with a match or soldering iron

SANDWICH METHOD FOR BUILDING A THROTTLE QUADRANT

3 After making an accurate replica of a Pratt and Whitney R2800 engine for the P-61 diorama, I decided to hang the engine in midair from a portable hoist where all the intricate detail can be appreciated. (For details, see text.)

4 Engine nacelle detailing for the P-61 is shown here in progress. The cuts in the nacelle area have been made, and the scratchbuilt engine support framework and fire wall are in place.

5 All of the various pipes, tubes, and wires on the engine mount of this derelict B-25 were made from small-diameter soft wire solder.

assemble research material. What does the engine look like—front, back, and sides? How is it mounted to the airframe? What does the nacelle look like with the engine removed? Is there a fire wall? What kind of electrical, hydraulic, and fuel connections are present? You should have answers to all of these questions before you begin.

The example shown is an exposed engine nacelle framework on the Monogram 1/48 P-61. Each engine assembly and mounting will be different, so the exact method will vary somewhat, but the basic principles and procedures remain the same. The first step was to cut away all of the engine nacelle panels that were to be removed, cutting along panel lines. This leaves a gaping hole in the wing that immediately makes you wish you hadn't done it. The next step on the P-61 was to install the fire wall. The fire wall was cut from .020″ styrene sheet to match the inside shape of the nacelle and glued in place. This left a narrow

rim showing around the bottom edge of the nacelle, which was drilled out to resemble framing. The fire wall was detailed with Plastruct framing and scavenged parts that duplicate electrical, hydraulic, and fuel connections to the missing engine. The panels near the leading edge of the wing were beveled to appear thinner, and a circular frame cut from styrene with sharpened dividers was glued in place. Additional framing was added using sheet styrene, and pieces of plastic drinking straw were used to simulate the air ducts.

Detailing engines by "creative gizmology." The next step on the P-61 was the engine, which was to be suspended from a hoist, completely clear of the aircraft. Starting with the engine provided in the kit, holes were drilled at intervals around the

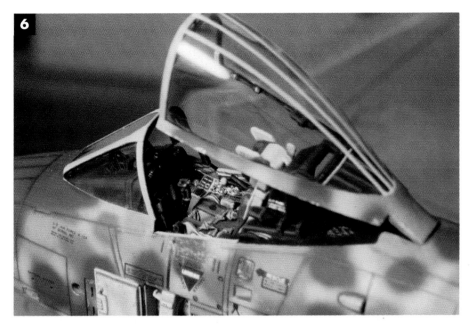

6 Cockpits, particularly modern ones, just cry out for superdetailing. Dave Smith's A-10 is an excellent example of the level of detail that you can achieve with careful work.

7 To make convincing bullet holes, first thin the plastic from the inside, then punch and twist the holes with a knife.

spool of very fine wire solder can cost upwards of $15, but if a group of modelers gets together to split the cost, the solder is well worth the expense and there will be plenty of the small-diameter solder to go around. The great advantage of wire solder over other wire is that solder is extremely flexible and stays exactly where you put it. It can be twisted and braided into cord or formed into other intricate designs.

To get back to our P-61 example, the gearbox behind the Wright Cyclone engine was made of Plastruct tubing, with nut-bolt-washers added around the rim and the end of an HO air reservoir used to cover the hole in the center. Wiring, hydraulic lines, oil reservoirs, pumps, and generators were built up from HO railroad parts. The air filter assembly was added using Plastruct tubing, with bolts, hooks, and other details by Grandt Line. The engine framing, which attaches to the fire wall, was made of brass rod and styrene. Additional details on the front of the engine included new covers for the magnetos and a governor assembly between them. Strips of stretched sprue were cemented around the prop shaft to provide the proper grooves.

Other mechanical details on aircraft can be modeled in much the same manner. On the P-61 the detailed areas include the gun bays and the nose radar. The P-61's guns were electrically loaded and fired, so there was a lot of gadgetry mounted in the real bays. Very little of this clutter would be visible in the finished diorama, but the bays looked unrealistically empty. No real effort was made to duplicate actual assemblies point for point; the goal was simply to create the appearance of a lot of gear when seen from the usual viewpoint. This is a rare case where "imagineering" is not only permissible, it is essential. Any effort made to get all of the details right in this area would be strictly a matter of personal satisfaction, because little of the work could ever be appreciated.

The "imagineering" approach was clearly out of the question for the radar gear, since it is right up front in plain sight. The gear provided in the kit was adequate, but seemed sparse when compared to photos of the real plane. A few railroad gizmos and some solder "plumbing" provided the required extra detail.

Cockpit details. Aside from the engine and mechanical equipment compartments, the part of an aircraft that cries out most for

bullet-shaped crankcase and fine wire solder glued into them. These wires were then cut to length and positioned to duplicate the ignition collars. Circular cowling frames were cut from styrene, drilled, and mounted on the cylinder banks. There should be two rows of fastening holes around the outer rim of the frame, but even with the smallest drills there is only room for one. The cowl flaps were cut from the kit and mounted on the second ring.

Final detailing of the engine involved an indispensable technique that I call "creative gizmology." This is the use of many plastic bits and pieces scrounged from various kits to simulate complex machinery. The most famous examples of this technique are the spacecraft created for films such as *2001: A Space Odyssey* and *Star Wars*. These models were detailed with parts scavenged from every plastic kit imaginable. The best source for gizmos is the model railroading department of your hobby shop. Cal-Scale, Grandt Line, and other firms offer brass and plastic detailing parts for HO scale railroad cars and locomotives. The brass pieces can be expensive if you need them in quantity, but the plastic items are cheap and the detail is simply amazing.

You will not want to use unmodified railroad parts often, because they soon become recognizable even to fellow airplane modelers, but you can cut them apart and recombine them to your heart's content, and this is really the crux of "gizmology." I offer no apologies for the modeling inaccuracies inherent in "gizmology," because the purpose of this technique is to simulate complex mechanisms that would be exhausting to make any other way; from a purely practical viewpoint, "gizmology" yields 90 percent of the results of painstakingly accurate modeling in only 10 percent of the time. This is not, however, a license to conjure up unlikely mechanisms out of thin air. The idea is to use available parts to represent mechanisms that actually existed, not to create new ones of your own.

Another important material for detailing complex mechanical systems is wire solder. This is the same solder used for wiring and working with brass. Hardware stores and electronics supply houses stock three or four sizes ranging from $\frac{1}{8}$" in diameter down to about $\frac{1}{32}$" Smaller sizes, down to .010", can be obtained from solder manufacturers, who will even make up spools to your specifications. A

8,9 Don't get carried away when modeling battle damage. Although this B-17 is in pretty rough shape, it is still flyable. Large hits require that you model some internal structure. The damaged engine on the same aircraft includes extensive flak damage in the cowl and prop.

superdetailing is the cockpit. Before you start, make sure that your efforts will be visible; the open cockpit of a fighter will show much more detail than the enclosed flight deck of a bomber. Make sure you have adequate reference material on how the real aircraft cockpit looked. Detailing is largely a matter of being resourceful and employing "gizmology." Use railroad parts, supplemented by solder wiring and piping, and scratchbuilt accessories. Make toggle switches by drilling holes in the instrument panel and inserting bits of stretched sprue from behind. If the switches stick up too far, they can be trimmed in place once the glue has dried. Throttles can be made by sandwiching sheet styrene and stretched sprue, and throttle knobs can be formed by holding the end of each lever near a soldering iron or candle. Gun sights are made from sheet styrene, a few railroad parts, and clear plastic. If the kit seat is wrong, a correct pattern can be made from wood and a proper one vacuum-formed, with cushions added from epoxy putty. Seat belts and parachute harnesses can be made with cloth adhesive tape. Waldron Model Products makes 1/72, 1/48, and 1/32 scale buckles, hinges, foot pedals, and other cockpit details.

Parachute stowage is an important aspect of cockpit detailing. Particularly on carrier-borne aircraft, the chute doubles as the seat cushion and the pilot buckles his harness to it

when he sits down. In other cases the harness is permanently attached to the chute, but the whole rig is left in the plane, spread over the back of the seat. Another practice is for the pilot to put on the entire rig, either a seat or backpack, before entering the plane. In larger multi-engine World War II aircraft it was common practice to wear only the harness and carry a detachable chest or backpack, which was stowed out of the way and clipped on only in an emergency. Find out which method was used on the aircraft you are modeling, and take the time to install it properly.

Battle damage for aircraft. Battle damage, either old or new, adds a lot of character to diorama aircraft, but be careful not to overdo it. Older damage usually takes two forms, patches on the skin of the aircraft (make these from .005" styrene, glued in place and sanded and steel-wooled down until they are barely visible), and replacement parts of different colors, either faded parts cannibalized from wrecks or freshly painted new ones. During the transition of U.S. aircraft from olive drab to natural metal during World War II, it was not uncommon to see both colors intermingled. The most famous example was the B-17 *Little Miss Mischief,* a silver plane that was olive drab from the wings back.

New battle damage consists mostly of bullet or flak holes in the plane's skin. The best way to make bullet holes is not to punch a hot needle through the plastic, but to thin the plastic out from behind until it is translucent, then punch and twist in the holes with a knife point. Entry holes should be punched from the outside so that the edges are pushed in, and exit holes punched from the inside, so that the jagged edges are pushed out. Larger

holes are made the same way, but bear in mind that where extensive damage reveals the plane's internal structure, the framework must be added to your model. Bent and twisted remains of structural shapes are easily made from plastic sheeting and strip. In a few cases it is easier to heat and twist the structures once they are in place on the model, but it is usually better to form them before installation.

Other indications of aircraft battle damage are catastrophic oil leaks from the engines and wide smoke streaks from failed engines. Engine malfunction, either as a result of enemy action or simple breakdown, can be indicated by feathering the blades of the prop, turning them 90 degrees to reduce drag. Simply cut the blades off the model prop and cement them back in the feathered position.

When adding battle damage to an airplane, think carefully about what you are doing. If your plane has crashed, you can simulate any kind of damage, but if the machine has returned home safely, make sure the wounds you inflict are not obviously mortal ones. The safest procedures are either to model your damage directly from photos of a single aircraft, or to research the design of the plane to ensure you don't damage too many vital systems at once. For example, the B-17 was famous for the punishment it could take and still fly home, and while the B-24 could absorb equal abuse in some areas, its Davis wing and awkward tail were quite vulnerable—extensive damage in these areas was usually fatal. Most multi-engine aircraft could fly on only one engine, although this frequently called for exhausting effort by the pilot.

The fuselage of most planes could absorb a great deal of damage without affecting airworthiness, and most "home on a wing and a

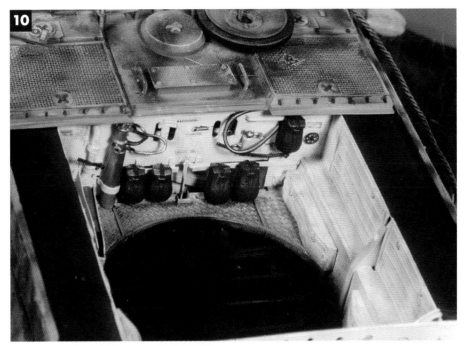

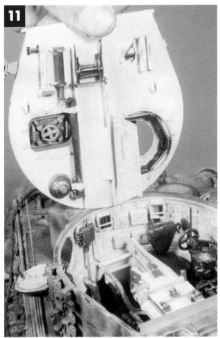

TRANSFERRING DETAIL TO A NEW HATCH COVER

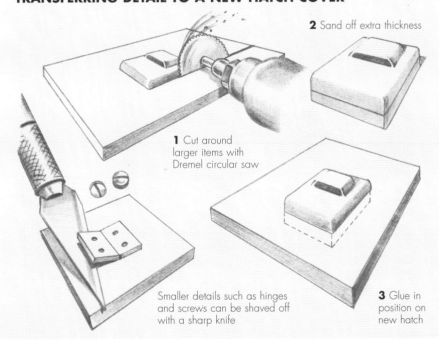

2 Sand off extra thickness

1 Cut around larger items with Dremel circular saw

Smaller details such as hinges and screws can be shaved off with a sharp knife

3 Glue in position on new hatch

DAMAGING AFV FENDERS

1 Cut through fender with Dremel tool

2 Heat fender with candle, bend with blunt end of pencil

3 Shave down edge with sharp knife

10, 11 This Tamiya Tiger I can be disassembled to show off the interior, so I went all out and added complete detail to the fighting compartment. Tanks are literally crammed with equipment, so detailing them presents a modeling challenge

prayer" cases suffered the bulk of their damage in the fuselage. The most vulnerable items in the fuselage were the control cables, which ran from the cockpit or flight deck aft to the rudder, elevators, and ailerons. These usually ran along the upper port side of the fuselage. A plane could still be controlled if only the cables running to the tail were cut, but if they were all gone, the plane could not fly.

Modeling fuel tank damage also calls for restraint. You can locate the fuel tanks by the round filler caps on the wings. It is all right to punch bullet holes in them, since nearly all tanks on Allied and German aircraft were self-sealing, but few planes could survive major flak hits in the tanks without bursting into flames.

Superdetailing armor interiors. Few armor kits contain interior detail, because such detail can rarely be seen. Even when the hatches are open, figures in them usually obstruct the view. Generally speaking, there is no reason to include detail that can't be seen, but there will be cases where you will want to open an engine compartment for maintenance or have hatches in the fighting compartment open, and interior detail will be required.

The first step is, as with aircraft, to assemble research material. The exact interior layout is different for each tank, but the general nature of the detail is pretty much the same, consisting of boxes and bins welded to the

12 Glancing blows like the ones that caused the shot damage on this Monogram Grant were not altogether rare, but they were unusual. Don't overdo such damage.

13 German skirt armor was only about ¼" thick, so it was quite susceptible to small arms and shrapnel damage.

turret walls and various other gear hanging on hooks. If only one hatch is open, a mere suggestion of an interior is sufficient, perhaps a simple gun breech, some plastic blocks glued to the inside of the hull, and a hint of wiring. You can duplicate the real vehicle item for item if you wish, but you'll find that in a dark interior, a "suggestive" approach is just as effective and a lot less work.

If all the hatches are to be open, the amount of work you'll have to do increases. There must be more to see, because more light will be admitted. The first step, however, may be to open the hatches themselves. While more and more kits come with separate hatches, sooner or later you will have to open a hatch that is molded shut. Use a thin-bladed circular saw in a motor tool, but do your final trimming with a knife. If the hatch cover is a separate molding, the job is pretty much done once the hole is cut, but if the hatch is molded on it will almost invariably be damaged by the cutting. Try to avoid damaging any of the surface details on the hatch. Most hatches are simple flat plates that you can make easily from sheet styrene, and details can be transferred from the original hatch to the new one. Shave off smaller bits such as screws and hinges with a sharp knife. Larger details, such as vision block covers and periscope housings, are more difficult to remove; in fact, it is often easier to remove the hatch from the detail rather than the detail from the hatch. Cut away the hatch from around the detail, leaving a small thickness of hatch. Sand away the excess material, and the detail is ready to glue in place on the new hatches.

Detailing the fighting compartment of a tank involves the same "creative gizmology" process used on aircraft. Various interior details can be made from raw plastic stock, but the judicious use of parts cannibalized from other kits will make the job a lot easier. Dashboards, steering wheels, and other parts from car kits are especially handy, and road wheels and other parts from tank kits are useful for making transmissions, elevation wheels, and similar gadgets. That limitless store of detail parts, the model railroad department, can provide all sorts of goodies. Unless you are determined to build a completely accurate interior, remember to check your work every so often to see what will actually be visible through the hatches. There is no point in detailing areas that won't

ever be seen, and you may also find a few areas you had overlooked.

Few modelers open the engine compartments on their tanks, but if you choose to do so, you don't have to build an engine from scratch. Truck and car kit engines can easily be adapted to tanks. The U.S. Lee, Grant, and some Sherman tanks used radial aircraft engines, which can be taken from 1/32 scale aircraft kits. Don't neglect the possibility of using in-line engines from 1/32 or 1/24 scale aircraft, either. You may have to do a bit of searching to find the engine that best suits your requirements, but there are plenty to choose from. (Engines are also available as aftermarket kits. See Chapter 12.)

One glance at a photo of a real tank engine compartment shows that it is crammed with wires, hydraulic lines, and accessory equipment. If you want to build a completely accurate model, you have a lot of work ahead of you. If, on the other hand, you

just want to create the appearance of the real tank, get a few photos or drawings to give you a visual impression to work from and start looking for parts that are close to the originals. The car or truck kit you swiped the engine from is an excellent source; hubcaps, for example, make excellent air filters. Ignition wire harnesses and hydraulic lines are best duplicated with wire solder.

Battle damage for armor. Tanks take a terrific beating in battle, and any armored vehicle that has been in the field for more than a few days will show wear and tear. Fenders and mud-guards are flimsy sheet metal, and they bend and twist easily. Damage of this sort must be built into the model before assembly because the process calls for heat, and you want to ensure that the only part distorted is the fender. Hold the fender over a candle and push on it with the blunt end of a pencil to determine when it becomes rubbery.

14 My completed Panzer IV E includes heavy desert weathering colors, open hatches and stowage bin, and open teeth on the spare tracks.

15 Particularly effective on this knocked-out Iraqi BRDM from the Gulf War by Italian Modeler Gian Luigi Benelli is the partially burned tire and small impact hole in the hull.

action, and it is not uncommon to see photos of vehicles with sections missing and the frames battered and twisted.

Knocked-out and abandoned tanks. There is little difference between a knocked-out tank and an abandoned one. Tanks are abandoned because of mechanical failure, and whenever possible they are sabotaged before the crew leaves. Thermite grenades are often used to freeze or explode the breech block of the gun or to burn out the engine. In other cases the oil is drained from the crankcase and the engine left running until the cylinders freeze up.

Before we discuss modeling knocked-out tanks, let's examine how they are knocked out. The most common antitank projectile during World War II was a high-velocity solid shot that was intended to penetrate the armor and then bounce around inside the tank. This shell created a small ragged hole at its point of entry, and unless it touched off a secondary explosion of the tank's ammunition, this hole would be the only damage visible from outside. Infantry antitank rocket launchers use a shaped charge that concentrates its entire explosive force on an area about the size of a coin, literally melting a hole through the armor and spraying the inside with molten metal. This, too, leaves only a small hole, but a hole with melted rather than ragged edges. A modern development is the "squash head" shell, which does not penetrate at all, but hits with such impact that it breaks lethal particles loose from the inside walls, ricocheting them around the interior. The actual mark of the fatal shot, therefore, is not hard to duplicate on a model tank. Doing so is simply a matter of drilling a hole and either chipping or beveling the edge.

Most photos of knocked-out vehicles show all the hatches open, which makes a considerable portion of the interior visible. Fortunately, you can smoke-blacken the interior, which greatly reduces what can be seen. Breaking loose some of the side-wall stowage gives a devastated look to the interior, and one of the most effective details, when viewed from outside, is a few loose wires hanging from the overhead. If the engine compartment has burned, the paint on the hatches will be blackened and peeling. This effect is easily duplicated by softening and wrinkling the

Then use the pencil to distort the fender into the desired shape. If the heat rounds off the edges of the plastic, scrape with a knife to restore the crispness of the edge. Do this only after bending, otherwise the heat will cause the thin edge to curl back unrealistically. Occasionally, sections of fender are torn off altogether. Modeling this is simply a matter of cutting off the required part and thinning the edge of whatever remains.

Damage caused by enemy fire usually consists of gouges or pockmarks on the surface of the armor plate. Although an occasional gouge is an effective and dramatic device, don't overdo it; try not to put more than one or two such marks on the same vehicle, and don't make a habit of it on every tank. Most tank battles take place at sufficiently short ranges that any hit is likely to be lethal, and glancing blows are the exception rather than the rule.

Nonarmored parts of the vehicle, such as fenders, stowage bins, and canvas mantlet cov-

ers, are highly susceptible to high-explosive, armor-piercing, and small arms fire. Shrapnel holes in the stowage bins are commonplace, and in some photos these bins have literally been blown to shreds. Distortion of non-armored features is accomplished using the same heat process used for fenders, while holes are made by thinning the plastic from behind, then punching and twisting the holes with a knife.

Most German vehicles in the latter part of World War II carried supplementary skirt armor along the sides. This served as protection against the shaped-charge projectiles of infantry weapons. These shells detonated on impact, and the skirts detonated them prematurely, dissipating the force of the explosion before it reached the main armor plate. This supplementary armor was about ¼" thick and hung in sections on frames welded to the sides and fenders of the vehicle. Skirt armor was frequently blown off in

16 If a 1/72 scale battleship is not the ultimate scratchbuilding project, it must be close to it! Lewis Pruneau, the Cecil B. DeMille of diorama builders, built this impressive USS *Texas* as part of his Pearl Harbor scene. The size of the case forced him to shorten the ship slightly because the manufacturer couldn't provide a single sheet of clear plexiglass long enough to cover the full length.

17 The two destroyers in Lewis's diorama, one damaged, one sunk. Few if any of us have the ambition to tackle a project this massive, but it is awe-inspiring to encounter someone who does.

paint with a little lacquer thinner, acetone, or liquid plastic cement.

When a tank burns out completely, the conflagration often spreads to the rubber on the road wheels and return rollers, and the rubber burns down to the steel rims of the wheels. To model this, remove the rubber portions of the wheel entirely by mounting the wheel in a motor tool and sanding. Road wheels with holes in them can be mounted on a screw-type mandrel; those without holes must be glued temporarily to a wood or plastic disc that can be mounted in the same manner. I use super glue for this purpose, because it is strong enough to hold under the stress of the work, yet can be dissolved later with acetone or nail polish remover. When grinding, work slowly so that the heat does not build up and melt the plastic.

One of the most common breakdowns associated with armored vehicles is throwing a track, either as a result of enemy fire or natural wear and tear. Most tracks are composed of individual links connected by pins. When a pin breaks, the vehicle will sometimes come to a stop immediately, but more often it continues until it runs out of track. On firm ground a tank may even continue some distance further, slewing sharply toward the damaged side. When modeling a thrown track, then, you are justified in showing no track at all, only part of the track (the rest being off the edge of the base), or the whole thing. Individual link traks are easiest to work with. Rubbery "loop" track is harder to control. Make sure, first of all, that the track is detailed on both sides, since both sides will be visible. When your vehicle is in place on the diorama base, position the track and secure each end with small pins. I use insect-mounting pins, because they have very tiny heads. Drill pilot holes slightly smaller than the pins in the base. Pin down each loop of track until you have the desired effect.

Tanks which have exploded are modeling challenges. Minor explosions usually do little more than lift the turret out of its ring, leaving it at a cockeyed angle, which is not at all hard to model and visually very effective. Larger explosions will crack and buckle the armor plate (armor plate does not bend), and occasionally pop open welded seams. The best way to duplicate this sort of damage is to scribe the desired cracks on the underside of the armor plate and then give the model a good whack with a hammer.

Finally, let me add a note of restraint. Catastrophic destruction caused by a major explosion will reveal the interior, which, even twisted and charred, will call for a lot of time and effort to model. There is a lot of wiring and equipment inside a tank, and when the vehicle is blown up it creates a mess that is harder to model than you might think. If it is to be done right, a shattered hulk is not a destruction job at all, but a difficult and exacting construction project involving extensive scratchbuilding. Don't try it until you are ready for it, and when you are, good luck!

CHAPTER EIGHT

The *Lady Be Good*

The luckless *Lady Be Good* has become one of the most famous aircraft of World War II. The B-24 was reported missing on its first mission, a bombing run to Naples from North Africa on April 4, 1943. No trace of the crew or plane was found, and they were presumed lost at sea. Seventeen years later, an oil search team came across the wreckage. It was 300 miles deep in the Sahara Desert.

The wreck was perfectly preserved by the dry desert atmosphere; the guns worked, coffee in the thermos bottles was still palatable, and the hydraulic systems were functional, but there was no sign of the crew. An aerial search turned up rescue markers set up by the crewmen as they walked across the desert, and slowly the pieces of the puzzle began to come together. After overshooting their base, the crew had made a navigational error, and

instead of turning back had flown deeper and deeper into the desert. When they were nearly out of fuel, the crew jumped. Ironically, they wore their Mae Wests and took their life rafts (they thought they were still over the Mediterranean), and the unmanned aircraft crashed into the desert.

As soon as the crew touched down on sand, they realized their error and began the long trek back toward Benghazi. How far they got was unknown until a year after the plane was discovered, when an exhaustive search located the bodies of five of the crew, 60 miles from the wreck. A diary found at the site revealed that three more crewmen had continued on, and two more bodies were found 30 miles beyond. The last crewman was never found.

Today, Robert Toner's moving diary can be seen along with other items from *Lady Be Good* in the Air Force Museum in Dayton, Ohio. The *Lady* herself rests un-

disturbed on the floor of the Libyan desert.

I had always wanted to build a diorama of the *Lady Be Good* and waited for a number of years for a model of the B-24D. An examination of the Monogram 1/48 B-24J revealed that conversion to the earlier "greenhouse nose" D version would not be difficult, and I decided not to wait any longer.

Research material on the *Lady Be Good* is plentiful. My primary sources were an article in *After the Battle* (No. 25), and one in the *International Plastic Modelers Society Quarterly*. There was some doubt as to whether the plane had a ball turret (which would have been visible at the break of the fuselage), but a phone call to the Air Force Museum revealed that it did not.

I decided to show the *Lady* as she appeared before discovery. Figures would only distract from her desolate mood, and after she was discovered, a lot of the equipment was stripped from her.

1 The first step in modeling the *Lady Be Good* is to mark out the break in the fuselage and the portion of the bottom that will have to be removed. Since the plane is somewhat down on the port (left) side, the starboard side of the fuselage should have a little less removed. The nose turret area is also to be cut off.

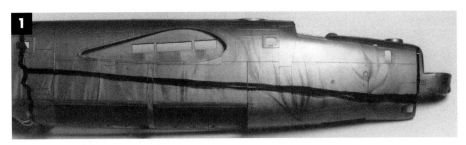

2 The rear part of the fuselage was the only part of the plane that called for interior detailing. The glass would all be frosted by sandstorms, and the break at the front of the fuselage is discreetly hidden by the tattered curtain (epoxy putty) of the radio compartment. Oxygen tanks from the Monogram B-25 were installed, two overhead forward of the waist positions and eight on the sides and overhead behind them. The distorted skin of the fuselage was accomplished by thinning out the plastic with a Dremel tool and steel cutter, adding wrinkles at the same time. Sheet styrene ribbing was then installed, and gentle heat applied to warp the surfaces.

3,4 One rudder has lost all its fabric covering and had to be built from scratch. The thick vertical spine and curved rim are assembled first, then oversize horizontal ribs are glued to either side. When the glue is dry, excess material is trimmed off and the final version sanded to shape, with the ribs tapering toward the rim. Note how a section of the rim has been removed where the trim tab would fit.

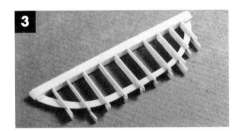
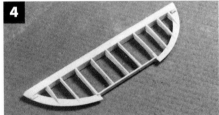

5 The wrinkles in the aircraft skin were made with a Dremel tool, then smoothed over with steel wool. The openings behind the dorsal turret are the life raft compartments. Also visible is the small sheet styrene rim added to the nose to support the clear nose bubble. The heavy bulging effect was created with epoxy putty. The B-24 was a notoriously bad "ditching" aircraft (the reason the crew jumped instead of going down with the plane) and in crash landings the fuselage often crushed like an egg.

6 At the time of the landing, the plane was flying on only the No. 4 engine, which wrenched from its mounts and kept flying for another hundred yards after the plane came to a stop. This picture shows the initial step in constructing the engine mount. The engine nacelle has been cut away, and sheet plastic has been installed along the wing.

7 The tail shows the extensive rotting of the fabric surfaces, done in the same manner as bullet holes—thin out from behind, and punch and twist the holes with a knife. The tail turret was slightly modified to the correct B-24D configuration by cutting away the glass near the guns and installing sheet styrene inner walls.

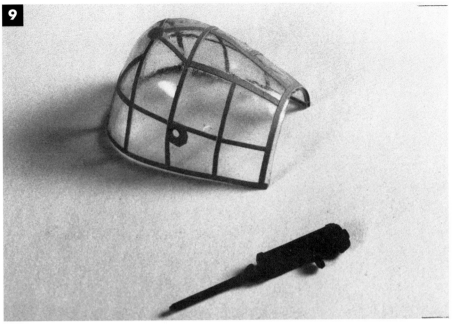

8,9 The most noticeable difference between the B-24J and the B-24D is the nose. A wood pattern was carefully made slightly smaller than the nose to allow for the thickness of the plastic to be formed over it. Clear ABS (Plastruct) plastic was then vacuum-formed over it. On the left is the wood pattern, on the right the formed nose. The ribbing on the nose was applied with strips of paper, painted chromate green on the inside and desert tan on the outside. These strips were glued in place with white glue—not very strong, but any excess can be neatly wiped off the clear plastic with a damp rag. Since part of the nose is buried in sand, only a partial nose bubble was needed.

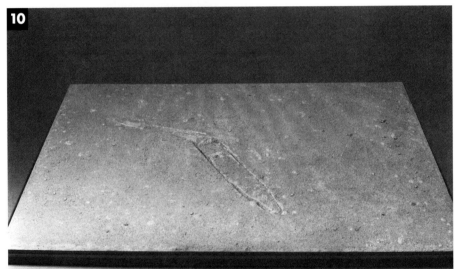

10 The groundwork is very plain, consisting only of Celluclay covered with sand. The fuselage halves were pressed into the surface and left there until the Celluclay was reasonably firm, then removed.

11 The small break in the nose bubble was made by grinding from the inside with a Dremel tool and steel cutter. The frosted effect on the glass was achieved by overspraying with matte varnish. Because no decals were available, the nose numbers and *Lady Be Good* were hand painted.

12 The rotten rubber peeling away from the deicer boots was achieved using the rubber cement masking trick used for peeling paint. The hanging sections of rubber were made from epoxy putty. This peeling effect is particularly striking on the tail section.

13 A closeup of the remains of the No. 4 engine. I had good photos to work from, and this detail is quite accurate. The straight cables and tubes are brass wire, the bent and twisted ones solder. Other than a few Grandt Line nuts, a little brass tubing, and some stretched sprue, that is all there is. The chipped paint effect was done with a brush and silver paint.

14 A closeup of the No. 2 engine. Notice the bent and feathered props, and the dents in the cowling.

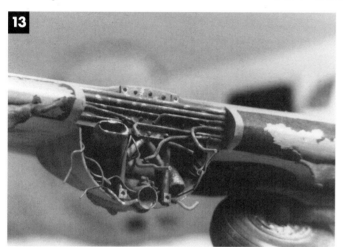

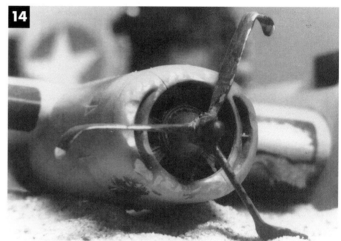

CHAPTER NINE

Farewell to the *Bonhomme Richard*

When I was first contacted by the designers of the U.S. Navy exhibit at the Museum of Science and Industry in Chicago about building a water-line model of John Paul Jones's famous flagship Bonhomme Richard, I was concerned that their imaginations had outstripped both their pocketbook and their schedule.

The original plan called for a battle scene showing the ship at the height of her death struggle with the *Serapis*. There were two problems with this concept. First, the battle took place at night with the two ships lashed yardarm to yardarm, which would entail building two ships, not one; and second, a

realistic battle scene with even one ship would call for over 200 figures visible on the upper decks. This was beyond their budget, and far beyond what could be accomplished in the short time scheduled to complete the project. I suggested they narrow the scope to something more realistic in the time frame available, namely the ship as she appeared after the battle, when the last party to leave the sinking vessel hauled down the colors for the last time. This would entail only a handful of figures on the poop deck, with perhaps twenty more in the longboat along side.

Even then, a sailing ship model of this size (³⁄₁₆″ to the foot) normally takes a good ship modeler two or more years to build, and we were looking at a deadline of less than nine months. There is an old joke that if one

woman can produce a baby in nine months, nine should be able to do the same in one month. With this dubious example in mind, we assembled a crew of experienced ship modelers to build the *Bonhomme Richard* in the same amount of time.

Research proved no problem. Jean Boudriot's *John Paul Jones and the Bonhomme*

Continued on page 90

An overall view of the finished model. The sails are intentionally "backed," to keep the sinking vessel from continuing to sail. For me, the mostly interesting modeling challenge was the battle damage. So far as I know, no one had ever modeled a sailing man o'war after a battle, much less one as shattered as the valiant *Bonhomme Richard*.

1 The partially completed model at one of the periodic "make sure it all fits together" meetings. To get the proper shape for the hull, Dick Williams found it easiest to build it with a full bottom; he said the most traumatic moment was when he had to run his masterpiece through a bandsaw to transform it into a waterline model!

2 Gus Agustin made the deck fittings. The chicken coops for the poop deck were so delicately modeled that I didn't have the heart to shoot them to pieces so I added just enough damage to keep them from looking pristine.

3 A close-up of the ship's hull during construction. The quarter deck has not been planked yet, so that the guns can be installed on the deck below. A cannon ball of the period could shoot through 24″ of solid oak at close range, so the damage to the hull over a period of two hours would have been horrific. Battle damage was started at this early stage, both to experiment with technique and to avoid breaking off delicate parts when handling the model later on. The holes were drilled with a standard household power drill, and then made ragged at the edges with a thin silicone cutter in a Dremel tool.

4 One of the most important lessons I learned from ship modelers was the value of using jigs. This simple stick and peg arrangement was designed to neatly coil rope over the pinrails. The ship line is coated with white glue so it will keep its shape when dry. The stick is greased so the glue won't stick to it, and one row of pegs is removable. A few finished coils can be seen in front of the stick, ready to hang over the belaying pins.

5 Bob Evans sewed and seamed the sails on a sewing machine, and dyed them in coffee for final color. It seemed a shame to cut holes in them, but it had to be done. One of HMS Victory's sails from Trafalgar is still in existence and I used that as a reference. Some experimentation proved necessary to discover the most effective way to simulate shot damage. After some experimentation with soldering irons, drills and such, I found the most realistic results came from bunching the fabric to a small point, cutting the end off with scissors, and fraying the edge of the hole with a steel cutter in my Dremel tool. The fraying is what really makes it look right. On the finished model, notice that most of the damage is to the lower sails: the Royal Navy intentionally fired low, to inflict maximum damage to the hull and guns.

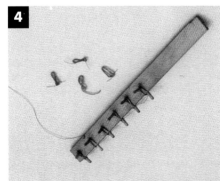

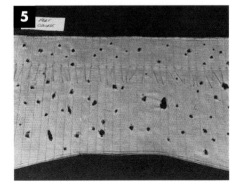

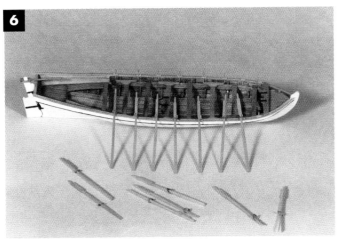

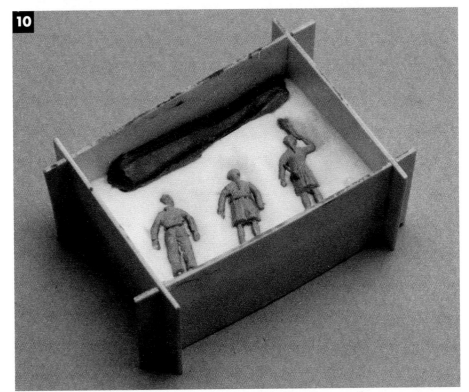

6 Frank Vitek's beautiful ship's boat. The oars were left loose so that they could be fitted to the figures once they were in place.

7 To pose the figures, I placed the boat in a tray of sand. This helped ensure that all oars would touch the water.

8 Making a mold to cast the figures. This is an alternate to the method described in Chapter 6. The patterns are embedded half-way into a bed of modeling clay. A strip of modeling clay forms the pouring sprue in what will be the top of the mold, while indentations pressed into the surface of the clay will create the locking lugs to align the two halves of the mold. The four sides of the mold box are laid flat prior to assembly.

9 The assembled mold box ready to pour the first half of the mold. The modeling clay, but not the patterns, has been coated with grease. Without this barrier, sulfur compounds in the clay would interfere with the curing of the rubber.

10 The first half has been poured and set. The mold is flipped over, and the clay bed is removed, leaving the former at the top for the sprue. The rubber is greased to prevent the second half from sticking to the first. Try not to remove your patterns from the first half if you can avoid it. Reseating them can be a problem and if they are not completely reseated, rubber from the second half can seep under the pattern, ruining the first half and forcing you to start all over again.

11 The figures were underpainted with hobby enamels prior to being painted in oils. Each figure is pinned through a foot. This pin is secured in a spring clamp, which serves as a handle for painting. Each clamp was numbered so that I could be sure to get each man back into his proper position in the boat when the painting was done.

12 This was my first experience using silicone caulk for water, so I ran some quick experiments to ensure that the technique would work.

13 The bottom of the base was reinforced to prevent warping.

14 The seas were formed of Celluclay, and then painted. Note the level space left for the ship, with the painted squares where water would be visible through the hatches.

15 The silicone caulk comes in standard caulking tubes. It applies white, but dries clear (I tried clear caulk, but found it was too thick to handle easily over such a large area).

16 The caulk was applied with the gun and textured with the fingers.

Continued from page 87

Richard (Naval Institute Press 1987), which is accompanied by an excellent set of plans, is the definitive work on the subject. By setting a whole team of modelers to work simultaneously, we were able to cut the time required substantially. While Dick Williams was building the hull, Frank Peterson was creating the masts and yards, Bob Evans was stitching the sails, Gus Agustin was working on the deck fittings, and Ed Urbanczyk and Ray Oswalt were assembling the ship's guns. Frank Vitek built a superb ship's boat, while Pete Kailus prepared the flags. I did the final assembly, "gingerbreads," battle damage, ocean, and figures. Every month or so, we got together to make sure the parts all fit together the way they were supposed to, and the project was finished on time. Without the efforts of the entire group, or had any one of us failed to fulfill his part, we could never have brought the project in on time. It is a credit to the cooperative effort of everyone who worked on it that we were able to carry it off with a minimum of aggravation, and all agreed that it was a worthwhile and enjoyable experience. (Although I am not so sure we'd volunteer to do it again!) This is one of the few dioramas that can actually be viewed. It is on display at the Museum of Science and Industry in Chicago.

17 Amidships. These was actually less damage to this part of the ship than there was farther aft. An important final touch for the battle damage was to was to glue jagged splinters of wood around the shot holes to give them a properly shattered look.

18 A closer view of the chaos on the gun deck, with debris, bits of sail, rigging, and dismounted guns. There are a few modest patches of blood on the deck.

19 The stern of the ship, showing the color party on the poop lowering the ensign, with the officers tipping their hats in salute. The flag is an unusual design but is based on an eyewitness sketch made shortly before the battle. The extraordinary size is typical of this period. Notice the extensive shot damage to the ship's side. Two lower deck guns exploded early in the battle, leaving a gaping hole near the waterline (already filled with water and just visible in this view), and the British guns firing at a range of only a few feet blew hundreds of gaping holes in the side of the ship.

20 The bow, showing the severe list of the sinking ship. The actual amount of list was limited by the space available for the case in which the model would be displayed. Aside from battle damage, the decks are bright and unweathered; it was standard practice for the sailors to "holystone" the deck every morning to give it a sparkling, almost white appearance.

21 The ship's head, showing the damage inflicted by the frigate *Alliance,* whose deranged Captain Landais repeatedly fired into his own flagship in the darkness.

22 The "gingerbreads" on the ship's stern, modeled in epoxy putty. The balusters on the rail were cast in white metal from patterns turned in brass. As I often pointed out to my colleagues during the project, the advantage of doing a battle-damaged ship is that the model work need not be perfect; any mistake that would flaw an ordinary model, such as a slightly crooked baluster, can simply be shot away. An unexpectedly tedious part of the job was applying tiny decals one letter at a time to form the ship's name on the stern. Why couldn't Jones have chosen a simpler name for his ship, like "Fury" or "Zeus"?

23 Although the ship was fatally damaged below the waterline, there was little damage aloft, so we were spared no work in that area. Just how much work there is in rigging a three-masted ship of this period is evident in this picture.

24 The commission pennant at the mainhead, like the other flags, was made of fine linen and painted. To make it fly horizontally, fine wire was glued to the edges of the underside.

25 The finished model is part of the U.S. Navy exhibit at the Museum of Science and Industry in Chicago.

CHAPTER TEN

Structures for Dioramas

Building structures is a rewarding extension of your modeling skills, and it opens a wide range of diorama subjects for you. Structures offer a whole new area in which to exercise your imagination, ingenuity, and eye for detail. There have been a number of excellent books on structures in the model railroad field, and these cover most of the basics. This chapter will deal only with the more specialized subject of war-torn buildings, the kind that are most often required for military dioramas.

Simple rural structures. The simplest form of structure to build, the type you will require most often, is a simple single-story dirt-floor farm building, usually a barn or outbuilding. The most significant difference between modeling structures in the common model railroad scales and 1/35 scale is the thickness of the walls. This thickness is

clearly visible in war-damaged buildings, and rules out using the time-honored method of building a shell out of cardboard, styrene, or basswood.

The easiest method of providing proper wall thickness is to use plywood. Either ³⁄₈″ or ¹⁄₄″ is satisfactory; ³⁄₈″ provides a 1/35 scale wall thickness of about 12″, while ¹⁄₄″ scales out to a thickness of about 8″. The first step is to draw up the plan of the walls on the plywood. If you made cardboard mock-ups while planning your diorama, these can be used as templates. The easiest way to cut the plywood is with a jigsaw, or you can do it by hand with a coping saw. You will have to drill starter holes for the windows so that you can insert the blade through the plywood.

An alternate method of building walls is to use precut strips of ¹⁄₄″ basswood (1″ width is most convenient), cut to length and glued together. This technique is fast and is particularly useful for buildings that call for a lot of evenly spaced windows. Be sure to

measure the parts carefully and use a miter box to cut the wood.

Once your walls are cut out or assembled, it is time to put the building together. If the structure is complicated, with limited access to the inside walls, it is best to do surface texturing and detailing before assembly. For simpler structures you can assemble the walls first. The easiest and most secure assembly method is to peg the parts together with toothpicks. Drill two or three ¹⁄₁₆″ holes in the edge of one of the walls and glue half of a round wood toothpick in each one. Trim these pegs to ¹⁄₄″ long and hold the wall in proper relation to the one it is to join. Mark the peg locations in the second wall, and drill ³⁄₃₂″ holes. The larger holes will give you some leeway in positioning. Next, glue the walls together and set them aside to dry. If an exact

A simple farmhouse like this one can be assembled in just two or three evenings, and the results are well worth the effort.

BUILT-UP METHOD FOR CONSTRUCTING BUILDINGS

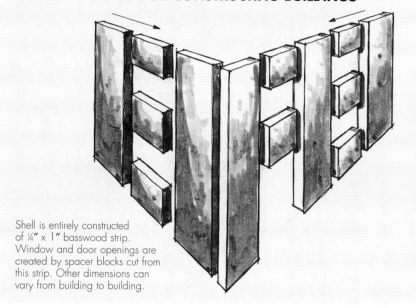

Shell is entirely constructed of ¼" x 1" basswood strip. Window and door openings are created by spacer blocks cut from this strip. Other dimensions can vary from building to building.

A SIMPLE FARMHOUSE

Basic walls are cut from plywood and covered with acrylic modeling paste

Detail of corner joint (toothpick pegs)

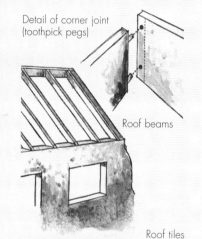

Roof beams

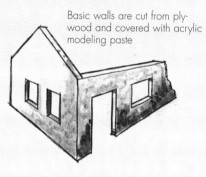

Planking the roof

Roof tiles and rubble

Plenty of broken beams, planks, and tiles

ROOF COVERINGS

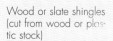

Wood or slate shingles (cut from wood or plastic stock)

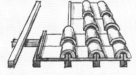

Mediterranean tile (individual tiles cut from tubing, and cast in sections)

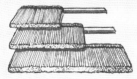

Straw thatch (hemp rope, unraveled and glued to battens)

---

90 degree angle is important, set the walls in the corner of a box to dry.

Texturing stucco walls. The easiest buildings to model are plaster-covered brick (stucco), and by a happy coincidence these are the most common type found on the European battlefields of World War II. The best material I have found for simulating stucco is acrylic modeling paste, available at art supply stores. Its qualities include nearly perfect texture, adequate working time, and excellent adhesion on a variety of surfaces. Apply the modeling paste with a putty knife, spreading it smoothly. Don't worry about the knife marks, since stucco on real buildings is rarely smooth, but try to eliminate obviously out-of-scale marks. Cracks, patches, and other flaws can be worked into the material while it is still wet, but bullet and shrapnel holes are best added after the paste has set. To pockmark the dried paste, use a Dremel tool with a drill bit or pointed cutter and simply bounce it at random across the surface.

Peeling and flaking stucco often reveals the brick or stone structure underneath. If you want to include this effect, brick or stone texture must be installed before the stucco is applied. The model railroad department of your hobby shop should have embossed plastic brick and stone sheets. Cut irregular patches and glue them in place on the wall, then apply modeling paste around them, overlapping the edges. All-brick buildings can also be built using embossed plastic sheet, but they involve a lot of work, so much work that they are rarely worth the effort. The brick courses must match at the corners, and each window must be carefully bricked in as well.

Adding the roof. A real roof usually consists of a timber framework that is planked over and then covered with shingles or tiles to make it waterproof, and the best material for model roof construction is wood. The first step is to prepare the wood by painting or staining it. Brown, gray, or a combination of the two, are good colors for the underside of a barn or shed roof. If you plan to have planks torn away from the beams, leave one side of each beam natural wood color. This surface, hidden by the planking, would not be subject to the same weathering as the exposed timber. Splinter the ends of broken beams and planks before assembly. It is easiest and fastest to create two splintered beams at once by breaking one long one in the middle. Heavily score the area to be broken with a knife, then snap it apart to make two splintered ends.

Use a T-square and ruler to draw up a plan of the roof beam spacing. Lay the beams in position on this plan and glue the planks across them, leaving gaps where planks have been torn loose or broken. Leave broken

1 Bullet pockmarks, shrapnel holes, and other superficial damage can be added to stucco walls using a motor tool with a steel cutter or drill.

2 To model the brick structure behind a stucco-covered wall, add small patches of brick to the plywood wall before applying the stucco texture (acrylic modeling paste) to it.

3 The farmhouse roof in this scene consists of individual styrene shingles applied over framing and planking made from individual wood strips.

DECORATIVE ACCENTS FOR URBAN BUILDINGS

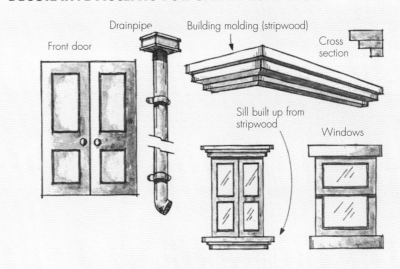

Front door • Drainpipe • Building molding (stripwood) • Cross section • Sill built up from stripwood • Windows

pieces hanging, and make sure you have enough pieces left over for rubble. When all beams and planks are assembled, go back over the beams and use a knife to gouge nail holes where planks have been torn loose. A final touch is to add bent nails made from brass wire sticking out of the fallen planks.

The next step is to install tiles or shingles. There are commercial plaster castings of roof tiles available that give an excellent effect for an intact roof but are less satisfactory for a shattered structure. When a real tile roof is broken the tiles break loose individually, not in chunks, so the effect of a broken plaster roof casting, while effective at a distance, will lack close-up realism. You can make your own flat tiles or slate or wood shingles fairly easily. Styrene is an excellent material for this, and a large number of tiles can be made quickly using the scribe and snap method. Each tile should be beveled and chipped around the edges with a Dremel tool, and don't forget to make a few broken ones. All tiles or shingles should be painted terra-cotta or slate gray before installation, and weathering can be done in place.

Complex tile shapes are harder to make, but if you are determined you can cast them in RTV molds using Hydrocal (a hard-setting plaster available in model railroad shops). Make up half a dozen master patterns of the desired design in wood or plastic, then make your RTV mold as described in Chapter 7. If you are ambitious the entire roof can be made up of individual cast tiles, or you can use them to supplement the commercial cast roof sections. You may even want to try gluing a group of your castings together, making a mold of these, then casting your own sections.

Thatched roofs, which were still fairly common in Europe during World War II, were built on the same beam structure as tiled ones. Instead of planks, horizontal wood batten strips were nailed or lashed to the beams about 2' apart and the thatching was lashed to these battens. The thatch itself is best made with unraveled hemp or crepe hair. If the underside of your roof will not be visible, you can get away with simply gluing the thatch to a sheet of heavy cardboard or plywood. If the underside will be visible, you'll have to install battens, wrap thin cord around them in a loose crisscross pattern, and then glue on the thatch.

To complete your rural building, make doors, shutters, and other wood trim the same way you made roof beams and planking. Stain or paint the wood, glue the pieces together, then add splinters and other details with a knife. Bullet holes are made the same way as nail holes.

Urban and residential buildings. Gutted urban building shells are actually easier than farm buildings because there is nothing to build but the walls, perhaps with some vestiges of flooring. Residential buildings that have suffered only blast damage are another matter. Here the interior walls and contents of the building will all be present, even if they are broken up and rearranged.

The basic construction method for walls is essentially the same as for simple buildings, except that there will be more windows and additional floors. There will be interior walls with doorways from room to room, and if there are additional stories, there will have to be floors for each of these. If the building is in a large city, its architectural details may be elaborate: windows will have sills and eaves, and there will be moldings and other decorative accents. Stripwood window sills, eaves, door framing, and decorative moldings can be added to basic stucco buildings, and the stucco worked around them. Fortunately, neatness is not essential in a shell-damaged building. You will find that pockmarks, bullet holes, and chipped plaster will cover a lot of sins.

If you build urban structures strictly to scale, they will be awfully large. Not only can you make your structures slightly undersize, they will actually look more to scale because they will not dwarf the scenes they are

4 Sharp-eyed modelers will note that there are nails and nail holes in the roof planking on this shattered farmhouse, but that there are no corresponding holes in either the broken or intact terra-cotta tiles, an unfortunate oversight on my part.

5 The inside of the wrecked farmhouse includes splintered roof beams and bullet-hole detail in the door.

6 Gutted shells are by far the easiest kind of urban structures to model, particularly when the scene calls for three or four of them. This diorama portrays the Battle of Arnhem.

7 Modeling an urban building that has not been burned out is a lot of work. This Monogram sturmpanzer IV diorama was my first attempt at modeling an urban setting. The iron balcony is a distinctly Mediterranean touch made by connecting the HO balcony railings at the top and bottom with strip styrene verticals.

8 This is but a sampling of the hundreds of model railroad architectural details available. You may not always be able to use these in their intended scale or for their original purpose, but they always come in handy for structure modeling.

supposed to support. When building multistory urban buildings, you can get away with making each successive story slightly smaller than the one below it until the top story is actually shorter than a man. This ruse works because we are used to looking at buildings from street level, where perspective makes upper stories look smaller. In modeling, the discrepancy in size will only be apparent if we actually hold a figure up to the window. A rule of thumb is that (assuming a 9' ceiling is standard) you can afford to drop one scale foot from the ground floor, and an additional foot from each additional story. This rule holds true for structures up to four stories tall.

Windows and doors. Residential structure windows need more than crude shutters to cover them. Each window opening must be lined with wood, and at least a few should show some vestiges of the window sashes themselves. The model railroad department of your hobby shop has a variety of windows that can be adapted. Look for windows that seem oversize for HO scale. The windows themselves will be too small, but you can cut them diagonally and vertically into fragments that will look like sashes from larger windows. The model railroad windows will have to be glued back to back with clear styrene sandwiched between them so that your windows will be framed on both sides. A substitute for clear styrene is the thin cover glass used for microscope slides. This material has the advantage that you can crack or break it, but the slide covers are very fragile and the broken glass is dangerous, so be careful with them.

Doors, too, require more elaborate construction. Paneled residential doors can be made by cutting the door from thin wood or .040" styrene and gluing strips around the edges to simulate framing. Doorknobs can be made from dressmaker's pins. By the way, most European doors have handles, which is why GI's overseas refer to the U.S. as "the land of the round doorknobs." Handles can be made from bent wire.

Floors, interior walls, and ceilings. Residential buildings have wooden floors,

not dirt ones, and when they are damaged, beams under the floor will be visible. Floors are made in the same manner as the barn roof. If the floor is for an upper story, it requires a ceiling for the room underneath. Such ceilings are plaster over wood lath. The lathing is easy enough to make with stripwood, and the plaster can be simulated with acrylic modeling paste, or, more simply, with index card stock. The latter method is very effective for plaster that is peeling away and hanging in strips. Coat the back of a piece of index card with fine sand, tear a ragged edge, and curl the edge back when you glue the card in place.

Interior walls will also have to be plastered. In rural structures you can get away with plastering and painting simple plywood walls, but city buildings require hollow interior walls. If any of the wall substructure is to be visible, the same plaster and lath method described for ceilings must be used.

Furniture making was discussed in Chapter 7. Urban furnishings should include rugs made from multi-ply tissue or scavenged from a miniature room shop, and curtains made with tissue, mounted on brass wire rods. Pictures on the wall can be cut from magazines and framed with HO windows or Plastruct shapes. The book and record club

advertisements seen in magazines are excellent sources for pictures for this purpose.

Rubble, streets, and sidewalks. It takes a lot of bricks, mortar, lumber, and other materials to make a building, and when it all falls to the ground it makes an impressive pile. It is important that a demolished building have enough rubble to justify the damage done to it, so it does not look as if an oversized charwoman has gone in and cleaned the place out. Nothing looks more disconcerting than a devastated building with only a few scraps of rubble scattered around it.

The most effective way to make rubble is to take the same material you used to detail the building and break it up. If you used cast masonry, take some reject castings and break them up with a hammer. If you don't have leftover masonry, pour plaster into the bottom of a plastic container, let it set, and shatter it. Another method is to use some of the larger stones in your gravel box. Avoid stones with rounded edges, and stay away from ones that are obviously too large for your wall thickness. Crushed gravel is best. Be sure to throw in some broken beams, planks, and tiles from your roof—that roof had to fall somewhere.

Install your building in its final location on your base, and carefully work Celluclay

9,10 These back views of the sturmpanzer diorama show how the interior was modeled. The downstairs living room includes curtains, pictures, furniture, rugs, flooring, and floor joists. The upstairs bedroom includes a scratchbuilt bureau, a family picture taken from a book club ad, and a crucifix made from styrene strips and an N scale railroad brakeman.

11 A fallen building leaves large piles of rubble, so be sure to include substantial piles around badly damaged structures.

12 Even when you use commercially available accessories, take the time to customize them. This realistic battered lamppost in Dave Smith's Tiger II diorama is an excellent example of a commercial part combined with a bit of extra work.

around it. Sprinkle and scatter the rubble over the diorama in a haphazard manner, pressing the pieces into the wet Celluclay, then sprinkle the whole affair with finer sand and gravel. Finally, overspray everything with a solution of white glue and water, and leave it to dry overnight. If the drying takes too long, you can hasten it with a heat lamp.

Urban boulevards, unlike country dirt roads, are paved, and have sidewalks, curbs,

13,14,15,16 This photo sequence shows the steps in building a rubble-covered cobblestone street. First, the cobblestone sections are positioned in the street. Then, Celluclay is applied over and around the stone sections to form the basic shapes of the rubble piles. Next, gravel and pebbles are applied over the Celluclay, and finally, sand and rubble are spread over the rest of the street, leaving only a few patches of realistic cobblestone texture showing through the debris.

17 I always liked the idea of doing a cannon inside a building. The church came about because I wanted a different kind of building, too. [This scene was done for Tamiya, who were requested to take it off display at a German trade convention because the management found the idea offensive.]

18 Building a simple cardboard mock-up of your building during the planning stages helps determine the basic dimensions and can help avoid placement and positioning problems later on.

and gutters. There will also be manhole covers and drains, street lamps, and signs. Asphalt streets are made the same way as runways (Chapter 2), and sidewalks can be added with ¼"-thick basswood or plywood. Scribe in concrete panels and curbstones, and add nicks, cracks, and other scars of day-to-day living or recent warfare.

Cobblestone streets can be made using HO model railroad fieldstone textured building sheet. Remember to make the "grain" run across the street, not along it. This often means using several sections, carefully camouflaging the seams between them. When a scene involves damaged buildings, you can cover most of the street with rubble, leaving only patches of cobblestone showing through. Be sure, however, that it looks like patches of cobblestone showing through, not rubble sprinkled along the seams between cobblestone sections!

Manhole covers can be cut from styrene and detailed with concentric rings by mounting the plastic disk in a motor tool and scoring the face with a file as it spins. Gutter drains are harder. You must first chisel a square hole out of the gutter, then paint it black before covering it with a styrene strip grille.

Wood and stone structures. Trees are a precious commodity in Western Europe and wooden buildings are rare, but this is not the case in Russia or the United States, where forests provide timber in abundance. Models of wooden buildings are constructed almost exactly like real frame structures.

A framework of beams is built first, then covered with plank siding. This construction is largely a matter of expanding the techniques described for building a roof. Wooden building construction is covered in great detail in model railroad books, and the methods

described for HO structures can easily be used for larger scales.

A wooden building is a time-consuming project, one I avoid unless the theme of the diorama specifically calls for it. Before construction, a full-size plan for the model must be drawn up on cardboard. Then, wooden spacer blocks and other locating devices are glued to the plan so that the framing pieces can be cut and positioned on top of the plan. The plan forms an assembly jig, and the frame is constructed and glued together right over it. When all the frames are assembled, they are removed from the jigs and assembled. This forms the shell of the building, and the siding can then be glued over the framework.

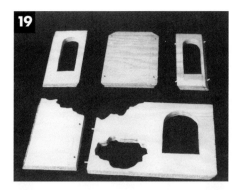

19 The plywood walls cut out and ready for detailing. Note the toothpick pegs and holes used to align the sections.

20 The finished walls in place on the diorama base. The stone sections were cast in a one-piece RTV mold and glued to the walls; the plaster was then laid on in the remaining areas and carried over the edges of the stonework. I used Liquitex acrylic modeling paste (from an art store) because it naturally shrinks and cracks as it dries. The area of the floor that will be visible is covered with a model railroad stonework plastic sheet.

21 The building from the "Green Line" diorama in Chapter 1 under construction. The walls were textured with spackle. Note that the balconies have been left off to give access when adding the rubble.

22 The finished building before painting. The corrugated shutters were made by pressing flattened sections of old paint tube onto a sheet plastic corrugated surface; this cracked the paint on the old tubes, which gave a realistic texture when painted as rust.

23 The back of the building. I didn't want the building to look like a hollow shell, so I had the collapsed concrete floors cover the back of the structure, the massive chunks of shattered concrete being held together by the steel reinforcing rods. The floors were cast in plaster in a shallow tray made of sheet plastic, with swirls of wire imbedded in the wet plaster. When the plaster was set, I smashed it up with a hammer, always leaving one corner intact to glue into the corner of the structure, and saving the loose chunks for use as rubble.

24 The finished building, ready to install. The walls were stained with multiple coats of thinned oil color. By alternately staining and wiping with a rag, some wonderfully subtle effects can be achieved.

Stone buildings add variety to your structures, whether they are rough farm buildings or fine masonry on a city block. Natural stone structures can be made using a mosaic method. You will need a lot of pebbles, so gather them ahead of time. The walls are cut from plywood, using thinner wood than usual. Pebbles are then glued to the surface with white glue. When the glue has set, apply standard tile grout over the pebbles to represent mortar. When the grout has set, follow the instructions provided to scrub away the surface grout, revealing the pebbles.

Cut-stone buildings are more time-consuming. Make the walls from plywood, and either cut grooves in the plywood surface or apply individual stripwood stones over it. Bevel the edges of each stone before gluing it in place. For more ornate stones, make one or two original patterns and then cast as many as you need in an RTV mold. You may want to use your first castings as patterns for a multiple mold, or even make a mold of a group of stones glued together to form an entire wall section. This casting technique is by far the best method if your building is to be badly damaged. Instead of casting thin veneer-like stone sections, cast full-thickness blocks. Then assemble the blocks to form the wall, or what's left of it, and break more blocks to scatter around as rubble.

25 The striking feature of this interior by Bill Taylor is the see-through wall of studs, lath, and detached plaster.

26 Bill added ivy to the outside wall with tea leaves, which look just right when painted and dry-brushed green.

27 Try to use distinctive architectural styles and unusual building features to your advantage, as Bill Chilstrom did here in a scene inspired by the movie *Full Metal Jacket*. The circular opening in the wall draws immediate attention to the figure standing on front of it, and his gaze starts the viewer's eye moving across the scene.

Weathering structures. Painting buildings is easier than painting vehicles, because you can make use of several techniques and apply them with a broader brush and a coarser touch. Stucco and stone surfaces can be weathered with a combination of washes and dry-brushing. I usually paint my buildings first with hobby paints, then follow with a wash of Polly S, thinned with denatured alcohol. Apply the wash liberally, then wipe it off with a rag, leaving color in the recesses. Then dry-brush the surface, first with a lighter version of the wall color, then with dusty tans and browns. Additional washes can be applied to tone down harsh dry-brush effects and to add subtle variety to the coloring. Finally, fresh bullet holes and pockmarks should be touched in with light tan or white, but older scars left dark.

To paint brick, first spray the walls with a uniform dull red (boxcar red is ideal), then apply a wash of Polly S gray and wipe it off, leaving the gray in the mortar lines between the bricks. Dry-brush irregularly with red and orange to vary the brick colors, then apply a brown wash. Add fresh bullet holes and pockmarks with a bright pinkish red.

While newly painted wood surfaces can be treated much like the materials and surfaces already mentioned, bare weathered wood is more time-consuming. Start by scribing and scoring the surface. Knotholes can be made either by pushing the scriber into the surface or by drilling a hole. For knots that are still in place, scribe a small circle or oval into the surface of the wood, or press it in with the end of a brass tube. Do the knots first, then scribe in the grain, flowing the grain lines around the knots. Use your knife to splinter board ends and split some of the boards.

Stain the wood first with a driftwood gray, then streak with browns by just touching the brush to the surface and allowing the cuts and splits to carry the stain in a natural manner. Fresh splits should be left a natural wood color or toned down with a tan or maple stain. Flo-Stain wood stains made by Floquil yield good results, but in a pinch you can mix up washes from any paint. Try staining at various stages during the scribing and splitting process. Finally, lightly dry-brush with gray, brown, or both. The rubber cement masking technique used for simulating peeling paint on aircraft (Chapter 8) works well on both wood and stucco walls.

In this chapter, emphasis has been on techniques, but before closing, I'd like to talk about designing the buildings themselves. Structures offer you the greatest freedom of design of any of the elements in your diorama, and it's a shame to let such an opportunity go to waste. A tank or airplane must look like its original, but a building can look like any of thousands of different types and styles seen in a particular theater of operations. Go through your reference library, looking not for military hardware but for the architectural styles of the buildings in the background. When you spot something unusual, make a note of it for future reference.

28 Bob Letterman is another master of the large diorama. Here is one of his World War II street scenes. The buildings all have interiors!

29 Another of Bob's massive undertakings, a 1/72 scale corvette in drydock, complete with rail lines, docks, and concrete bunkers.

30 Structures aren't always buildings. An experienced ship modeler, Larry Hubbell built his 1/35 scale section of the Titanic out of wood. Notice the effective use of detail at each level to hold the viewer's attention.

CHAPTER ELEVEN

The Road to Damascus

This diorama depicts a typical moment toward the end of the Yom Kippur War of 1973. Shown is an intersection in Quneitra, the principal Syrian city in the Golan region. The town, abandoned since the 1967 war, was recaptured by the Syrians during the first few days of fighting, then overrun once more by the Israelis during their counteroffensive. By the end of that counteroffensive, the Israeli armored forces were within striking distance of Damascus, and Quneitra was in the wake of the Israeli advance.

The Israelis are famous for their practice of scavenging battlefields, and they salvage absolutely anything that might be of value. In

this scene, a damaged M-51 Sherman tank is being transported back to the depot on an M-26 armored tank transporter and recovery vehicle. Like the Sherman, the transporter is a rebuilt American relic of World War II. The Israeli "super Shermans" are remarkable tanks. Up-gunned with an awesome French 105mm gun and powered by a 500-h.p. diesel, these 30-year veterans were able to hold their own against Syrian T-62s, then the latest tank in the Soviet arsenal.

Although the scene is set before the arrival of the United Nations peacekeeping forces on the Syrian front, the U.N. had maintained observer teams in the Middle East since 1948, and one of these units is seen watching the proceedings. Their white Land Rover and famous blue berets provide the

only touches of bright color in the diorama.

This diorama is a good example of a project that, like Topsy, "just sorta growed." The tank transporter, the centerpiece of the scene, did not figure in the original design at all. I have always been fascinated by the souped-up Sherman tanks used by the Israeli army. My original concept was to do a scene of such a Sherman replenishing ammunition in an Arab town, but when I saw the kit of the tank transporter in a hobby shop, I realized I had to include it. Including the transporter meant eliminating the ammo idea, and posing the transporter in the act of negotiating a difficult corner developed instead. The knocked-out T-62, the Israeli weapons carrier, and the U.N. Land Rover were added as planning progressed.

1 This is the initial planning layout, with boxes representing the buildings. The vehicles and buildings were positioned first, then the figures were posed to fit, one by one. Until well into the construction phase of this project, I had considerable doubts as to whether this many vehicles could be integrated into a scene of reasonable size without looking like a parking lot. The layout was constantly checked and analyzed as the vehicles were constructed.

2,3 The figures are all Tamiya, taken primarily from the British stretcher party, modern U.S. command set, and various U.S. World War II sets. Most have been converted to a new pose. During the 1973 war, the Israelis frequently wore their shirttails out, and this detail was added with epoxy putty. The net texture on the helmet covers was achieved by covering the helmet with putty and pressing it with an old T-shirt. In these photos, two figures are missing. The ground guide in the center of the diorama and the fellow munching a matzo were last-minute additions.

4 Cardboard mock-ups were made to establish the exact designs and dimensions for the buildings. The Max tank transporter was extensively rebuilt with parts from a Life-Like Atomic Cannon, Monogram 1/24 scale Mack truck, and Monogram M-8 armored car. The Sherman was built using the hull and turret from an Italaeri-Testors M4A1 and the suspension from a Tamiya M4A3E8. The big 105mm gun was built up from telescoping brass tubing, epoxy putty, and sheet styrene. The other vehicles in the scene were built, with minor modifications, straight from the box.

5 The parts for the smaller of the two buildings. The walls were cut from ⅜" plywood and covered with acrylic modeling paste. Note the toothpick pegs.

6, 7 The assembled building. Shrapnel marks from several wars have been added and the building sprayed tan overall. Rubble has been added to the floors and roof and glued in place with a generous overspray of diluted white glue.

8, 9, 10 Construction of the larger building is identical. After assembling and texturing the walls and painting them light tan, a dark brown wash was applied, then wiped off where necessary with a tissue. The entire surface was dry-brushed with several shades of tan, and Arabic lettering applied to the walls. The buildings in the Golan region had been abandoned since the Six-Day War, so there would be little left of the furnishings.

11 The finished buildings in place on the diorama base, with landscaping completed. The sand in northern Palestine is distinctly gray, accounting for the grayish tan colors used on Israeli armor.

12 The extensively rebuilt transporter and Sherman after weathering.

13 The road signs are provided here actual diorama size. I made originals using rub-on Hebrew lettering. These were copied down to the correct size on a copy machine, then the signs were cut out, glued to plastic sheet, and weathered with pastels.

14 The completed Sherman. Notice the enormous size of the gun, which is, believe it or not, in scale. I am told that when the gun is fired, the crews frequently put the transmission in neutral and let the whole tank absorb the recoil! Stowage bins on the side are sheet styrene, and the searchlight is a spare road wheel covered with sheet styrene. Also noteworthy are the tissue mantlet cover, smoke grenade launchers (brass tube), and unusual jerry cans, which are black rubber and have only one handle. The tactical signs and telephone poles were not part of the original design. When all of the planned elements were in place, something was still missing, and the signs added the needed spark to the scene.

13

תיקון תותחים	תחנת מקלחת	חדר-מתים
תחנת דפבת		
צורה דאשׂונה	מחסן	קצין
✡ תחנת ✡		תחנת נוהיות
קצין חיצע הזיה	הזיה	בומר מלכוהי
	מחנה כידוד	

16,17 Note the winch rollers on the front of the trailer, and the yarmulke on the crewman (during the Yom Kippur War, many soldiers wore them as a sign of faith). The shutters were added at the last minute because the buildings looked too plain, and a touch of color was needed. One pattern was made, and the rest were cast in Tuf-fil/polyester.

18 Placing figures in conversational groups like this is an effective design device. The downed power lines are black thread, stiffened in place with white glue.

19,20 An important final touch is the way the ground color is carried up onto the vehicles and boots of the figures. This is partly the way they were painted, but also a result of a final application of pastels after the figures were glued in place. This is important, because it gives the diorama visual unity that might otherwise be lost.

CHAPTER TWELVE

Resin, Plaster, and Other Aftermarket Kits

The past few years have seen the introduction of a wide variety of diorama accessories in a variety of materials—some new, some old. This is particularly true of the so-called "aftermarket" kits, superdetailing kits that do not make a stand-alone model at all, but are designed to supplement a vehicle or aircraft kit already on the market. Also available is an impressive variety of diorama accessories, ranging from weapon sets to complete buildings and bridges.

Although these new kits make diorama building much easier, they do create a bit of a problem for the modeler who wants to put his own distinctive mark on his work: an experienced audience of fellow modelers will be able to look around the scene and quickly identify

all of the kits that have been used to create it. This is particularly apparent with buildings.

If this doesn't bother you, don't worry about it. But if you like to put a strong personal stamp on everything you do, a practical solution is to use the parts that come in the kit, but to recombine them in such a way that the final result looks distinctly different from the original kit. We'll discuss ways to do this, but first let's take a look at the new materials we will be dealing with and some of the special techniques needed to work with them.

Resin kits. Polypropylene resin is a popular medium for models of all sizes, to the extent that it has revolutionized the hobby in recent years. Vehicle and figure kits of extraordinary quality have been produced by a variety of manufacturers, and modelers have discovered

that these models are not much more difficult to assemble than the traditional styrene ones.

Resin kits are produced from silicone rubber molds, which allow greater detail and much deeper undercuts than the steel dies used to produce styrene, and at a much lower manufacturing cost. This means that makers can produce kits of more exotic subjects, since they have to sell fewer of them to cover their production costs.

One of the most welcome changes in modeling over the past few years has been the introduction of superdetailing kits for armor and aircraft. These kits are usually produced in resin, photoetched brass, or a combination of the two. There are also kits specifically for the diorama builder. Included in the assortment shown here are plaster and resin architectural pieces and groundwork materials.

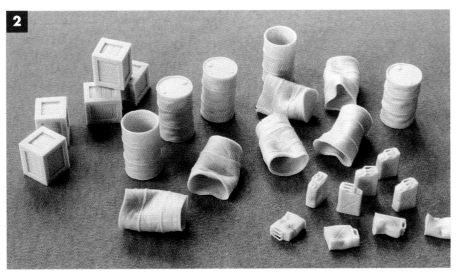

Resin kit parts are usually produced in one-piece molds, with a large sprue at the top (if you are really interested in the mechanics of this process, see the discussion of mold-making in Chapter 6). This means the parts have no parting line to remove, but it also mean that there is a fairly large pouring sprue that has to be cut or ground off.

Fortunately this is not difficult. You can cut the sprue with a razor saw, or more easily still, grind it off. Modelers who do a lot of work with resin kits often use a table model belt or disk sander, which is great if you have one. A model builder's jig or scroll saw, either hand or power driven, is also very useful for cutting off large sprues.

I usually use a Dremel tool with my favorite attachment, the Merit Sanding disk attachment with quick change disks—I can use a coarse disk to rapidly remove the bulk of the material and quickly switch to a finer disk to smooth the final surface. Whatever you use, it is a good idea to wear a face mask when sanding resin; the dust smells like insecticide, and that's not a good sign. I also have some smaller disks I got from a jeweler's supply house that are excellent for working with smaller and more delicate parts.

You may find that removing the sprue reveals small air bubbles on the surface of the casting. These can be filled with modeler's green putty and sanded smooth when dry.

Polypropylene resin is not soluble and cannot be glued with plastic solvents designed for styrene. Resin can be glued well, however, with cyanoacrylate "super" glues and five-minute epoxies. It can be filed, sanded, and carved as easily as styrene. It can be made temporarily flexible by heating, and will hold the shape it has been bent to if allowed to cool in that shape. A disadvantage is that small thin sections like gun barrels and sword blades have an annoying tendency to warp over time, and while they can be heated and bent straight, the material seems to have a memory

1 Some resin kits are virtually "dioramas in a box", like this ingenious sewer fighting scene from Warriors.

2 Resin aftermarket kits are particularly helpful and convenient when your scene calls for a lot of something—be they crates and cartons or battered oil drums or jerry cans (courtesy Armand Bayardi Models).

3 Because they are cast in flexible rubber molds, resin kits have surprisingly few parts. The most obvious characteristic of these parts, and the most inconvenient for the modeler, is the large sprue block on each piece. Courtesy of Warriors.

4 The Merit clip-on sanding disc is an essential tool for covering metal figures. The coarse disc removes the old detail in seconds, while the fine disc smooths the surface for redetailing.

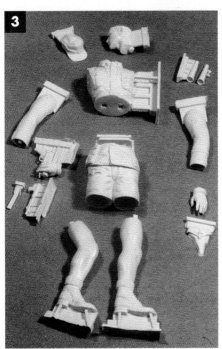

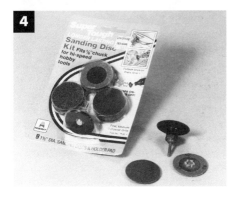

and will sometimes warp again. This is why many makers are now producing the smaller parts in white metal.

Resin models can be painted with the same paints used on styrene and metal kits. A coat of primer is recommended but not absolutely necessary.

Plaster and expanded foam building kits. Plaster building kits have been popular with model railroaders for years and are now available for military modelers as well. A number of materials actually come under this heading: plaster of paris, Hydrocal, and Hydrostone. Plaster is a fairly straightforward material to use.

An advantage of plaster as a material for brick or stone buildings is that it is so close to the material you are trying to portray—it chips, shatters, and gouges just like real masonry. It can be sanded and carved easily and can be worked with virtually any tools—saws, knives, sandpaper, files, and grinders. It can be glued easily with white glue, but you

can also use super glue or epoxy. For carving, you can soften it by wetting the surface thoroughly and allowing time for the water to penetrate. Don't worry—unless you immerse it in water for hours at a time, it won't dissolve.

Plaster is also extremely versatile when it comes to painting. You can use hobby paints (both water and spirit based), artists oils, and

5 The block can often be cut from small parts with a pair of nippers.

6 A hobby scroll saw gives you a lot of control when cutting resin sprues and is particularly good at following multiple contours, such as the soles of these boots.

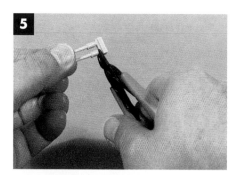

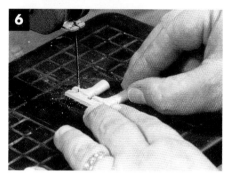

even stains, marker pens, or watercolors. You can also use some or all of these materials in conjunction with each other. For example, you can stain the plaster with watercolors, weather it with a wash of thinned acrylic modeling paint, and dry-brush the details with artist's oils.

It is also easy to cast your own plaster buildings and accessories in open-face molds, using plaster of paris from an art supply store or Hydrocal from a model railroad shop. Both materials mix with water and pour easily—again, see Chapter 6 for information on making the rubber molds.

Expanded foam buildings are also a popular aftermarket item. These are manufactured by mixing a liquid plastic base with its catalyst and pouring it into a mold; the reaction with the catalyst causes the material to expand rapidly into a foam, which forms an outer skin and presses that surface into the detail of the mold. The material is light and takes detail beautifully, and the foam interior is not visible unless you break or cut through the outer skin. Expanded foam buildings are not quite as versatile or as easy to paint and weather as plaster, but they are still very effective. Because they are lighter, they are more practical on large urban scenes.

Whatever kit buildings you use, don't hesitate to cut them apart and reassemble them to meet your needs. Not only does this allow you build the scene the way *you* want it to be, but it also adds a strong personal touch that sets your diorama apart from those of other modelers.

Photoetched brass. This is a particularly popular medium for advanced aircraft and armored vehicle kits, particularly the superdetailing, modification, and conversion kits being offered on the market today.

These pieces take advantage of the photoetching process used to make electric circuit boards. It starts with a large black-and-white drawing, which is then reduced to the appropriate size and converted to a photographic negative. The negative is then projected or contact-printed, like a photographic print, onto a sheet of brass coated with a photosensitive material. When this "photo" is developed, parts of the image remain coated while others are stripped down to the brass. The brass sheet is then immersed in an acid solution, which eats away all the exposed brass, leaving the coated areas untouched. The process can be repeated one or more times,

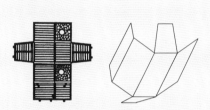

The artwork for Bob Hayden's ingenious photoetched HO scale lobster trap. The flat photoetched piece is folded into a box as shown in the drawing. Bob needed a large number of these for the docks on his railroad layout, and this proved the perfect way to make them.

creating several levels of detail on a given part.

The advantage of this process is that it permits certain types of detail that would be difficult or impossible by any other method. Brass parts are an important part of modern ship models, allowing delicate and precise handrails and radar screens in scales where they could never be achieved by more traditional modeling methods. Another good example is the ring-sights used on anti-aircraft guns, which were a major modeling headache until this method came along.

While the advantages of this process are considerable, it does have limitations. Designers are limited to flat objects, with one or two stepped levels of detail. The process does not allow fully rounded three-dimensional objects. It can produce an excellent armor plate, for example, with rivets on the surface, but it cannot produce a figure's face.

Modelers being the ingenious types they are, however, they soon discovered that objects could be etched flat and then bent to the required shape. Ship modelers like John

Photoetched brass is also good for making stencils. The artwork shown here was used for the carpet in "A Stillness at Appomattox" (see photo in Chapter 14). The carpet was naturally red; I masked and airbrushed a light green checkerboard over it, and then used this stencil to spray the black pattern over both red and green squares.

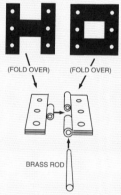

Photoetched hinges. The drawing for the flat parts is shown above. Fold each part over the brass rod separately as shown, then mate the two parts of the hinge and slide the rod into place. For ease of handling make the rod longer than needed and trim to length once in place. The screw holes in the drawing can be left as holes, or raised as rivets (or screw-heads, with a slot in them) on a second level of etching.

Leyland, for example, photoetch the tiny figures they use on 1/700 scale ships; a hundred or more figure can fit on a single sheet, and they can be bend with needle-nosed pliers to whatever pose is needed. A coat of white glue rounds them off just enough before they are painted. Another good example of this sort of thing is the working hinges shown above; this way fully functional hinges can be made for building doors and vehicle hatches.

Photoetched parts can also be used as stencils for painting. The patterned carpet in "A Stillness at Appomattox" (see picture in Chapter 14) was painted using an airbrush and a series of etched metal stencils. I don't

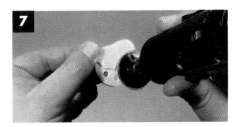

7 Sometimes the sprue is actually bigger than the part, which is when the Merit Sanding Disc really comes in handy.

8 With a bit of practice, you can even remove blocks from delicate parts with the sander, although it is wise to switch from coarse to fine grit for the final moments.

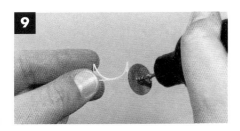

9 I also use small jeweler's sanding discs for final touch-up on delicate or small parts.

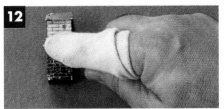

10 A final alternative is a disc or belt sander. Modelers who do a lot of work with resin develop a deft touch and swear by this method.

11 Resin architectural features before and after painting, and a finished plaster wall. The finished plaster wall is done much the same way, with some additional dry-brushing of red to restore the brick color.

12 A quick and easy way to finish brick walls is to paint the entire surface brownish red with oil-based hobby enamels. When the red paint has set (not just dry to the touch—give it at least 24 hours), brush on some slightly thinned gray so that it covers everything, including the space between the bricks. While it is still wet, or immediately after it has dried, wipe the surface with a rag moistened in thinner, revealing the red but leaving the gray in between the bricks.

13 Photoetched parts are an essential tool of the trade for modern ship modelers, who use them for railings, radar screens and dozens of other tiny details that would be almost impossible to make any other way. Even the figures on 1/700 scale ships can be photoetched, as in this model by John Leyland. The tiny figures are coated with white glue before painting to give them a more natural rounded appearance.

think it could have been does as well or as easily any other way.

I had the stencils custom-made to my design, which bring us to one of the best things about photoetching: you can do it yourself. Several companies offer a custom photoetching service. For years I have had my work done by a company called Fotocut, Box 120, Erieville, NY 13061.

You have to provide camera-ready black-and-white artwork for each level of etching. Fortunately, this can be done several times actual size, so any mistakes you make are much less evident when the drawing is reduced. You may be able to find ready-made artwork, but sooner or later you will have to draw your own. You can do this the old-fashioned way with pen and ink, but a computer is an ideal tool for this process, providing perfect circles, squares and straight lines every time. If you are doing multi-level etching, draw or print out the drawings on tracing paper so that you check the alignment of the different levels.

Many of the newest kits use a combination of these materials: resin for solid parts, plaster for very large ones, and photoetched brass for extremely delicate or sheet metal pieces. It doesn't take much adjustment to get the hang of working with these new materials, and when you do a whole new world of modeling will open up for you.

CHAPTER THIRTEEN

The Hornet's Nest

During some of the bitter fighting on the Eastern Front in World War II, it was not unusual for both sides to incorporate knocked-out vehicles into their trench lines. Tanks offered comforting overhead protection against anything but a direct hit by large caliber artillery and they often became strong points in a defensive line. A diorama of a machine gun nest under a knocked-out tank was an idea that had been germinating in the back of my mind for years. I had originally thought of doing it in 1/35th scale but worried that it would be too hard

to see the figures under the vehicle. Modeling it the larger 1/15 size would solve this problem and make a more physically impressive model as well. When I encountered the resin T34 designed by Mike McCauley for Frontline Miniatures, I realized that this would be the perfect vehicle for this project.

When I start working on a diorama, I usually have a picture in my mind of what it is going to look like. The picture may be fuzzy in some of its details—exact number of figures, poses, and so on—but the basic concept and overall shape is there. As work progresses and the details flesh themselves out, they often trigger new ideas, some of

which end up being worked into the scene. In this case, I knew there would be a machine gun crew under the tank, but I had no clear idea of the poses until I actually started working with the figures. I also knew there would be some figures outside the tank, but again, I let the available kit pieces determine the actual number of figures and their poses.

This was a pretty straightforward modeling project—no major figure conversions or special effects. Resin figures and vehicles kits require some new techniques for preparation and assembly, but once they are put together, painting, detailing and weathering are the same as with plastic or metal.

1 I used the Merit sanding disk to grind the rubber tires off the road wheels on the burned side of the vehicle. The coarse disk is powerful enough to remove a complete tire in less than a minute, so the job is less daunting than it appears.

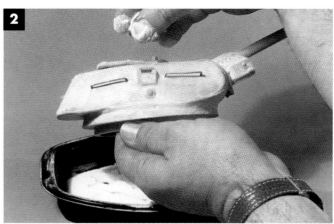

2 To get the proper rusted texture I coated the "burned" areas with varnish and sprinkled on baking soda.

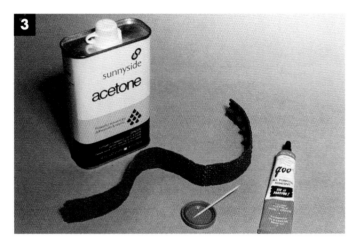

3 I found the most effect way to assemble the individual linked tracks was to glue them with Walthers Goo, which is fairly flexible when it dries. When additional flexibility is needed, you can brush on a bit of acetone to soften the Goo.

4 The figures for the scene, assembled and ready to paint. The figures are all Verlinden kits, with the parts swapped around. The machine gunner and the prone sniper, for example, have essentially swapped arms and weapons, while the assistant gunner is straight out of the box. The other two figures were a matter of trial and error, to a point where I can't clearly remember which parts came from which kits.

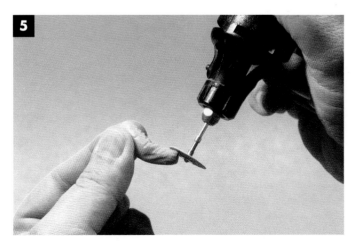

5 Some of the arms used with the figures in camouflage smocks had regular tunic cuffs. To transform them into the drawstring cuffs used on smocks, round off the cuffs with a fine sanding stick.

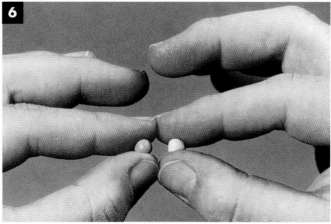

6 To mix epoxy putty, cut two small bits of parts A and B, roll them into balls to ensure they are about the same size, and then knead them together thoroughly.

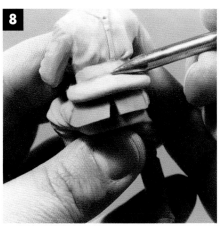

7 To add the skirt of the smock, which had a drawstring in the bottom and tended to ride up on the tunic underneath, start by rolling a sausage of epoxy putty and press it into place below the figure's waist.

8 Next, use a pointed sculpting tool (a cosmetic orange stick works fine) to press the putty up under the belt.

9 Use the same tool to press the pleats and folds into the bottom of the smock.

10 Priming your figures not only gives the paint something to stick to, it also helps you spot seams, sanding marks, and other flaws you missed during assembly. In this case I found a seam at the shoulder, which I filled with a dab of epoxy putty before painting.

11 Before you start to paint, hold the underpainted figure under a direct light and study the shadows it casts. This will tell you where the shadows and highlights should be painted.

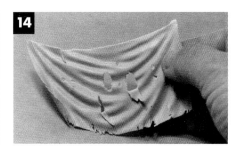

12 To get a realistic drape to the flag, I sculpted the folds into a block of modeling clay.

13 Then I mixed and flattened a blob of epoxy putty, sandwiched it between two sheets of waxed paper coated with talcum powder, and rolled it very thin with a dowel. After sitting for 45 minutes or so, it had started to stiffen up noticeably. I peeled it off the waxed paper, cut it to shape with scissors, cut some tears and holes in it with an X-Acto knife, and pressed it down onto the modeling clay folds.

14 When the putty has set, peel it off the modeling clay, and this is what you get.

15 Planning was done in a box of sand to establish the contours of the ground.

16 Use a ruler to measure the depth of the sand at various points.

17 Cut the contours of the ground from styrofoam insulation. The best thing to use for gluing styrofoam is five-minute epoxy (white glue takes days to dry, and virtually anything else dissolves the stuff).

18 I put the vehicle and figures into place to confirm the styrofoam contours.

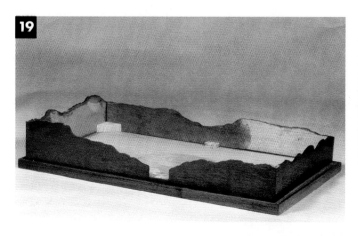

19 The side boards were cut from basswood, stained, varnished, and glued in place. Note the reinforcing blocks on the sides and in the corners.

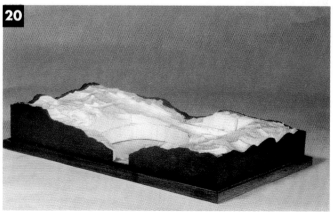

20 The base ready for landscaping.

21 Landscape and paint the area under the tank first, because it will be inaccessible once the vehicle is in place. Do this in the usual manner, with Celluclay and gutter gravel. Note the ammunition cases used to shore up the sides of the emplacement.

22 The second stage of the landscaping completed, before painting.

23 The finished diorama. Several people have asked how the tank got past the tree right behind it. The answer is that a moving tank that suddenly loses a track tends to swerve violently to one side, and that is how it would wind up in this position.

CHAPTER FOURTEEN

Shadow Boxes

A shadow box is a diorama set into a box and viewed through an opening in one side, and its effect is essentially that of a three-dimensional painting. In many ways, the shadow box is the ultimate form of the diorama. This is because of the degree of control over all aspects of the display that a shadow box affords the modeler. In a shadow box you can dictate the viewing angle, lighting conditions, and, most important, the atmosphere and mood of the scene.

Because it is contained in a box, a shadow box must have its own lighting system, a requirement that is both an awful nuisance and a golden opportunity. A certain working knowledge of electricity is essential in building shadow boxes, but you need not be an electronics expert. The small-time electrical system in a diorama is strictly kindergarten level when compared to even the simplest model railroad layout.

Planning a shadow box. Building a shadow box is more work than other dioramas, especially if you spend time backtracking to correct mistakes. The scene involves several disparate elements, each of which must be constructed separately and coordinated to fit into the final display. Careful planning can save you a lot of headaches later on.

The first step is to ensure that your subject is workable in the format. Shadow boxes lend themselves most readily to enclosed settings. Wide-open outdoor scenes are possible and have been done well, but they require the ability to paint a realistic backdrop and the means to blend it with the three-dimensional foreground. If you're just starting out, limit yourself to scenes that are set indoors or in locations surrounded by walls, trees, or other enclosing devices.

Make sure that your topic is suited to a single viewpoint. Subjects with a lot of detail or a hopelessly obstructed view of the main event require all-around viewing for the scene to be effective. Don't fall into the trap of confining such a scene to a shadow box just because you feel like building a box.

A shadow box is best planned from the inside out. Start by arranging your figures. Check different arrangements and viewing angles to determine which you like the best. Once the final figure arrangement is set, lay out the scene around it.

Next, decide the sizes of your viewing window and borders. Make sure the aperture is not too small for the box (a border of 2"–4" is best; anything over that us usually wasted space) and that the scene inside will be

This 1/18 scale scene of the turret of the Monitor is approximately 14" across. I managed to illuminate it evenly by using a pair of 8" fluorescent tubes.

1 Candlelight creates unparalleled moods and dramatic effects. In this 1/18 scale scene of Napoleon at the tomb of Frederick the Great, the candles are PFM bulbs in a brass candelabrum. Wires run down the arm, body, and leg of the figure.

2 Outdoor scenes are hard to handle in shadow boxes, because the confines of the box are so obvious. Dennis Levy got around this problem by concealing the horizon behind sand dunes and using a plexiglass dome for a background, lighting it from behind.

compatible with the "apparent value" of the box. A big box calls for a big scene.

The overall size of the shadow box has a lot to do with the size of the border around the viewing window. The exact size of your border is usually dictated by the side of the scene that needs more space than the others. For example, in a scene with a high ceiling, the wide border needed to mask this element will be what determines the dimensions of the other three. Likewise, a scene in which a room is canted at an angle rather than viewed straight on requires a wide border on one side. For a simple, straight-on scene the only border width requirement might be the 2″ clearance needed underneath to accommodate the lighting transformer. Your shadow boxes will be more attractive and have more of a picture effect if the viewing aperture is centered on the front of the box, with an equal border all the way around. You can occasionally get away with making the bottom border ½″ wider than the others, but I would not carry it any further than that.

Now draw up a complete set of plans for your scene. Start with rough sketches less than actual size, but make the final detailed set of drawings the same size as your model. These drawings don't have to be beautiful, just detailed. Draw up an overall top view of your shadow box, a side view, and a front view. Take the time to work up actual-size drawings of each interior wall, including all details. Drawing these plans actual-size gives you a feel for the project and allows you to transfer measurements directly from the plan to the model, saving time and possible errors.

When the drawings are done, check them carefully. Plot sight lines from the edges of the viewing aperture to ensure that the viewer cannot accidentally see what he is not meant to see. Make sure that you have allowed enough room for light fixtures and that they will not be visible. Other practical problems will still turn up during construction, but the more of them you can eliminate at this stage, the easier the later going will be.

Constructing the scene. The shadow box is also built from the inside out. Build the

PLANNING A SHADOW BOX

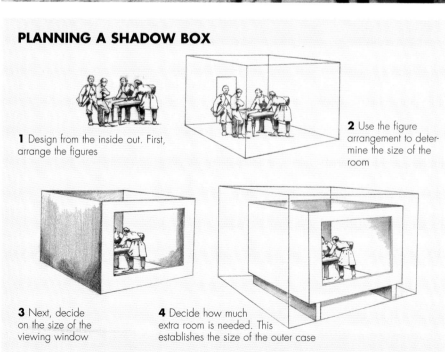

1 Design from the inside out. First, arrange the figures

2 Use the figure arrangement to determine the size of the room

3 Next, decide on the size of the viewing window

4 Decide how much extra room is needed. This establishes the size of the outer case

3 I normally don't favor copying paintings for dioramas—I'd rather work to my own designs than someone else's, even if that someone happens to be Rembrandt. But I was drawn to his "Night Watch" because I wanted to see how the composition and overall effect of the scene would change when transferred from two dimensions to three. When it was finished, I concluded that Rembrandt would have been a pretty good diorama builder!

4 The assembled scene before painting. The "Night Watch" called for over 30 figures, each of which had to be precisely posed and positioned to duplicate the painting.

5 Positioning of the figures called for a lot of trial and error: each toothpick fills a hole drilled in the wrong place!

6 The back of this completed shadow box frame shows the short toothpick pegs that retain the mat and glass, and the mat itself. The basswood strips were added around the edge to make it a snug press fit into the front of the box. Screws to hold the frame are then optional.

scene first, saving the outer case for last. This way you are free to make changes as construction progresses. The scene itself should be built on a simple plywood shelf that can slide in and out of the case. This allows full access to the modelwork during construction, and ease of repair when it is completed. Other than the sliding shelf, the scene is constructed just like any other diorama, except for one cardinal rule: DON'T WASTE TIME ON WHAT CAN'T BE SEEN. This means painting only the visible sides of figures and accessories. This rule is the great timesaver that makes up for the time devoted to the other aspects of the shadow box.

Building the case. This is the frame that sets off your scene, so you want it attractive, but not ostentatious. Unless you are a cabinetmaker, you also want it to be easy to build.

The sturdiest material for the case is plywood—$\frac{1}{4}''$ plywood is sufficient for most

boxes. Those more than 24" high, wide, or deep may require $\frac{3}{8}''$ material. The basic shell is constructed as shown in the drawing. Again, draw up a plan and figure out exact dimensions for each piece, compensating where necessary for the thickness of the adjoining sides. Nail the box together with small brads, and glue reinforcing strips into the inside corners. The nails should be set and the holes filled with putty. Fill all seams and surface flaws and sand the exterior smooth.

The outside of the case can be finished in a number of ways. One popular covering is self-adhesive vinyl, and many modelers use walnut wood grain vinyl. I find it easier (and a little less "plastic") to simply paint the entire box an unobtrusive gloss black, both inside and out. A final touch is to attach four small supporting blocks to the bottom of the box to raise it about 1" from table level.

Only a few fittings are required inside the case. A 1" x 1" rail should be glued to the left and right inside walls to support the scene. A $\frac{1}{4}''$ hole should be drilled at the bottom back for the main power cord, and a larger ($\frac{1}{2}''$ or $\frac{5}{8}''$) hole drilled near the front for the on-off switch. If you are going to use plug-in electrical connections, you will need a simple wood mounting plate for the required plugs. Finally, you will have to drill mounting holes for the lighting transformer.

Don't worry if your first shadow box case is less than a masterpiece. Your carpentry skills will improve with practice, and there is more than a little truth to the rationalization that if the viewer spends all his time noticing flaws in the case, the scene inside must be pretty dull!

The frame. The next step in preparing the case is the frame. Don't try to make this at home; invest in a custom frame, or go to a frame-it-yourself shop and build your own. You will want the inner frame mat board to show, but not much of it; about 2" is generally the limit. The area covered by the mat can be reduced by choosing a fairly wide frame and using a fabric-covered liner.

You can cut the frame mat yourself if you have a mat cutter, or you can have the frame shop do it. They won't charge much to cut it for you and will probably do a better job. Have the glass cut at the same time. I always put the glass behind the mat, but it can be done the other way around too. Drill holes around the inner edge of the frame and insert toothpick pegs to hold the mat and glass in place. This arrangement allows both the mat and glass to be removed for cleaning or replacement.

The back of the frame should have a ridge or rim that is a force fit into the front of the case. Some frames include such a ridge as part of the molding, in which case you can order the frame custom-made to an exact fit. Otherwise, glue strips of $\frac{1}{2}''$ square basswood to the back of the frame to make the ridge. This ridge has several advantages. First, it allows you to install and remove the frame quickly while you are working; second, it prevents light from escaping around the edges of

SHADOW BOX OUTER CASE

1" x 1" shelf support, one on each side

1" x 1" supporting blocks under box

7,8 Back and front views of one of the central figures, before and after painting. One of the best things about box dioramas is that you can save time by not painting or detailing the backs of the figures (or anything else, for that matter), since this won't be seen.

ASSEMBLING THE SHADOW BOX

Sliding the scene into the case

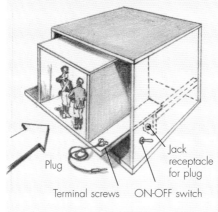

Plug

Terminal screws

ON-OFF switch

Jack receptacle for plug

THE INNER FRAME OR REVEAL

Cover shaded areas with black velvet before assembly

Toothpick pegs

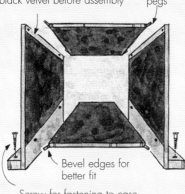

Bevel edges for better fit

Screw for fastening to case

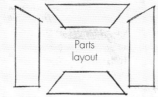

Parts layout

(Opposite pieces must be identical)

---

the frame; and third, it can easily be secured with small screws at either side of the case.

You may want to install an inner frame, called a "reveal," as well. This device allows you to set the scene back farther into the box, which will cut down on room light spilling into the scene (an important consideration for night scenes) and give the viewer some focusing distance between himself and the models. The reveal also provides a convenient place to mount lights, allowing you to illuminate the scene from an oblique angle while casting light on the front of the figures.

The inner frame is a square funnel, narrow at the scene end and growing wider as it nears the frame. The narrow end should be the same size as the opening in the mat, and the other end about 2″ wider on each side.

To build the reveal, draw up a plan to establish measurements and construct the frame as shown in the drawing. The edges where the top and bottom contact the sides should be beveled. Opposite pieces must be exactly the same size and shape, and positioned at exactly the same angle. The reveal is held together with toothpick pegs, much the same as the buildings described in Chapter 10.

Before assembly, the four pieces should be covered with velvet. Velour paper will do, but velvet fabric is better. I use black velvet because it remains totally neutral even when exposed to direct light, but other colors might work just as well. Cut the velvet to size allowing for an overlapping flap on the inside edge, and glue in place with spray adhesive or white glue. Since it is important that all visible sur-

faces be covered, glue the material in place slightly oversize, then trim it with a knife after the glue has set. Next, apply glue to the joints and assemble the reveal. Use a stack of books on either side of the frame to hold it in position, and make sure that the opening on the frame is exactly square. Let it dry overnight.

When the inner frame is ready, position it inside the case to check the fit in relation to the scene. Blocks can be glued to the bottom of the inner frame so it can be screwed to the bottom of the case, or simple retaining blocks can be glued to the case to hold the reveal.

Lighting system basics. This is the subject that most frightens would-be shadow box builders. Fortunately, the knowledge you need is so specialized that it is very limited in scope. Shadow box lighting systems are simple.

Although there are a number of lighting systems that could be used for dioramas, I prefer a 12-volt system for a number of reasons.

First, 12-volt bulbs can provide lots of illumination without generating appreciable heat. Second, the low voltage makes the system safe to use; short circuits might smoke and scare you a bit, but they won't electrocute you. Third, 12-volt systems are standard in model railroads, dollhouses, and full-size automobiles, giving you an extremely wide range of miniature lamps and fixtures to choose from.

Let's look at a simple 12-volt lighting system that consists of a power source, an on-off switch, and a lamp. Current flows from the power source, through the lamp, and through the switch, back to the power source. When the switch is on, the circuit is complete and

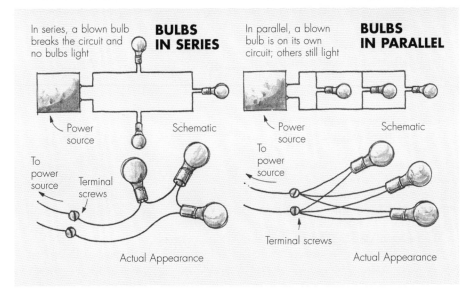

In series, a blown bulb breaks the circuit and no bulbs light

BULBS IN SERIES

Power source

Schematic

To power source

Terminal screws

Actual Appearance

In parallel, a blown bulb is on its own circuit; others still light

BULBS IN PARALLEL

Power source

Schematic

To power source

Terminal screws

Actual Appearance

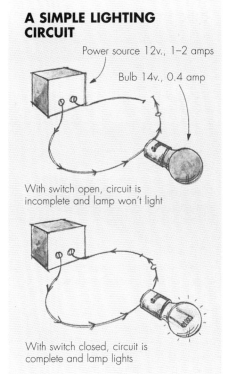

A SIMPLE LIGHTING CIRCUIT

Power source 12v., 1–2 amps

Bulb 14v., 0.4 amp

With switch open, circuit is incomplete and lamp won't light

With switch closed, circuit is complete and lamp lights

USEFUL BULBS FOR SHADOW BOXES

LAMP	SOCKET	CANDLE-POWER	AMPS	VOLTS	LIFE (HOURS)
CM 1815	min.bay.	1.4	.2	14	3000
CM 57	min.bay.	2	.24	14	500
GE 89	auto bay.	6	.58	13	750
GE 97	auto bay.	4	.69	13.5	5000
GE 1003	auto bay.	15	.94	12.8	200
GE 1156	auto bay.	32	2.1	12.8	1200
GE 1195	auto bay.	50	3	12.8	250

CM—Chicago Miniature Light   GE—General Electric
Code number of bulbs is generally the same from manufacturer to manufacturer.

9 "Stopping the Slave Trade" shows how lighting can affect composition. The bright light coming down the hatchway immediately draws the viewer's eye to the main action, even though it is at the back of the scene.

10 "The Capture of Redoubt Number Ten at Yorktown." This was a night assault illuminated, according to survivors' memoirs, "by the flash of British muskets and grenades." The explosions and lit fuses were achieved using the same technique described for "The Death of Jim Bowie" in chapter 16.

the current flows, lighting the lamp. When the switch is off, the circuit is interrupted and the flow stops. Note that it doesn't matter whether the switch is before or after the lamp in the system; the circuit must be complete for the system to work. Don't worry about the direction of the current flow; this makes a difference in motors, but not with lamps.

In our example, the power source (a transformer) is rated at 12 volts and 1.2 amperes, and the light bulb at 14 volts and 0.4 amp. Since the power source supplies only 12 volts, the lamp will not burn quite as bright as it would at 14 volts, but it will last longer. Since the one bulb draws only one-third of the current produced by the power source, two other bulbs can be added to the circuit. Then, three bulbs at 0.4 amp each will match the output of the 1.2-amp transformer. Additional bulbs (beyond three) would require more current than the power source can provide, and the transformer would burn out.

CIRCUIT TESTER

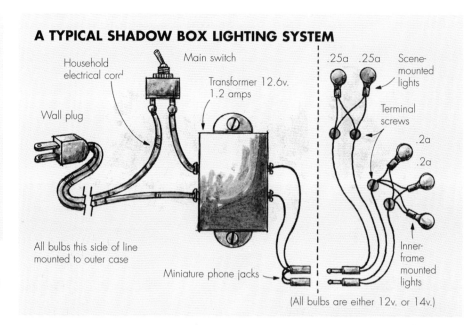

One lead longer than the other, to avoid accidental contact

18v. bulb and socket

Small alligator clips

A TYPICAL SHADOW BOX LIGHTING SYSTEM

Household electrical cord

Main switch

Transformer 12.6v. 1.2 amps

Wall plug

.25a .25a Scene-mounted lights

Terminal screws

.2a

.2a

All bulbs this side of line mounted to outer case

Miniature phone jacks

Inner-frame mounted lights

(All bulbs are either 12v. or 14v.)

11 The Yorktown diorama during the posing and positioning stage, using modeling clay and plywood boards for the ramparts.

12 The base before landscaping, showing how the ramparts were built up with wood. the correct position holes for the figure are circled; as with the "Night Watch," you can see a number of holes drilled by mistake.

13 Checking the sight lines, with the figures positioned on the base and two strips of cardboard tacked on either side to indicate the edge of the viewing window.

Now that we have three bulbs in our system, burning at 12 volts, each drawing 0.4 amp, let's diagram the circuit. There are two ways to connect the bulbs in the system and still have a complete circuit. The first is to connect them in series, so current flows from one bulb to the next and back to the power source. This is a workable system, but it has an important drawback. If one bulb burns out, it interrupts the circuit, extinguishing all the bulbs, and the only way to find the culprit is to exchange each bulb until they all light again. A better method is to connect the lamps in parallel. In a parallel system each bulb has its own circuit to the power source, so if one burns out, the others are not affected.

Components. First, you will need a 12-volt power source. The most convenient source of this type is a transformer, which converts standard 115-volt household current to 12 volts. Transformers are available at Radio Shack or any electronics supply store; the usual ratings are 1.2 amps, 3 amps, and 5 amps. To determine which transformer rating you need, add up the ampere ratings of your lamps and make sure that they do not total more than the rating of the transformer.

There are hundreds of bulbs and several types of lamp sockets for you to choose from. There are three basic types of bulbs. The most familiar has a miniature screw-in socket and

comes in several sizes. The second type is the bayonet-base in which the bulb is pushed and turned into the socket. Very small bulbs simply have two wire leads and do not use a socket. I use the bayonet-base sockets and bulbs most often, because there are only two standard sizes and I can fit all of the bulbs I usually use into one or the other. Miniature bulb sockets usually are not rated as to volts or amps, so a given socket will do as well for a 3-volt bulb as for a 12-volt bulb.

The table on page 121 lists the bulbs I have found most useful in shadow boxes. I have omitted grain-of-wheat and smaller bulbs because they vary so widely in size and ratings. You can generally figure a current requirement of .08 amp for a grain-of-wheat bulb. Candlepower is a measure of brightness. You will notice that not all bulbs are rated at exactly 12 volts. A 14-volt bulb is actually preferable, because even though it will not burn at quite its full brightness, the voltage "cushion" will double or triple its life.

Shadow box lighting installation. Now let's install a lighting system in a shadow box. The best way is to start at the wall plug and work your way through, step by step. You will need a wire stripper, pliers, and a screwdriver. A soldering iron is also recommended,

but not absolutely necessary. While you can mount the components in the box as you go, it is often easier to assemble the whole rig first, before installation.

The great bugaboo of every novice electrician is the short circuit. A short circuit is caused by the outgoing and ingoing lines from the power source coming into direct electrical contact. When this happens, the contact point becomes an accidental heat and light source; at low voltages it just smokes a bit, but at higher voltages, it can cause fire, sparks, and intense heat. Never touch the bare parts of both outgoing and ingoing wires at once; if you do, you become a short circuit, and at high voltages you can electrocute yourself. At lower voltages you will just get a mild shock, but it is still best to be careful.

MINIATURE SPOTLIGHTS

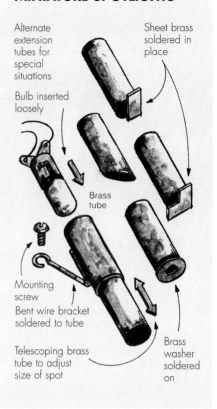

Alternate extension tubes for special situations

Sheet brass soldered in place

Bulb inserted loosely

Brass tube

Mounting screw

Bent wire bracket soldered to tube

Telescoping brass tube to adjust size of spot

Brass washer soldered on

14 "A Stillness at Appomattox." Often the most telling moment of a historic event occurs before or after the event itself. In this case I felt that the deep sadness of General Lee waiting for Grant, knowing he had no choice but to accept whatever terms were offered, was more moving than the actual surrender. His aide Colonel Marshall stands by the mantel wiping his glasses, while Grant's representative, Colonel Babcock, looks out the window for the arrival of his boss.

15 "To a Fair Wind . . . and Victory!" On the eve of his greatest triumph, Trafalgar, Admiral Nelson dined alone, but before the Battle of Copenhagen, he gathered with his captains for a final meal. A significant design problem was positioning Nelson, who was of small stature, so that he could be seen. The solution was to have the men rising for the toast: those in the center foreground conveniently happen to be a bit slower to rise than the others, giving a clear view of the Admiral (the Royal Navy's privilege of drinking toasts seated was not granted until after Nelson's time).

16 A close-up, showing the faces of the figures.

DIMMER INSTALLATION FOR A SINGLE BULB

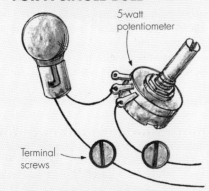

5-watt potentiometer

Terminal screws

The "Golden Rule" of electricity is this: NEVER TOUCH OR WORK ON THE SYSTEM WITHOUT UNPLUGGING IT. You can't get a shock if there is no current in the system.

Start assembling the system with the main power cord. This should be long enough to reach from the transformer through the hole in the back of the box, with three feet to spare. This length requires an extension cord to connect the shadow box to a wall socket, but you will probably need one anyway. Standard household lamp cord is fine, and a quick-connect plug is easy to install. Strip about ¾" of insulation from the other end of the cord, split the two conductor wires apart for about 8",

and twist the wire strands to form more manageable wire ends.

The two leads are connected to the 115-volt side of the transformer. One lead will run directly to the transformer, and the other will run to the main power switch and then to the

CANDLES

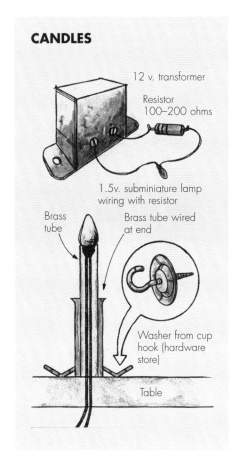

12 v. transformer

Resistor
100–200 ohms

1.5v. subminiature lamp
wiring with resistor

Brass tube

Brass tube wired at end

Washer from cup hook (hardware store)

Table

transformer. Twist the wires around the terminals; then, for a secure connection, solder them. Once you have experience soldering models (Chapter 6), electrical soldering is a snap. There's only one new wrinkle—acid flux is never used for electrical soldering.

Now move to the 12-volt side of the transformer. All wiring from here on is done with two-conductor model railroad or hi-fi speaker wire. Cut a piece long enough to reach from the transformer to one side of the box (with a bit to spare), strip about ½″ of insulation from the ends, and connect the leads at one end to the two outside posts of the transformer (nothing is connected to the center post). Connect the other end of the wire to the female receptacle of a miniature phone jack. The jack affords a quick plug-in connection for the lighting system mounted on the scene. Since most lighting systems will also call for lights mounted on the inner frame, install two jacks. Connect them in parallel as shown in the drawing. The electrical installation for the outer case is now complete.

Now cut a piece of wire long enough to reach from the jack plug to the lights on the scene, and another piece to run to the lights on the inner frame. Connect each of these to the jack plugs. The other end of each line should be connected to a pair of screw terminal posts installed in convenient locations on the scene and inner frame. Strip the wire ends, wrap them securely around the terminal posts,

and tighten down the nuts. These terminals permit you to experiment with various styles and numbers of lights without having to dismantle the entire system.

Make wire leads for each of your light fixtures, connecting the leads permanently to the fixture and securing them with nuts to the terminal posts at the other end. Most light fixtures have some sort of mounting bracket, but you may have to devise some mounts yourself from wood or sheet brass.

What to do if it doesn't work.
Your lighting system is now complete. Connect the jacks, plug in the main power cord, turn on the switch, and see if it works. If you have followed the steps carefully, everything should be fine and all the lamps should light. If they don't, immediately unplug the main power cord. Sniff for smoke and feel the wires and connections for heat. If the problem is not a short circuit, it means that the current flow is interrupted because (a) there is a loose connection somewhere or (b) you have goofed while connecting the wires, leaving a gap.

To locate the trouble spot, start at the main power cord and check each element of the system. Plug another appliance into the wall socket and extension cord to make sure these are good. Make up a 12-volt test bulb as shown in the drawing on page 122, unplug the phone jacks, and clip the test light to the 12-volt terminals of the transformer. If it

17 This was a pretty elaborate setting, with fine furniture, silver, and paneling in the cabin. The cabin was built of plywood, with basswood strips for the paneling, with thin brass rod for the gilt mouldings. I made one chair in several parts and cast the others from it.

18 Another shipboard scene, "Mr. Christian!" shows the cabin of the Bounty after Captain Bligh has just discovered a dead breadfruit tree. The brown color of the plant (in contrast to the green of the others) and the obvious dismay of the gardener help tell the story.

lights, the system up to that point is good; if it does not, you have narrowed the problem to the transformer, the plug, or the switch. Isolate each in turn until you find the culprit.

If the transformer, main power cord, and power switch are good, move farther down the line, checking the circuit at each point until you locate the problem. Sometimes it is an improper connection, sometimes a faulty fixture. Remember, unplug the transformer from the wall each time you work on the system.

Optional features. A fuse is a piece of metal enclosed in a glass tube that forms part of the circuit; when too much current flows through it, the metal melts, breaking the circuit and preventing further damage. This safety option will protect the components of your lighting system from damage caused by a

19 Dennis Levy's diorama of German para-troops exiting their aircraft makes clever use of the distinctive corrugated fuselage of the JU-52 aircraft as part of the outside frame.

short circuit and prevent your shadow box from becoming a fire hazard. Fuses and fuse brackets can be obtained at model railroad and miniature room shops and electronics supply stores such as Radio Shack. Choose a fuse to match the rating of your transformer. Simply connect the fuse in series in the line between the transformer and the jacks.

Larger lights are another option. To brightly illuminate a scene, especially a large one, you may want to use standard 115-volt bulbs and fixtures. Electronics supply stores sell fluorescent tubes and fixtures as small as 6″ long and these are useful. Small incandescent bulbs (7, 15, and 25 watts) can be obtained, with fixtures, at hardware stores.

All 115-volt appliances should be wired into the lighting system between the switch and the transformer. In-line connections of this sort are easy; just twist the three cord ends together and secure them with a wire nut, available at your hardware store.

Establishing lighting effects. Now that we know the basics of building a lighting system, let's talk about what you want to do with it. The reason phone jacks and terminal screws are worth the time spent installing them is that effective lighting is a matter of experimentation. You will have to vary the number of lights, their positions, and their brightness until you get the effect you want.

There are three basic lighting effects, and they can be used alone or in combinations. These are single (pinpoint) source, diffuse, and focused. Light from a pinpoint source, such as the filament of a light bulb, casts sharp, distinct shadows, and several pinpoint sources can cast conflicting shadows. Diffuse light from a single wide source, such as a fluorescent tube, casts fuzzy, indistinct shadows. Focused light, such as the light from a spotlight, is directed to a narrow location. These are the lighting tools you have to work with.

First, decide how you want to handle the general illumination of your scene. General illumination can be provided with one bright pinpoint light, several smaller pinpoints, or a diffuse fluorescent light. If you are using a strong pinpoint light source, you may find the contrast between the highlights and shadows too great. This can be cured in a number of ways. First try installing reflectors made of white cardboard or crumpled aluminum foil. Position these so they bounce light back up into the shadows. If this is not satisfactory, install small fill lights to illuminate the shadows. The fill lights should only be strong enough to bring out detail in the shadows without casting conflicting shadows of their own.

Use focused illumination to brighten certain parts of your scene more than others. If a wide area is to be illuminated, try adding small pinpoint light sources in the right places. Another method of focusing light is to cut a paper mask that will fit in front of the light source and block light from certain areas.

If a more restricted pool of light is called for, you will have to shield the light source in some way. The best method is to build miniature spotlights. These need be nothing more than brass tubes with a lamp inserted at one end. The inside of the tube should be bright (not blackened) so the light pattern will be a fuzzy spot instead of a sharp ring. The spotlights can accommodate a telescoping extension tube to vary the area covered with light. These extensions can be made with various rims and shades to suit specific situations.

Spotlights can be used both as main lights and fill lights. Spotlight tubes are particularly handy for grain-of-wheat bulbs, because these bulbs have no other mounting devices.

Dimmers. There are special situations where you will want to increase or decrease the brightness of your lighting. A shadow box that looks good in a dark room, for example, may not have enough light for viewing in a bright room, and vice versa. Dimming all the lights in the system is quite simple, and can even be done as an afterthought. Hardware stores sell inline dimmers that can be wired

into your extension cord. Dimmers vary the current transmitted to all lights in the box, increasing or decreasing their brightness.

Eventually, you will want to dim lights individually to adjust them for just the right effect. This is something that must be planned into the lighting system during its construction. At an electronics store you can buy 5-watt potentiometers, called "pots," which are dimmers about 1½″ in diameter. These can be wired into the system between the lamps and the terminals. A 5-watt pot can handle one or two .25-amp bulbs.

Don't automatically install a separate pot for each lamp in your system, because half of the bulbs usually have to be turned up to full brightness anyway. Instead, set up all your lights for full power, and then install pots on those that need to be toned down.

Colored lights. Occasionally you will want to use colored lights in your shadow box. The colors can range from overall deep blue tones for night scenes to subtle warming colors for daylight. Unless the light source will be visible, stay away from colored bulbs—their available range is limited, and the color may not be permanent. For hidden lights, all that is needed is a simple color filter in front of the light.

Tinted gelatin or plastic filters, called gels, are used in the theater, television, and movies, and any place that sells theatrical lighting equipment should have them. The range of available colors is staggering, so ask for a sample book. When in doubt, buy the lighter of two colors. You can always use two or three thicknesses of a light tint to make a deeper color, but there is no way to lighten a single thickness that is too dark. Since a single 2′ square gel is more than enough to last you a lifetime, an ideal source for miniature gels is the sample book itself, which contains sheets about 1″ x 2″. The theatrical supply house should be able to sell you a sample book, or you can send away for one.

If your bulb will be visible, achieving the right color is more difficult. You can buy red, green, and amber bulbs in various sizes from a model railroad shop, but the colors are harsh.

20 Like "Napoleon at the Tomb of Frederick the Great," "The Last Survivor" is a mood piece, with the tone of pathos established by dramatic lighting. The wounded horse Comanche, the only survivor of Custer's command at the Little Bighorn, was nursed back to health as he returned to Fort Lincoln on the riverboat Far West.

21 "Is That You, Daddy?" is a good example of how well fantasy subjects are suited to dramatic lighting possibilities, as a small boy in his pajamas fearfully looks out his back door, with the terrible monsters of his imagination lurking among the trees at the edge of the yard (model by Spencer Van Gulick).

22 Another example of how lighting can be used. Dennis Levy copied this Franco-Prussian War composition from a painting by Antoine de Neuville, called "Combat in a Church."

Bulb coloring kits are made for scientific and automotive purposes, but it may be hard to find them. Avoid using ordinary paint, since it will discolor from the heat.

Fireplaces and candles. Open flames in a fireplace can be simulated by hiding a grain-of-wheat bulb behind the logs. Surround the bulb with crumpled orange, yellow, and red gel filters for flames, and add crumpled aluminum foil for coals.

Candles are more awkward. Pacific Fast Mail offers excellent subminiature bulbs for model railroad use that give an excellent candle effect, but they are expensive and

temperamental. The bulbs are rated at 1.5 volts and run well off a standard flashlight battery, but batteries always die out at just the wrong time. If you want to incorporate 1.5-volt subminiature bulbs into your 12-volt system, you will have to install resistors in line with the bulbs. A resistor is an electrical "sponge" that soaks off enough current to drop the voltage to the desired level. Resistors are available in various ohm ratings at any electronics store. My experience is that a 1/2-watt, 100- to 200-ohm resistor is about right for use with PFM bulbs, but you will have to test to be sure, so buy an assortment of resistors.

Hook up the bulb to the transformer with the resistor connected in series with the bulb. Start testing using a resistor with a high ohm rating, and gradually work your way down. At first nothing will happen because the resistor is soaking off too much current, but as you reduce the ohm value, the bulb will start to glow. When you have an acceptable glow, stop; these bulbs burn out very suddenly. When you have found the proper resistor, install it permanently in the system. You can also add a potentiometer to the line if you want to vary the brightness of the candle.

Construction of a simple candlestick and candle is shown in the drawing. Brass is the best material to use because of the heat generated by the bulb. Make sure that when you design your scene you devise some way to run the wires out of sight. To keep the bulb in the proper position, tack it lightly in place with white glue. The glue can be dissolved with water to replace the bulb.

Other lighting tricks. As you become more deeply involved in lighting shadow boxes, the electronic aspects of the projects take on a fascination and challenge of their own. New and sometimes not-so-new developments in lighting are always potentially useful to you, and it is worth keeping up with them. The light-emitting diode (LED) was originally developed for digital readouts in calculators and monitor lights for stereos. An LED is best described as a colored bit of plastic which lights up when current is applied to it. Since there is no filament to burn out, LEDs last practically forever, which makes permanent installation possible. While they don't throw much light, they do glow nicely and are excellent as miniature lights in a scene. Modelers have recently discovered that LEDs are perfect for navigation and instrument lights on model aircraft, and the effect when the navigation light is connected to a flasher unit is most impressive. LEDs can be permanently built into a model at the time of construction, without having to worry about replacement, and, in series with a resistor, they can be operated by anything from penlight batteries to a standard 12-volt lighting system.

Model railroaders are frequent beneficiaries of new developments in miniature lighting techniques, and the electrical aspects of dollhouses are only beginning to be explored. One dollhouse innovation is the use of flat metal tape instead of wire. The tape can be run along the surface of a wall to a light fixture and is so thin that it can be hidden by wallpaper or even a couple of thick coats of paint.

CHAPTER FIFTEEN

The Meeting of the Admiralty Board

uring the 300 years that Britannia ruled the waves, the nerve center of British naval power was in the Board Room of the Admiralty in London. It was the Admiralty Board, presided over by the First Sea Lord, that made the strategic decisions and gradually amassed the empire on which the sun never set. The Admiralty Board was also responsible for approving the design and authorizing construction of all ships built for the Royal Navy. Since the time of Samuel Pepys in the reign of Charles II, it was mandatory for the designer to submit a model of the proposed vessel along with his plans. These Admiralty models were exquisitely crafted and are the most sought-after antique ship models.

In the scene, the Admiralty Board is meeting to discuss the merits of a new 104-gun three-decker, a first-rate ship of the line. It might even be HMS *Victory*, whose keel was laid in 1765. The First Sea Lord is at the far end of the table, deciding whether the occasion calls for a little port, while the other members, with varying degrees of interest, examine the latest proposed addition to His Majesty's fleet.

Although the Admiralty Board has long been on my list of desirable subjects, it was chosen for this book because it could be built using furniture and figures that are available in kit form. Phoenix Model Developments of England has produced several series of diorama-oriented 54mm figures, and their eighteenth-century Tavern group

is one of their best. The character of the figures is marvelous, and the poses are ideally suited to a subject like the Admiralty Board. Sufficient furniture is also available to fill out the scene, leaving only the walls and details to be constructed.

The complexity of the Admiralty Board scene is about average for a shadow box diorama. The modeling challenges in this project include the rigged Admiralty model on the table, the bookcases full of books along the rear wall of the room, and the two large globes housed in the center bay between the bookcases. Although the Admiralty Board Room still exists, it has been redecorated several times since the scene I wanted to re-create took place, so I used an eighteenth-century print as reference.

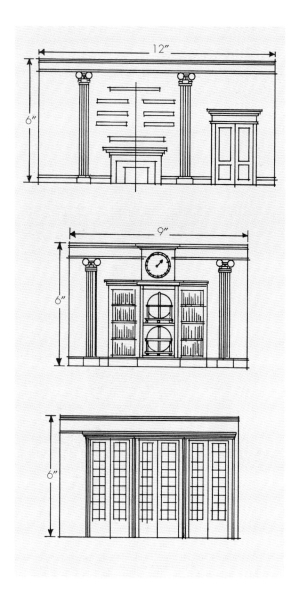

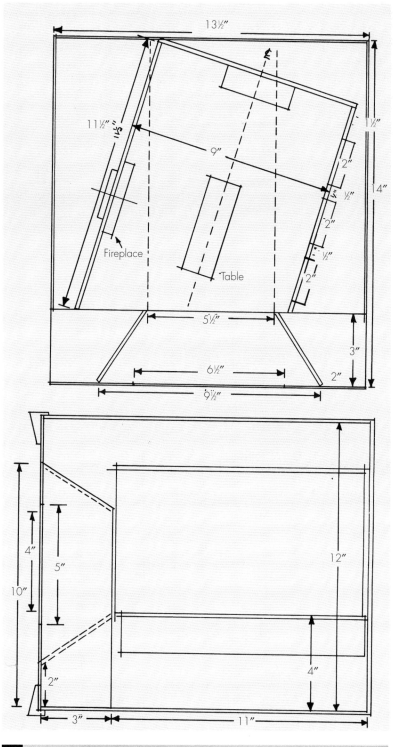

1 The first step, as always, is planning. Here the figures and furniture are laid out to establish the floor plan. Some of the furniture will be relocated in the course of construction, but the overall effect is very close to the finished version. Having the viewer look at the table from the end means that figures can be placed on both sides, but it also means that they must be carefully positioned if all of them are to be seen through the window.

2 The outline of the walls is traced onto the base. There is still some doubt as to the exact angle of the walls, a problem that will be dealt with later.

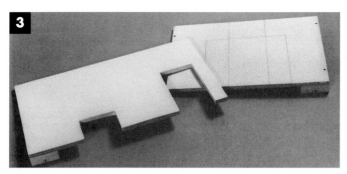

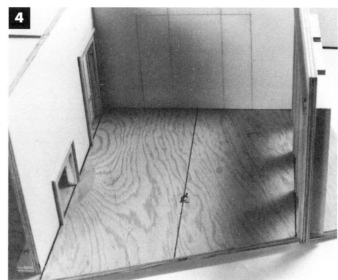

3,4 The walls were cut from ¼" model aircraft plywood and brushed with several coats of artist's gesso. The location of the large bookcase has been marked on the back wall As soon as the walls were cut, they were mounted on the base to check the fit. Notice that one wall is a little short for the base, while the other is a little long. This is due to a last-minute adjustment in the angle of the right wall. The discrepancy will not show once the scene is in the box.

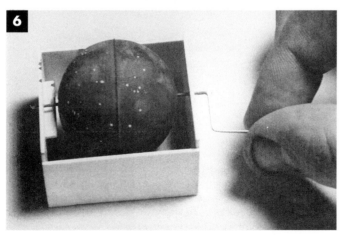

5,6 I expected the two large globes, one terrestrial, one celestial, to be a challenge, but they came off without a hitch. The globes themselves are cheap rubber balls that I bought at the dime store. The molding seam makes a nice equator. The frame consists of HO porch pillars and circular parts cut from sheet styrene with the aid of a pair of dividers. In order to draw the latitude and longitude lines on the globes, I built a simple fixture. The rubber balls were mounted on pins that passed through holes in the box. By sliding a pencil across the side of the box, I made longitude lines, and by holding the pencil stationary and rotating the globe, I made perfect latitude lines.

7,8 Here, the walls are almost completed. The pilasters were glued in place first, and the moldings fitted around them. The fancy-looking cove moldings are nothing more than layered stripwood. The double door is heavy illustration board paneled with stripwood. The fireplace is lined with illustration board, and the bookcase is basswood. A disc of styrene was added to the bookcase for the wind direction indicator. The floor is scribed basswood sheet, glued down with contact cement to avoid warping.

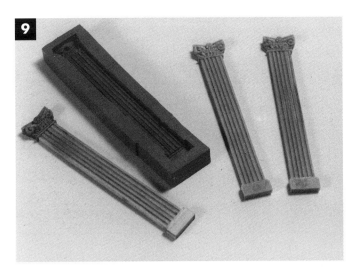

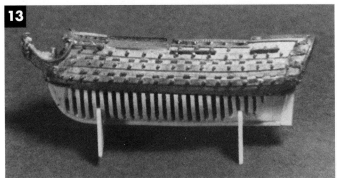

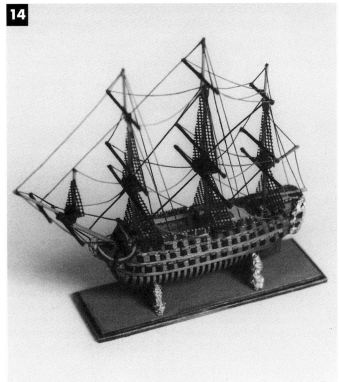

9 The Corinthian pilasters add a classical eighteenth-century touch, so it was worth the effort to cast them. The pattern was a basswood backing with strips of two thicknesses glued to it to form the grooves. The capital was then sculpted from epoxy putty. From left to right, the pattern, the mold, and two castings. Linear shrinkage, which is unavoidable, means that the cast columns are about 1/16" shorter than the pattern, so I had to make allowances for this in the pattern.

10,11 All window framing on the right wall is stripwood. If you look closely, you can see that the window moldings are only detailed on the side that can be seen from the viewing window. The glass is a single sheet of clear styrene held in place with wood battens screwed to the wall.

12,13 The ship model is the center of attention in the scene. Fortunately, an appropriate ship was available, part of Valiant Miniatures' line of wargame models. All that was needed was to add the portion below the waterline. It was traditional for Admiralty models to have the planking stripped away below the waterline to show the inner structure of ribs. I modeled this by gluing together wide and narrow pieces of sheet styrene sandwich-style, forming a solid block as long as the ship. This block was cut and ground down with a Dremel tool, and final shaping was done with sandpaper and a sanding block.

14 I rigged my model, but Admiralty models were also made unrigged, with stump masts. The rigging was done with strands of fine electrical wire, cut to length and glued in place with white glue. The masts are brass wire, held together with super glue. The ratlines are model railroad expanded aluminum screening, and the base and supports are styrene, with golden dolphins made from epoxy putty.

15 Each shelf of books on the back wall is an identical resin casting, painted to look different. The strange device over the bookcase is a wind gauge, which was attached to a weather vane on the roof of the building and which told their lordships whether the wind was right for the fleet to sail. Its hand is a watch hand scavenged from a watch repair shop.

16 Details on the left wall include map cases made from Plastruct tubing and brass wire rods. There is a small hole at the back of the fireplace for a grain-of-wheat bulb for the fire.

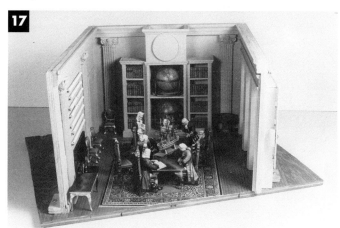

17 The assembled scene. The wind gauge and ceiling have not been installed, but all other elements are in place. Although the figures were painted all the way around, the greatest care was taken only with the side that would be seen.

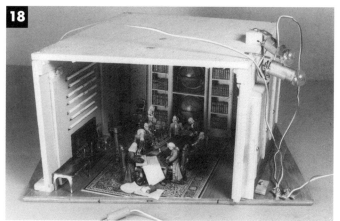

18 The ceiling is held in place by four screws. A single GE 1003 bulb was later substituted for the two GE 97 automotive lamps shown here because they cast conflicting shadows. The lead running over the top is for the fireplace light, which is masked with crumpled red cellophane. Later, the wires were taped down so they would not be seen through the windows. A filler light was installed on the top of the inner frame in addition to the lighting shown here.

19,20 Above, the scene has been installed in the outer case. Note the transformer, on-off switch, and shelf supports. Below, the completed shadow box after the frame and inner frame have been installed on the front of the case looks like this. The brass title plate is not yet attached to the mat.

21 The plans scattered on the table and floor were lightly drawn in pencil on paper that had been dipped in weak coffee. The servant call cords overhead are twisted solder wire with Historex trumpet tassels at the ends.

22 The elaborate carpet is a trimmed-down dollhouse item. The wine glass on the servant's tray consists of a bowl made by carefully cutting off a grain-of-wheat bulb, and a stem turned from a small piece of plexiglass rod. The wine itself is a liquid stained glass product sold for use in the miniature rooms and dollhouse crafts hobbies.

CHAPTER SIXTEEN

Mirrors, Forced Perspectives, and Other Special Effects

Special effects are the fun part of box dioramas. They allow the frustrated movie director that seems to reside in all of us to come forth and work out his fantasies on a little sound stage of his own, without the frustrations of dealing with a cast, crew, and multi-million dollar budget. Some special effects are simple, others are complicated. And the pleasure of having fooled your audience, if only for a moment, more than makes up for the effort required.

Fire and explosions. Pyrotechnics are not as much fun as they are in the movies, but they are a lot safer and less complicated. Whatever the size of your explosion, at the heart of it will be a light bulb, or for a really big

bang, perhaps a cluster of light bulbs. The next step is to hide the fact that it is a light bulb. I do this with fiberglass insulation, the kind that is sold in rolls for insulating houses. The glass fibers carry the light, creating a fireball effect. Pull off a small clump of material and stretch it out, forming it into a loose ball. Carefully wrap this around your light bulb, turn it on and check the effect. Make adjustments if necessary and, when satisfied, glue the ball in place on the bulb. You will probably want to color the bulb red or orange, or a combination of the two. Ordinary paint turns black with the heat, but you can buy bulb coloring sets at electronics stores that will do the job nicely.

If you want to add smoke to your explosion, stretch out some cotton, lightly color it gray with an airbrush, and wrap it gently around your fireball.

Bright fireballs are really only appropriate for night scenes. In daylight, only the intense center of the explosion is visible, and that only for a brief fraction of a second. So resist the temptation to have your infantry advance through a maze of towering orange fireballs.

A simple but striking special effect, especially in a night scene, is the explosion of a gun going off, as seen here in "The Death of Jim Bowie." It is achieved with a model railroad grain-of-wheat bulb at the end of the pistol, with the wires running along the back of Bowie's arm and down through the floor. The fireball is formed of a small clump of fiberglass home insulation, carefully spread and shaped for the desired effect. Note the flash in the pistol's pan, which is a model railroad micro-mini bulb poking from a hole drilled in the pistol from the back.

The scene was quite dark, but as you looked at it you became aware of the flickering light of fireflies in the night, each a fiber optic strand leading back to a light behind the scene. A slowly rotating mask in front of the light illuminated only one or two strands at a time, and those for only a brief moment. The effect was perfect, and created a wonderful atmosphere for the scene.

Forced perspective. Forced perspective is the use of foreshortening, making items seen in the distance grow smaller in a shorter distance than they naturally would.

With figures, it is simply a matter of using larger scale figures in the foreground and smaller ones in the background. With 1/15 scale figures in the foreground, 1/35 scale in the middle, and 1/72 scale figures in the back, an apparent scale distance of several hundred yards can be crammed into a space less than a foot deep.

Unfortunately, everything else in the scene has to grow smaller at the same rate as the figures. Small individual objects like trees, telephone poles, and the like can be scaled to

Only gasoline or napalm explodes this way (high explosive is little more than a large puff of smoke), but Hollywood can't resist the dramatic effect it creates on film—I'm always amazed at how they can pack five gallons of gasoline into a hand grenade.

Model railroad micro-mini bulbs are useful for all sorts of things—the lit fuses on the hand grenades in "Redoubt No. 10 at Yorktown," the flash in the pan in "The Death of Jim Bowie," or (in a scene yet to be built) the distant muzzle flashes of enemy rifles firing at an attacking line of troops.

One of the neatest tricks I have ever seen with fiber optics was in a scene by Hans Reuters of pirates burying treasure at night.

1 The overall illumination for "The Legend of Sleepy Hollow," like the Yorktown diorama, is given a bluish color with a blue theatrical gel filter placed over the light fixture. The jack-o-lantern has a grain-of-wheat bulb inside it.

2 When posing figures, it sometimes helps to have a model. My friend Joe Berton (the closest I could find to an Ichabod Crane physique) ran down the sidewalk several times while I snapped a series of pictures. This one was just the pose I was after and served as the pattern for the figure.

3 Fantasy and special effects naturally go together. In "The Swamp Ogre," the ogre's eyes are grain-of-wheat bulbs (colored red with bulb coloring). The bubbles of swamp gas on the surface of the water are clear plastic navigation domes from model airplane kits. People have told me this is based on their favorite Frank Frazetta painting. In fact, it's not based on any single painting but combines elements of half a dozen of them. I knew this was likely to be my only foray into fantasy, so I packed all the Frazetta choiceness—horned helmets, snakes, skulls, swamps and monsters—into one scene.

FORCED PERSPECTIVE

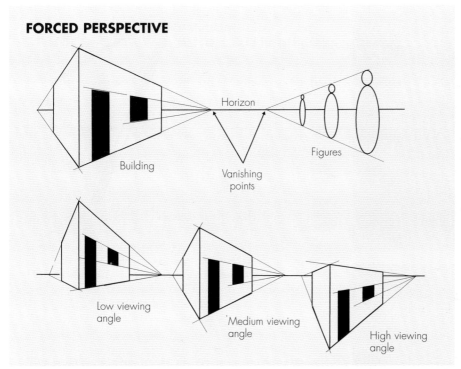

Building

Horizon

Figures

Vanishing points

Low viewing angle

Medium viewing angle

High viewing angle

4 Forced perspective can give your box much greater depth than it really has. Hans Reuters and Gregg Volke used 100mm figures in the foreground and 30 and 20mm figures in the back for "The Force Grows Weak, Old Man!" The secret of forced perspective is correctly angling the receding walls and restricting the viewing angle so that the illusion works from all possible viewing positions: left, right, above, and below.

5 Gregg Volke also use forced perspective for his dramatic "Egyptian Queen," which is based on a Frazetta painting.

High viewing angles are the most common problem. The solution is to frame the scene in such a way that when the viewer gets too high, his view is cut off by the top of the viewing window.

When working with forced perspective, it pays to make a cardboard mockup of your scene, so you can check the results from all possible viewing angles. Make adjustments if necessary and continue to check your work as the model progresses, particularly if you make any changes to the original design. The worst thing that can happen is to finish your diorama only to discover that one of your forced perspectives doesn't work.

There is a lot more to forced perspective than can be covered here. Whole books have been written on the subject—if you want to learn more, check the art or mechanical drawing section of your local library.

Mirrors. Mirrors have long been used by magicians to fool their audiences, and you can use them, too. I have used them a number of

the figures and present no serious problem, but a building or large receding object needs to be carefully worked out.

For this you need a rudimentary knowledge of perspective. Look at the drawing on this page. Study the various angles carefully. The natural flat horizon (i.e., discounting any intervening trees, hills, or buildings) is always at eye level. Objects receding from the viewer always recede toward a point on the horizon. Establishing for each object the precise location of this "vanishing point" along the horizon is important in drawing or painting, where there is only one point of view. In a diorama, where the viewer can move his head from side to side, precise calculations are less important, and for most

purposes you can simply follow your instinct without getting into too much trouble.

Buildings in forced perspective have funny angles. A square window becomes a trapezoid, and the more the perspective is forced, the more acute the angles of the trapezoid become. And the more balconies, doors, windows and other features your building has, the more angles you will have to work out, so try to keep things simple in the beginning.

With a bit of practice, you'll be surprised at how well forced perspective can work, even in extreme cases. But forced perspective is an illusion, and it will succeed in a boxed diorama only if the sight lines and vanishing points work from all possible viewing angles.

THE SECRET BEHIND THE GHOST OF HAMLET'S FATHER

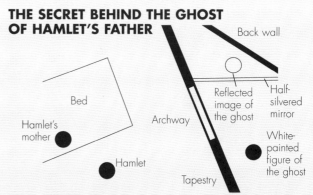

The illusion of a fully three-dimensional ghost is accomplished with a half-silvered mirror (the kind used to look into rooms without being seen). The layout above shows how the scene is laid out. The figure of the king is located behind the tapestry to the right; what Hamlet and the viewer see is the reflection of the figure on the surface of the mirror. Because the figure is three-dimensional, the reflection is, too. And since the mirror is only half-silvered, we can see past the ghost through the mirror to the wall behind. By using dimmers to raise and lower the separate illumination on the figure and the wall, we can control the transparency of the ghost. With no light at all behind the mirror, the ghost appears solid; as the illuminates behind the mirror gets brighter, the ghost becomes transparent,

CREATING THE GHOSTS FOR "SON OF THE MORNING STAR"

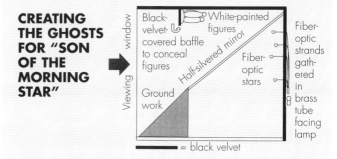

This side view shows how the mirror is set, with the figures secured to the overhead behind a baffle. The box duplicating the night sky is lined entirely with black velvet so that none of the seams is visible. The stars are fiber optics leading back to a single light bulb in the back of the box. The fiber optic strands poke through the black velvet sky at different lengths; this way, the bright spots at the end of the strands (the stars) seem to float three-dimensionally in space, and the sky appears to have depth.

6 Three-dimensional transparent ghosts are a great effect, and not too difficult to accomplish. In "A King of Shred and Patches" Hamlet sees the ghost of his father. As the viewer moves from side to side, he sees the ghost as a three-dimensional image, but he can also see right through it to the stonework and staircase behind.

7 The ghosts of Custer and his men in the night sky in "Son of the Morning Star" are achieved in the same way, although the mirror is angled differently. The groundwork is a good example of forced perspective. The hill itself is only 3" deep, but by using rapidly diminishing tombstones, the impression of a much greater distance is achieved.

8 The inner scene from "Morning Star." Visible here are the velvet covered walls of the "night sky" and the angled mirror.

9 The figures concealed in the overhead. Everything is constructed backwards so that the reflection reads right. The figures were sprayed overall gray, then airbrushed from above with white to create "instant" shading.

10 Fiber optics are also used for the reflections of the campfire in the wolves' eyes in "The Remnants of an Army," a scene from Napoleon's retreat from Moscow. This is an example of timing in a diorama: the viewer's eye is first drawn to the large bright object, the campfire, and only after absorbing that does it follow the figures' gaze over to the wolves, which form the "punch line" of the scene.

11

12

times, and it is always fun to see what can be done with them.

My first attempt was with the gun deck of HMS *Victory*. Mirrors at each end of the scene reflected each other, multiplying two model cannon to create the illusion of the entire length of the gun deck, fifteen guns in all. The same mirror trick was used in "Stopping the Slave Trade" (page 121) and the B-26 assembly line (page 64). For this purpose you will need special mirrors. Ordinary household mirrors are silvered on the back of the glass so the glass protects it from scratching. This is a good idea for most purposes, but it means that when you press an object such as your finger up to the glass, there is a gap the thickness of the glass between the object and its reflection. what is needed for this kind of illusion is a "front-silvered" mirror, with the silvering on the *front* of the glass. These are manufactured for scientific purposes and can be quite expensive—I bought slightly flawed ones at a scientific surplus store for a lot less money. Since the silvering is on the front, when you touch your finger to it, your finger actually touches its reflection, with no gap in

between. In the case of HMS *Victory*, this means that the planks of the deck continue unbroken from the scene into the mirror, and the illusion is complete.

A second use I have found for mirrors is to create three-dimensional ghosts, fully round figures that you can see through. The trick here is to use a "half-silvered" mirror (also called "one-way glass"). The mirror reflects the image of a figure placed in form of it, but because the mirror is only half silvered, objects behind the mirror can be seen as well. By using dimmers to raise and lower the separate illumination on the figure and the wall, we can control the transparency of the ghost. With no light at all behind the mirror, the ghost appears solid, but as the illumination behind the mirror gets brighter, the ghost becomes increasingly transparent. By putting separate dimmers on the figure light and the background light, you can raise and lower them until just the right degree of transparency is achieved.

These are a few of the tricks I have discovered. I hope they inspire you to go out and develop ones of your own that you in turn can share with me.

11 Nick Infield's "We'll Always Have Paris" shows the filming of the final scene of the movie classic *Casablanca*. The special effect that really makes this scene is the plane visible through the mist in the background.

12 A close-up of the airplane, taken from a high angle to show how small it is (1/72 scale) and how it appears through the mist, which is created by lighting spraying a sheet of glass in the hangar doorway with matt varnish.

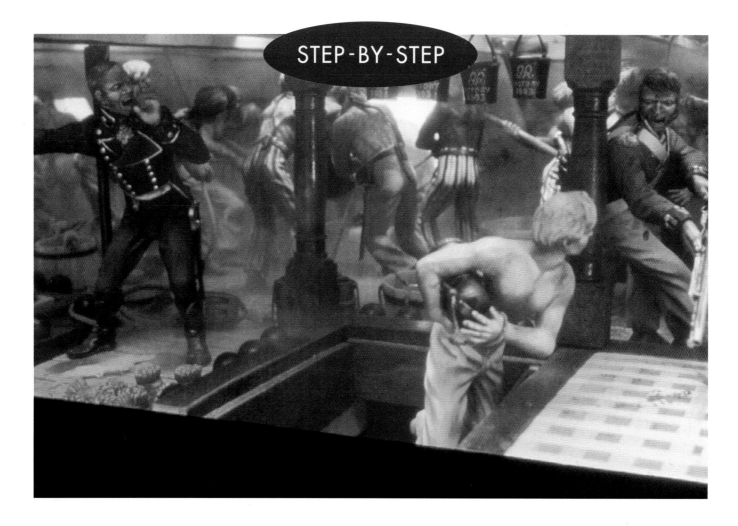

STEP-BY-STEP

CHAPTER SEVENTEEN

The Gun Deck of HMS *Victory*

I have always been fascinated by the age of fighting sail, and a boxed diorama showing the turbulent action on the gun deck of Nelson's flagship at Trafalgar had been in the back of my mind for some time. The impetus for its construction came when I realized I could use mirrors to create the appearance of the full length of the deck, extending on each side well beyond the limits of the box. The secret to completing this illusion was to use front-surface mirrors, which would give the appearance of a continuous deck without breaks or gaps.

This was a significant construction project, one that required a lot of research and planning. Working in 100mm (1/18 scale) meant that virtually everything had to be scratchbuilt—figures, guns, and the ship's interior. Drawing up a set of full-size plans made the job a lot easier. Not only could I

work out a lot of problems before construction began, but I could also check the measurements of parts by laying them directly on the plan.

At some point during the planning stages, the idea occurred to me to make the ship actually roll with the sea. I had never made a model move before, and wasn't sure if I could pull it off—making the deck move might only draw attention to the fact that the figures were motionless—but I decided to design and install the system anyway, with the idea that if the illusion failed, I could always just leave the system turned off. As it turned out, the idea was successful beyond my expectations: the motion was slow enough that few viewers noticed it until they had been looking at the scene for several minutes, and their surprise and delight as they gradually realized what they were seeing more than justified the work that went into it.

Looking back, I can now see that the motion of the deck succeeded because it was not part of the action, but part of the setting. Providing movement for the French ship in the opposite plane was the final touch—it gave an eerie floating sensation that a number of people swore made them seasick!

In all, the project consumed about four months of part-time work. It was a challenge from beginning to end, and one of my most enjoyable modeling experiences.

"The Gun Deck of HMS *Victory* at Trafalgar" shows why the shadow box is the ultimate form of the diorama. The dramatic effects possible when the viewpoint is restricted and the lighting is controlled cannot be achieved in an open scene. The scratchbuilt 1/18 scale scene has mirrors at each end to provide the illusion of a full-length gun deck and a motorized motion that gives the illusion of floating on the ocean.

MOTION SYSTEM FOR THE GUN DECK

MOTION SYSTEM FOR THE BACKGROUND SHIP

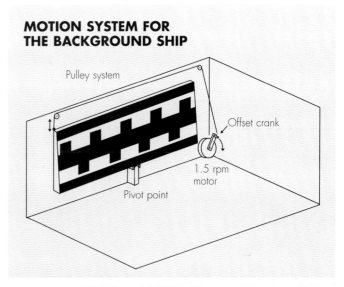

1 There are only two cannons in the model. This view of the gun deck without the figures shows how the mirrors reflect each other to create the illusion of the deck extending each direction. In this view, the only real cannon is the one on the far right; the others are all reflections. By looking at the pillars you can spot the location of the mirror, between the two black iron posts.

2 The first pieces built for this scene were the large overhead beams. A friend came to visit that day and as we talked, his dog was happily gnawing on the beams. They had to be made over, of course, but I saved the chewed rejects, and when the time came to model the shot holes in the side of the ship, the dog made his contribution—I could never have made miniature splinters as realistically as he could! The moral of the story: don't miss a chance to take advantage of happy accidents.

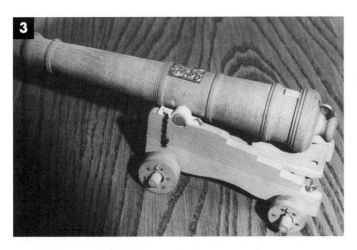

3 Most of the construction was in basswood. This is a cannon, showing the barrel turned on a lathe. The Royal cypher on the gun was photoetched.

4 Also made of wood is the side of the French ship *Redoutable* visible through the gun ports.

5 There is a lot of detail on the deck itself: match tubs, cannon balls, grapeshot, powder pass boxes, water tubs, ropes and pulleys, etc.

6 The scene draws its sense of frantic action from the posing of the figures and the expressions on their faces.

7 The scene is filled with telling little details, such as the flogging scars on this man's back. The drops of sweat are five-minute epoxy.

8 Some of the figure groups turned out so nicely it seemed a shame to coop them up in a box. This trio could easily have stood on a base of their own as a small vignette.

9 The same group as installed in the scene. The abundant blood on the deck, while realistic, is more than I would normally put into a diorama but is more subdued when seen from eye level through the viewing window.

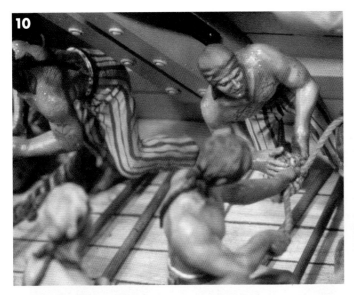

10 You can often have fun with the mirrors. The tattoo "Ajax" on the arm of the figure on the left is actually painted backwards on the arm of the figure on the right!

11 You can play clever tricks with the mirrors, too. The viewer eventually concludes that there has to be a mirror at the end of the scene, but in searching for its precise location, his eye inevitably looks past this pair of figures. In fact, there is only one figure and half a bucket; the other figure is his reflection (if you look closely, you can see a thin line where the mirror meets the deck). To achieve this degree of deception, you need a "front surface" mirror, one with the silvering on the front of the glass rather than the back. These are used for telescopes and other scientific purposes and are available from a scientific supply house. I bought mine surplus, which is a lot cheaper; the minor scratches that made them unsuitable for the scientific work were perfectly acceptable for my purposes.

12 Another view looking down the deck, showing the effect of the mirror.

13 A view into the outer case with the gun deck removed. In the foreground are the two blocks on which the front of the gun deck rests. To the left, behind the transformer, can be seen the motor (with its eccentric crank with the cord looped over it). On the far right is a similar looped cord, which hooks onto the lead ingot just below it when the gun deck is in place and suspended from the motor cord. In the back is the French ship, with its cord and motor to the right. Because the French ship is hinged and balanced at the center, it does not need a counterweight.

CHAPTER EIGHTEEN

Photographing Your Dioramas

Taking pictures of your dioramas adds a new and exciting dimension to your hobby. Aside from keeping a record of your work—important if you part with your dioramas—photography allows you to take a fresh look at scenes. Photography also allows you to achieve special effects not possible in a static display, such as night scenes, dramatic lighting, and the smoke and dust of battle. In some cases you'll like the photographs better than the dioramas and may even find yourself building scenes with particular photographs in mind.

The purpose of this brief chapter is to acquaint you with the bare essentials of model photography, and to outline the minimum tools required to take decent pictures. With the equipment described here—and a little practice—you should be able to take pictures suitable for publication.

Equipment. Model photography is a specialized field that requires a certain amount of special equipment, but not nearly as much as you might expect. These are the minimum essentials:

· *Camera.* If you don't already have a suitable camera, this will be your biggest investment. When selecting a camera, consider its usefulness for family and other types of photographs, as well as its model photography use. A single lens reflex (SLR), the most common type of 35mm camera sold today, is practically a must. This type allows through-the-lens viewing, which means that what you see through the viewfinder is exactly what you'll get on film. Most SLRs come with a built-in, through-the-lens light meter. This is a desirable feature, because it frees you from having to measure the light and compute the correct exposure. The 50mm lens that comes with the camera is fine, although you will have to buy a set of inexpensive close-up lenses that

screw onto the front to allow it to focus at close distances. A tripod is also required, because you will be shooting at slow shutter speeds and must keep the camera steady. Screw-type camera elevation on the tripod is very handy. A cable release, which allows you to click the shutter without touching the camera, is also helpful.

· *Film.* The films I find most dependable are Kodak High Speed Ektachrome (Tungsten) for color slides and Plus-X for black-and-white. Color is more expensive and less forgiving of mistakes, so it is much cheaper to learn with black-and-white film.

To make your pictures appear as if they were taken by a real photographer standing on the ground, place the center of the camera lens at scale eye level. Placing the lens even lower will make the model appear larger and more dramatic. The model is a 1/35 (yes, 1/35!) scale B-52 by Louis Pruneau.

1 This typical 35mm SLR is easy to use, and because it is a common type of camera, a wide range of accessories is available. The screw-on closeup lens shown here is one of the most useful extras.

2,3 These photos show the relationship of lens opening to depth of field. The setup and focus in both was identical, but the photo on top was opened up to f2.8, while the one at bottom was closed down to f16.

· *Lights.* Nothing fancy here. Camera shops sell inexpensive photoflood bulbs that are good enough for what we are doing. These bulbs look like ordinary light bulbs and fit standard sockets. You will need two sizes: 500 watt and 250 watt. Make sure that the bulbs you buy are color balanced at 3200 degrees K to match your film. Ordinary clamp-on fixtures are fine, although you may want to invest in light stands later on. You will also want a 10" reflector for each light and a plastic or fiberglass diffusion screen to cut down the harshness of the shadows.

· *Background.* You can use your imagination here, but a good way to start is to purchase two pieces of light blue mat board, one to go under the model and one to go behind it.

· *Optional equipment.* As you learn more about photography, you may want to consider adding specialized gear to your equipment. A macro lens is especially designed for close-up photography, providing closer focusing distances and sharper pictures without the aid of close-up lenses. A telephoto lens will allow you to photograph from farther back, and to zero in on details at the back of your scene. A strobe flash unit provides more light than photoflood lamps and generates less heat.

Setting up. Allow plenty of room for photography. You'll be surprised at how much room it takes to photograph even a single figure, and you don't want to trip over anything. The drawing shows a typical setup. In the beginning, position your main light (the 500 watt) above and to one side, slightly toward the front of the model, and about 3" away from it. Place the second light (the 250 watt),

A SIMPLE SET-UP FOR PHOTOGRAPHING YOUR DIORAMAS

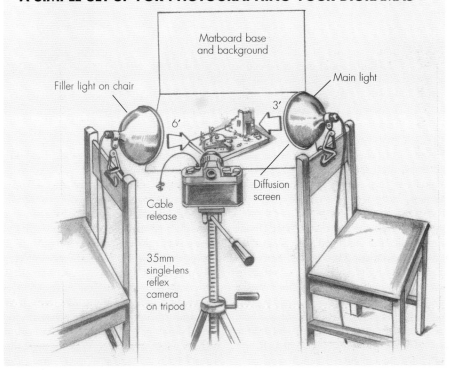

Matboard base and background

Filler light on chair

Main light

Cable release

Diffusion screen

35mm single-lens reflex camera on tripod

6'

3'

4 To add smoke effects, blow smoke at the model just before tripping the camera shutter. Because the smoke is hard to control, take several shots at each angle so you can pick the best one.

your fill, level with the model and on the opposite side from the main, twice as far away. This light will help fill shadows, but watch that it is not bright enough to cast conflicting shadows of its own. If it does, move it farther away. Keep the lights on only when you are looking through the viewfinder or snapping the shutter, because they give off a lot of heat, enough to warp and melt plastic models.

From here on, lighting is strictly a matter of

experience and experimentation. Try something, and if it doesn't work, try something else.

Exposures. The primary problem in miniature photography is achieving adequate depth of field (depth of focus). The closer you move your camera to an object, the narrower the camera's range of focus becomes. In this respect the camera is the same as your eye; hold your finger 12″ in front of your face, and you cannot focus on both the finger and the background at the same time. The controls on the camera allow you to select a center of focus, but things will start to go fuzzy behind and in front of this center. When you get the camera really close, say 3″ or 4″ from the

model, the maximum area in sharp focus will be little more than 2″ deep. On a 54mm figure with an outthrust musket, this area of sharp focus barely covers the figure and the length of the bayonet.

We can't overcome depth of field limitations completely, but we can learn to live with them. The critical factor in achieving satisfactory depth of field is this: The smaller the lens opening (f stop) the greater the depth of field. Always shoot with the lens set at minimum aperture. On most cameras this will be f16 or f22, although some macro lenses will stop down to f64. This means varying only the shutter speed to control exposures. Set your aperture, turn on your lights, read the meter in the viewfinder, and adjust the shutter speed for proper exposure.

With the lighting I've described, you will usually shoot at shutter speeds between $\frac{1}{15}$ and $\frac{1}{2}$ second. When focusing, bear in mind that the depth of field extends $\frac{1}{3}$ in front of the focusing point and $\frac{2}{3}$ in back of it, so focus slightly forward of the center of your subject. Some cameras have a depth of field preview button that allows you to check focus. An out-of-focus foreground is more distracting than an out-of-focus background, so take care of the foreground first.

Now you are ready to click the shutter. Bracket your exposures by shooting one picture at the exposure indicated by the meter, then at one f stop above it, and one stop below. Although the camera meter is usually accurate, it can be fooled, and bracketing exposures provides some insurance. Professional photographers bracket their exposures—one reason they always come back with the picture.

Special effects

· *Night scenes.* These are easily achieved by underexposing the film, possibly using a blue filter as well. You will have to experiment to get just the right degree of night effect.

· *Bright desert sun.* This is the opposite of a night scene, so overexpose the film one stop.

· *Grainy "combat" appearance.* The grainy appearance of most combat footage is a result of the cameramen using high-speed film, which has coarse grain. To duplicate this effect, use a high-speed film such as Tri-X for black-and-white or Ektachrome 400 for color. The grain effect may not be noticeable until you make enlargements.

· *Smoke and dust.* These are created by blowing cigar or cigarette smoke through a tube onto the scene. Experiment with different angles and pressures. If you blow hard, the effect is hazy; if you blow very softly, the smoke will float gently across the scene, hugging the hollows like ground fog. Shoot each pose at least three times, because smoke is an accidental effect—you may find only one of the shots is just the effect you want.